ACKNOWLEDGMENTS

I'd like to thank the following people for agreeing to be interviewed for this project:

Peter B. Lewis, Tom Schiller, Sean Kleefeld, Luke François Murray, Robert Michelson, Andrew Madigan, Jay Cronley, Dean Poulos, Jeff Santo, Joe Nicchi, E. J. Rumpke, Raheel Gauba, Vadim Birstein, David Walton Smith, Gary Lachman, and Larry Basil.

The inimitable James Robert Parish provided crackerjack research assistance.

Finally, many thanks as always to Jason Rekulak, Andie Reid, Jane Morley, Nicole De Jackmo, Eric Smith, and everyone else at Quirk Books. That is one nutty publisher.

NOTA BENE

Despite the author's best efforts, this unauthorized biography was produced without the direct involvement of Bill Murray. Nevertheless, we have taken every precaution to ensure the information contained herein is accurate and correct. A list of sources begins on page 269.

Library of Congress Cataloging in Publication Number: 2014956799

ISBN: 978-1-59474-801-1

Printed in China
Typeset in Eames Century Modern and Futura

Quirk Books staff (and their favorite Bill Murray performances)

Designed by Andie Reid (*Lost in Translation*)

Edited by Jason Rekulak (*Groundhog Day*) and Jane Morley (*Zombieland*)

Production management by John J. McGurk (*Quick Change*)

Cover photo © Matthias Clamer/CORBIS OUTLINE
Interior and back cover photos courtesy of the Everett Collection

Quirk Books
215 Church Street
Philadelphia, PA 19106
quirkbooks.com

10 9 8 7 6 5 4 3 2 1

THE BIG BAD BOOK OF BILL MURRAY

A Critical Appreciation of the World's Finest Actor

By Robert Schnakenberg

QUIRK BOOKS

PHILADELPHIA

"NOTHING PREPARED ME FOR BEING THIS AWESOME.... IT'S KIND OF A SHOCK TO WAKE UP EVERY MORNING AND BE BATHED IN THIS PURPLE LIGHT."

—BILL MURRAY, to an interviewer who asked "What's it like to be so awesome?"

STALKING THE MURRICANE

"'You may seek it with thimbles—and seek it with care;
You may hunt it with forks and hope;
You may threaten its life with a railway-share;
You may charm it with smiles and soap—'"

("That's exactly the method," the Bellman bold
In a hasty parenthesis cried,
"That's exactly the way I have always been told
That the capture of Snarks should be tried!")

—LEWIS CARROLL, *The Hunting of the Snark*

BILL MURRAY seems to be everywhere these days—or at least he seems capable of turning up anywhere at any time. According to a widely disseminated urban legend, he's liable to pop up behind you as you're reading this. He'll put his hands over your eyes, or give you a noogie, then whisper that "no one will ever believe you" if you try to tell them what you've seen. He's like a mischievous Keyser Söze.

There are websites devoted to chronicling Murray's sudden public apparitions—from sandlot kickball games to drunken bachelor parties—and entire Twitter accounts made up of impromptu photographs taken with him in airport lounges, hotel lobbies, and minor league baseball stadiums. It's hard to remember a time when he was just a famous actor and not the world's most celebrated gatecrasher.

Yet for all his ubiquity, we know very little about the real Bill Murray. Like Lewis Carroll's elusive Snark, his true nature remains shrouded in mystery. Although he's been an internationally recognized star for more than thirty years, no one has tried to publish a book-length biography about him. Murray's own 1999 memoir, *Cinderella Story*, was written with tongue planted firmly in cheek. It is a rough roadmap to his early life, but it's hardly comprehensive. And God help the humble researcher trying to arrange an interview with him. Murray stays zealously cloaked behind his fabled 800 number, which restricts telephonic access to a few close friends and Hollywood insiders. Believe me, I know. I tried to contact nearly every one of them. No one is giving up those digits.

In a way, it feels like I've been stalking "The Murricane"—as he's known among his intimates—my whole life. I'm old enough to have watched the arc of his career. When I was a child, it was considered bad form to show up to school on Monday mornings without having memorized that weekend's *Saturday Night Live* sketches. While most kids gravitated toward tentpole recurring characters like the Coneheads or Roseanne Roseannadanna, I found myself mesmerized by the subtler work being done by a certain mustachioed newcomer from Chicago who replaced Chevy Chase. Over the course of Murray's three and a half seasons on *SNL*, a handful of his one-shot characters imprinted themselves indelibly in my comedy consciousness: a crazed Richard Dawson bellowing "Show me Romaine Lettuce!" during a parody of *Family Feud*; the oleaginous host of the Mexican game show *¿Quién Es Más Macho?*; and his exquisite Earl of Sandwich in the "Lord and Lady Douchebag" sketch—arguably the high-water mark of the show's forty-plus-year run, if not of the history of American humor.

As I grew older, my tastes (hopefully) matured. Lo and behold, so did Murray's. He graduated from the exuberant juvenilia of *Meatballs* to the existential mind-tripping of *Groundhog Day*. He drew on an untapped well of pathos in *Rushmore* and became the embodiment of middle-aged loneliness in *Lost in Translation*. In interviews, he was less snarky and more gnomic; the stories about his private behavior involved fewer drunken escapades and more Zen pranks. Before my eyes, Bill Murray became the rare celebrity who got more interesting—and more mysterious—the longer he was in the public eye. He was a fascinating jigsaw puzzle, begging to be solved.

The Big Bad Book of Bill Murray is the closest we may ever come to a written record of the Murricane's life, career, and philosophy. Using insights derived from published accounts and Murray's own on-the-record utterances dating back to the mid-1970s, I have tried to create a complete contextualized picture of the man, his work, and his unique approach to life. Included are Murray's observations on everything from the afterlife to underwear, Mark Twain to Mr. Magoo. I interviewed more than a dozen of Murray's colleagues and associates for this project, from high school friends to Hollywood screenwriters. I even spoke to his body double, who told me stories of on-set antics I'd be scared to repeat even if I could corroborate them. All of them supplied insights that greatly enriched my understanding of the man, his movies, and the personal and professional choices he has made.

For the record, no one I spoke with had an unkind word to say about Bill. As a matter of fact, time and again, the portrait his friends painted looked an awful lot like the image of Bill Murray we know from photo-bombs: the rumpled, wisecracking rapscallion with an impish gleam in his eye. The guy whose bear hugs and bawdy jokes enliven any party he deigns to crash.

When I asked him to explain Murray's outrageous public behavior, *Saturday Night Live's* Tom Schiller likened him to a Buddhist trickster figure, a reincarnated peripatetic monk who uses humor to awaken and enlighten. "These kinds of masters come around only once every thousand years," Schiller told me. If so, it has been my privilege to trail behind the master, relaying his teachings to a world yearning to understand.

A NOTE ON THE TEXT:

All words in bold are cross-references to other entries within this book.

Each of the feature films in *The Big Bad Book of Bill Murray* is rated for overall quality on a four-star scale. I've also included a "Murray rating," which grades each movie according to Murray's performance and its importance within his cinematic oeuvre. The key for those ratings is as follows:

★★★★ = ESSENTIAL. IF YOU CONSIDER YOURSELF A BILL MURRAY FAN, YOU MUST SEE THIS MOVIE.

★★★ = NOTEWORTHY. A GOOD PERFORMANCE OR IMPORTANT MILESTONE IN THE GREAT MAN'S CAREER.

★★ = NONESSENTIAL. OF INTEREST TO COMPLETISTS ONLY.

★ = SKIP IT. A CAMEO, CURIOSITY, OR OTHERWISE FORGETTABLE MURRAY PERFORMANCE.

All opinions, of course, are the author's own. Your mileage may vary.

ABOUT LAST NIGHT

Murray was under consideration for the role of Danny Martin, the restaurant-supply salesman played by Rob Lowe, in this 1986 big-screen adaptation of David Mamet's play *Sexual Perversity in Chicago*. At various points in the development process, **John Belushi** and Nick Nolte were to costar as Danny's friend Bernie Litgo. That part went to James Belushi, who had played the character on stage. Negotiations with Murray apparently broke down after a disastrous meeting between Murray and Nolte in New York.

ACADEMY AWARDS

At the seventy-sixth Academy Awards ceremony in 2004, Murray was the odds-on favorite to win the Oscar for best actor for his work in *Lost in Translation*. But he lost to Sean Penn of *Mystic River*. When Penn's name was announced, cameras caught a visibly disappointed Murray frowning in disgust at his table. "Pissed off? You bet I was," he later admitted. "I don't approve of award ceremonies, so I was wondering what had persuaded me to attend that one. I was pissed at myself."

The best actor loss was just the latest item in a dossier of Oscar snubs Murray had been compiling since the mid-1990s. "Comedy never gets the Oscar," he groused. "*Groundhog Day* was one of the greatest scripts ever written. It didn't even get nominated for an Academy Award. And a movie called *Dave* won, which was a rehash of a movie about a Spanish dictator who died and had an actor replace him. How can that be the best original screenplay? Laughter and the lighter moments of life always seem easy to deliver. I don't expect those giving out the **awards** to understand." (In fact, *Dave*—directed by Murray's old *Ghostbusters* collabora-

> **"I FEEL THAT IF YOU REALLY WANT AN OSCAR, YOU'RE IN TROUBLE. IT'S LIKE WANTING TO BE MARRIED— YOU'LL TAKE ANYBODY."**
>
> —MURRAY, on the pursuit of Academy glory

tor **Ivan Reitman**—did not win the Oscar for best original screenplay in 1993. *The Piano* did. But it's true that **Groundhog Day** was passed over.)

Justified or not, Murray's loss deprived television viewers of the chance to hear one of the most original and insouciant acceptance speeches in Oscars history. As Murray told PBS talk show host Charlie Rose in a 2014 interview: "I was going to say, 'When I heard I'd been nominated with,' you know I'd name these other people [Sean Penn, Ben Kingsley, Johnny Depp, and Jude Law], 'I really thought I had a pretty good chance.' I just thought no one had ever given that speech. . . . I didn't have **agents**, I didn't have managers, I didn't have any of that stuff. So I wouldn't have to give that ordinary speech of thanking everyone. I'd just go out there and entertain. I always figure, if you're on a TV show where there's a billion people, show up and do something, okay? Give those folks in Bombay something to talk about."

It took nearly half a year for Murray to recover from the shock of hearing Sean Penn's name being called instead of his own. About six months later, he said, "I realized I'd come down with something. That prize-winning stuff. I'd sort of had a low-grade infection of liking winning the prize and wanting to win the prize. I thought, oh, good. You've seen when people do win the prize, and then for the next couple of years they really struggle. Because they're sort of stuck. 'Hey, I'm an Academy Award winner. And now what do I want to do?' They get all messed up. And that could have happened to me." In recent years, Murray has taken solace knowing that many people think he actually *did* win the Oscar for *Lost in Translation*. "I never try to say, 'No, that isn't true.' I just say, 'You're so kind.'"

AGENTS

Murray is famously disdainful of professional representation. In 2000, he fired his agents—reportedly for calling him on the phone too often—and replaced them with an automated **800 number**. "I said I didn't ever want to speak to them again, and I never did," he says. "I like to cut my own lawn now. I don't need a landscaper."

Filmmakers who wish to pitch projects to Murray must leave a message on his voice mailbox, which he rarely checks. When he *is* interested in a script, Murray demands that it be faxed to him care of his local office supply store. This unique arrangement has resulted in Murray missing out on a number of high-profile job offers, including the roles of Willy Wonka in *Charlie and the Chocolate Factory*, Frank Ginsberg in *Little Miss Sunshine*, and the title role in *Bad Santa*. "We wanted Bill to consider a role in *Iron Man*, but nobody could find him," observed Robert Downey Jr.

When asked to explain his decision to represent himself, Murray will often cite a quote attributed to actress Ellen Burstyn: "I had a dream that I was being drowned in a flood and I realized it was a flood of people." According to

Murray: "When you have an agent, the phone rings all the time because there's someone there whose job it is to get so-and-so on the phone, and so they dial the number, and they'll let it ring seventy-five times. You can be in your house and be like, 'I'm not answering that phone . . .' and all you can really think is, 'I really don't want to meet the person that lets a phone ring like that.'"

AGING

Murray began making the transition to dramatic roles in his late forties, in part because of fears that his comedic prowess would diminish with age. "As you get older, you have less chance to be funny," he once declared. "That's where most comedians lose it. Very few make it all the way to the end, like Jack Benny or George Burns." During a 2014 press junket to promote *St. Vincent*, Murray mused on what the end stage of his career might look like. It involved graduating to insect roles. "If I keep living, I will probably play a grasshopper someday," he said. "Hopefully there's some kid someday who played with grasshoppers as a kid and will write a script about it and cast me."

AIR AMERICA

Murray was filmmaker Richard Rush's first choice to play the role of Billy Covington in this 1990 comedy about a hotshot helicopter pilot who takes a job flying covert missions for the CIA during the Vietnam War. Sean Connery was originally tapped to play Covington's wizened mentor, Gene Ryack. After Rush was ousted as director, the film was retooled as a vehicle for Robert Downey Jr. and Mel Gibson.

AIRPLANE!

Murray turned down an offer to play the lead role of Ted Striker in this 1980 comedy from the creative team of Jim Abrahams, Jerry Zucker, and David Zucker. The part, which David Letterman also declined, eventually went to Robert Hays. Murray later cited *Airplane!* as an example of a movie that he passed on even though he knew it would be successful.

> ## "THIS IS GONNA WORK, BUT IT'S NOT FOR ME."
> —MURRAY, on reading the screenplay for *Airplane!*

ALL YOU NEED IS CASH

Murray has a scenery-chewing cameo in this 1978 TV mockumentary chronicling the career of the Rutles, a fictitious British pop band modeled on the Beatles. His character, bellowing radio deejay "Bill Murray the K," is loosely based on self-proclaimed "Fifth Beatle" Murray Kaufman, aka "Murray the K." Also known as *The Rutles, All You Need Is Cash* was expanded from a sketch that originally aired on the BBC program *Rutland Weekend Television* in 1975. Excerpts from that skit were shown on the October 2, 1976, episode of *Saturday Night Live*, hosted by Monty Python veteran and Rutles cocreator Eric Idle. A number of *SNL* cast members from the period, including **Dan Aykroyd** and **John Belushi**, also have cameos in the film.

ALPHA HOUSE

Since 2013, Murray has had a recurring cameo on this Amazon Original comedy series from *Doonesbury* creator Garry Trudeau. He plays Vernon Smits, a U.S. senator imprisoned for unspecified improprieties at an amusement park. Trudeau was able to snag Murray for the role through the good offices of his wife, former *Today* show anchor Jane Pauley, whom Murray had befriended around the NBC craft services table during his days on *Saturday Night Live*.

ALVIN AND THE CHIPMUNKS

Murray turned down the role of David Seville in this dreadful 2006 film based on the screeching cartoon musical group of the 1950s. Jason Lee eventually took on the burden of playing the chipmunks' beleaguered human companion.

ANDERSON, WES

Texas-born film director in whose unofficial repertory company Murray enlisted in the late 1990s. To date, Murray has appeared in all but one of Anderson's eight increasingly idiosyncratic features, and he would have been offered a role in the eighth—1996's *Bottle Rocket*—had he bothered to answer the director's phone calls. Judging from his public comments, it's safe to say Anderson tops the list of filmmakers with whom Murray most enjoys working. "I really love the way Wes writes with his collaborators," Murray has said. "I like the way he shoots, and I like *him*. I've become so fond of him. I love the way that he has made his art his life. And you know, it's a lesson to all of us, to take what you love and make it the way you live your life, and that way you

bring love into the world." Anderson was among the first to exploit Murray's potential for pathos on film, beginning with 1998's *Rushmore*. After several years spent flailing in lowbrow comedies like *Larger Than Life* and *The Man Who Knew Too Little*, Murray welcomed the chance to stretch his acting muscles. Of Anderson's approach to using him, he once observed: "Wes really knows what he wants. It's not like, 'Get the ham out there and let him oink.'"

"THERE'S USUALLY A WARNING SHOT ACROSS THE BOW, LIKE 'I'M GOING TO BE DOING SOMETHING.' YOU KNOW, JUST A LITTLE BIT OF TALK. I NEVER KNOW IF HE MEANS, 'ARE YOU INTERESTED?' OR 'ARE YOU ALIVE?' IT COULD BE BOTH."

—MURRAY, on how he knows there's a new Wes Anderson movie in the works

ARMAGNAC

Aromatic French brandy favored by Murray in his mid-twenties. He has referred to Armagnac as "truth serum." Murray and his *Stripes* costar Warren Oates got falling-down drunk on Armagnac during a 1980 visit to the grave of character actor Strother Martin.

ARTHUR, BEA

The legendary star of *Maude* and *The Golden Girls* met Murray when she hosted the November 17, 1979, episode of *Saturday Night Live*. In a 2008 interview with film critic Elvis Mitchell, Murray confessed that he did not look forward to working with Arthur, considering her an "old dame" whose antiquated, declamatory acting style wouldn't mesh with his more improvisational approach. "I wouldn't have thought I'd give a hoot and holler about Bea Arthur," he said. But she won him over with her commitment to her performance. "I was very impressed with her," he admitted. "She was amazingly professional. She was game. She had all kinds of chops and could do anything."

ASSASSINATION

In a 2014 interview, Murray revealed the reason he does not surround himself with an entourage as other celebrities do: fear of assassination. "The first time I was ever given a bodyguard, I thought, 'Oh, my God, I'm going to be assassinated,'" he told the *Detroit Free Press*. "It made me think I was going to be shot. So I never liked it. I never liked the sensation of it."

AUTOGRAPHS

Murray hates signing autographs. Besieged by autograph seekers during dinner with a magazine interviewer in 1989, he reacted angrily, calling the imposition "an assault." "Why do some people want your autograph when it's plain that they don't give a shit about you?" he complained. "At least let a guy finish his dinner. Sometimes I feel people think, 'What the hell, this bum is getting all that dough—let's make him earn it.'"

When he does give in, Murray has been known to append slyly menacing notes for his **fans**. One six-year-old who requested his signature at the height of *Ghostbusters* mania was greeted with the message: "Sidney, run away from home tonight—Bill Murray." At other times, Murray has made a point of signing Jim Belushi's name instead of his own. During a vacation in Mexico in 1988, Murray was pestered by one "overdressed" female fan who "kept ordering me to give her autographs . . . like I was her personal trinket." He responded by dumping the woman—"furs, designer clothes, and all"—into a swimming pool.

AWAKENINGS

Director Penny Marshall considered Murray for the role of catatonic Leonard Lowe in this 1990 film based on the casebook of neurologist Oliver Sacks. But with Robin Williams on board as a fictionalized version of Sacks, Marshall was reluctant to add another comic actor to the cast. Robert De Niro took the part and received an Academy Award nomination for best actor. Murray went on to play a bearded neurologist, loosely based on Oliver Sacks, in 2001's *The Royal Tenenbaums*.

AWARDS

Over his long career, Murray has amassed numerous acting prizes and nominations, including an Emmy for outstanding writing on *Saturday Night Live* and a Golden Globe for best actor in a musical or comedy for *Lost in Translation*. In 2004, he was famously passed over for an Academy Award for best actor in favor of Sean Penn. He is one of only a handful of actors to be nominated for both the Oscar and its Canadian cousin, the Genie Award. Despite all the accolades he's received, Murray has a professed aversion for the pursuit of awards, a desire he once likened to a "low-grade infection."

See also **Academy Awards**.

AYKROYD, DAN

Web-footed, heterochromic Canadian comic actor whom Murray credits with being one of the only people to write sketches for him during his difficult first season on *Saturday Night Live*. A gifted impressionist and character actor, Aykroyd collaborated with Murray on two *Ghostbusters* films and helped grease the wheels for the greenlighting of Murray's magnum opus, *The Razor's Edge*, in 1984. Both men also had small roles in *Mr. Mike's Mondo Video*, *All You Need Is Cash*, and *Nothing Lasts Forever*.

> **"AWARDS ARE MEANINGLESS TO ME AND I HAVE NOTHING BUT DISDAIN FOR ANYONE WHO ACTIVELY CAMPAIGNS TO GET ONE."**
>
> —MURRAY, on awards fever

Murray has called Aykroyd "a hell of a guy" and once claimed he was the only one of the ex-ghostbusters with whom he socialized regularly. Despite their longstanding friendship, Murray has resisted all of Aykroyd's entreaties to join him in a proposed third *Ghostbusters* movie.

TALES FROM
MURRAYLAND

№ 1	Crashing E. J.'s Bachelor Party

On Memorial Day weekend in 2014, Murray was dining with friends at Oak Steakhouse in Charleston, South Carolina, when a group of revelers from Washington, D.C., real estate developer E. J. Rumpke's bachelor party asked if he would join them upstairs and say a few words to the groom-to-be. After initially declining, Murray ambled on up to the restaurant's second floor and began dishing out relationship advice to the assembled partygoers. "You know how funerals are not for the dead, they're for the living?" Murray told an astonished Rumpke and twenty of his Boston College buddies. "Bachelor parties are not for the groom, they're for the unmarried." He then shared his secret for finding your soul mate:

"If you have someone that you think is the One, don't just sort of think in your ordinary mind, 'Okay, let's make a date. Let's plan this and make a party and get married.' Take that person and travel around the world. Buy a plane ticket for the two of you to travel all around the world, and go to places that are hard to go to and hard to get out of. And if when you come back to JFK, when you land in JFK, and you're still in love with that person, get married at the airport."

BAD SANTA

Murray was the original choice to play Willie T. Stokes, a lowlife shopping-mall
Santa Claus, in this 2003 comedy from director Terry Zwigoff. According
to Zwigoff, Murray made a verbal agreement to do the film, but when the
time came to sign his contract, he was incommunicado. "I was told by one of
the producers that he really wanted to do it — just tell him where and when
and he'd be there," Zwigoff said. "I left several messages on his answering
machine, but after a few weeks of hearing nothing, we eventually moved on."
Jack Nicholson was also under consideration for the role, which eventually
went to Billy Bob Thornton.

BALL, LUCILLE

Despite a self-professed predilection for "funny females," Murray is not a fan
of the wailing red-headed comedian who starred in the eponymous 1950s sitcom *I Love Lucy*. "Lucy never really made me laugh," he told film critic Elvis
Mitchell in a 2008 interview. "Lucy was never my girl."

BALLHAWKS

DIRECTED BY: Mike Diedrich

WRITTEN BY: Kyle McCarthy, Terry
Cosgrove, and Joe Sciarrotta

RELEASE DATE: April 27, 2010

FILM RATING: ★ ★

MURRAY RATING: ★

PLOT: A documentary filmmaker turns
his camera on the rabid Chicago Cubs
fans who chase home run balls as they
fly out of Wrigley Field.

STARRING BILL MURRAY AS: Your humble
narrator

Murray's brother Joel served as executive producer for this reverent sports
documentary, which was shot during the 2004 and 2005 baseball seasons.
Murray recorded his deadpan narration track in 2009, inside his suite at the
Sunset Tower Hotel in West Hollywood.

NEXT MOVIE: *Get Low* (2010)

BANKS, ERNIE

The Hall of Fame shortstop known as "Mr. Cub" is Murray's all-time favorite baseball player. Murray gave his firstborn son the middle name Banks in his honor.

BARK

Rambunctious golden retriever owned by Murray in the mid-1980s.

BASEBALL

Murray is a lifelong baseball fan who grew up rooting for his hometown Chicago Cubs. "The saddest day of the year," he once said, "is the last day of the baseball season."

As a child, Murray played Little League ball for his local Lions Club team—until he was kicked out for getting into a fight with an opposing player. He was also the ringleader of his neighborhood pickup league. "My childhood summers were all about baseball," he said. "I played nearly every day. We'd ride an hour from home on bikes to find a ballpark with home run fences. I'd spend hours at night making phone calls to round up eighteen players. That was the ultimate—two full teams for a pickup game."

Each season, when the Cubs inevitably fell out of the National League pennant race, Murray transferred his allegiance to the Milwaukee Braves. In 1957, on the day the Braves clinched the National League pennant, Murray's father drove the entire family up to Milwaukee to join in the celebration. Decades later, Murray could still recite from memory the entire starting lineup of the '57 Braves.

As an adult, Murray continues to follow the Cubs, although most of his passion is channeled into the minors. "Minor league baseball is very seductive," he has observed. "The magic is that this is how you remember baseball from when you were young." He called the atmosphere at minor league games "a calming, relaxing, soothing environment" and praised it for its restorative powers. "They should definitely close the state hospitals and make more minor league baseball," he once remarked. "It's very good for the brain."

It also appeals to Murray's love of showmanship—and underdogs: "I like rejects, and I like the carny part of minor league baseball." Murray has at times been a part owner of the Texas City Stars, Grays Harbor Loggers, Utica Blue Sox, Salt Lake City Trappers, St. Paul Saints, Charleston RiverDogs, Hudson Valley Renegades, Brockton Rox, Miami Miracle, Catskill Cougars, Charleston Rainbows, and Williamsport Bills. The common thread uniting all of Murray's teams is a lack of success. "I've always owned teams of players nobody wants," he said. "There's a lot of good will that comes from being the mutt." Murray has called his yen for owning bush league franchises "a fun way to disappear," likening it to **Dan Aykroyd** and **John Belushi**'s desire to form a blues band in the 1970s. In 2012, Murray was inducted into the South Atlantic League Hall of Fame in recognition of his efforts to promote minor league baseball.

In 1993, *New York Times* columnist Robert Lipsyte tried to sell Murray on the idea of becoming commissioner of Major League Baseball. "I will accept the job," Murray told Lipsyte, "if you give me unlimited powers."

BATMAN

Murray was briefly considered for the title role in director Tim Burton's 1989 big-screen adaptation of the long-running DC Comics series. Mel Gibson, Kevin Costner, and Pierce Brosnan were among a who's who of '80s icons in contention for the part, which went to Michael Keaton. Playing the Dark Knight would have been a major career coup for Murray, who had only recently returned to Hollywood after a four-year **sabbatical** from moviemaking.

B.C. ROCK

DIRECTED BY: Picha

WRITTEN BY: Jonathan Schmock, James Vallely, Joseph Plewa, and Christine Neubaur

RELEASE DATE: May 21, 1980 (as *The Missing Link*)

FILM RATING: ★

MURRAY RATING: ★

PLOT: The story of human evolution as told from the perspective of a sex-crazed caveman.

STARRING BILL MURRAY AS: A gassy dragon

Murray did uncredited vocal work on the English-language dub of this 1980 animated feature from Belgian cartoonist Jean-Paul "Picha" Walravens. A raunchy comedy in the spirit of Ralph Bakshi's *Fritz the Cat, B.C. Rock* was originally released in France as *Le chainon manquant* (*The Missing Link*). The film was redubbed twice in English: once in 1980 with a script from *National Lampoon* contributor Tony Hendra; and again in 1984 in a more sophomoric American version retitled *B.C. Rock,* with new dialogue by the comedy duo Jim Vallely and Jonathan Schmock. Murray supplies the voice of a flying dragon who farts fire. In a scene that is sadly representative of the level of comedy on display in the film, the hero "cures" the dragon of his explosive flatulence by stopping his anus with a cork. As bad as *B.C. Rock* is, it is a marked improvement over Murray's previous collaboration with Picha, 1979's *Shame of the Jungle*.

NEXT MOVIE: *Caddyshack* (1980)

BEAT

Abortive Murray movie project of the mid-1990s that was meant to be the actor's second directorial effort. Cowritten by Murray and his *Scrooged* collaborator **Mitch Glazer**, *Beat* was an Americanized re-do of a 1994 French feature, *Grosse fatigue*. (Oddly enough, Murray's directorial debut, 1990's *Quick Change*, was also a remake of a French film.) The surreal black comedy would have chronicled the travails of a world-famous actor bedeviled by a lookalike whose outrageous behavior threatens to ruin his reputation. Enthused about the prospect of playing a dual role, Murray was very high on the project. But the studio mysteriously bailed on him. "Disney was gonna do it," he said, "and they said it was the best script they'd read in five years. And then, two days later, some guy said, 'We don't make this kind of movie anymore.' And I was like, 'What?' It just took the wind out of my sails for working. I was just so disappointed." Eleven years later, in 2008, Murray was still gushing about the screenplay to the *Chicago Tribune*. "It spoke very much to the celebrity culture we have now," he said. "Everything we wrote has come true. I think it still plays. I do want to direct it.... I'm confident I can do it. But if there was somebody who was really funny and wanted to haul off and do it very quickly, I'd let them do it."

BELUSHI, JOHN

Falstaffian Albanian American comic actor who served as Murray's role model during the early stages of his career. Murray has called Belushi "the best actor I've ever seen" and "a powerful powerboat" paving the way for his own ascent to stardom. In interviews, he repeatedly praised Belushi's improv technique, likening it to "a martial art." "He was really free on the stage,"

> **"HE WAS A BIG, BIG HUMAN BEING. HE HAD EXTRAORDINARY APPETITES AND EXTRAORDINARY TALENTS. HE WAS LIKE BABE RUTH. HE COULD EAT FIFTY HOT DOGS AND HE COULD HIT SIXTY HOME RUNS. HE COULD DO IT ALL. YOU NEVER THOUGHT ANYTHING COULD REALLY STOP JOHN."**
>
> —MURRAY, on John Belushi's larger-than-life persona

SNL

Saturday Night Live, 1978

Murray once said. "Belushi always made active choices rather than word game choices," he told MTV.

The two men first met at **Second City** in **Chicago** and began working regularly together on *The National Lampoon Radio Hour* in New York. Murray and Belushi roomed together on the road when *The National Lampoon Show* went on tour in 1975. "We drank a lot of Rolling Rock in those days," Murray said. They also perfected their recipe for the **Champa Tampa** cocktail, an inexpensive alternative to the hard drugs they couldn't afford at the time. In 1977, after **Chevy Chase** left *Saturday Night Live*, Belushi lobbied for Murray's addition to the cast. Belushi and Murray both appeared in the films *Shame of the Jungle* and *All You Need Is Cash*, though they never shared any scenes together. After Belushi's tragic **death** from a drug overdose in 1982, Murray delivered a memorable eulogy at his memorial service. He later incorporated his funeral remarks verbatim into a scene in *The Razor's Edge*. In 1984, Murray replaced Belushi in the lead role in *Ghostbusters*.

BILL MURRAY'S CELEBRITY CORNER

Recurring *Saturday Night Live* segment that served as a showcase for Murray's smarmy, stargazing movie-critic character. Murray first performed *Celebrity Corner* on the October 14, 1978, show hosted by Fred Willard. The character was rumored to be modeled on TV entertainment reporter David Sheehan, although Murray has always denied it. "A lot of people talk like the *Celebrity Corner* guy," Murray said in a 1979 interview. "I can do him for hours. He's the reviewer who puts himself on a first-name basis with the stars, who don't know him from Adam. . . . He's the guy who'll say, 'You're fabulous, you're the greatest.' The guy who goes on a talk show and interrupts when another guest is introduced, 'Excuse me for a second . . . can I say something about this man right here, he is so terrific.' In the meantime he's taken up a whole segment." One of Murray's most popular *SNL* characters, the *Celebrity Corner* host provided a vehicle for the actor to vent his hatred of **critics**.

BOOGIE NIGHTS

Murray turned down the role of adult film director Jack Horner in this 1997 movie about a well-endowed porn star. Sydney Pollack, Albert Brooks, Harvey Keitel, and Warren Beatty also passed on the part, which earned Burt Reynolds an Oscar nomination for best supporting actor.

BOTTLE ROCKET

Murray was director **Wes Anderson**'s first choice for the role of small-time crook/landscaper Abe Henry in this idiosyncratic 1996 caper film starring Luke and Owen Wilson. But Murray was traveling the country in a Winnebago at the time the film was being cast and never saw the screenplay. "I had agents then who had never heard of [Anderson]," Murray said, "so that script never got to me, because as far as they were concerned I was a movie star and this was some kid from Texas." The part eventually went to James Caan instead.

After *Bottle Rocket* became an indie sensation, Murray found himself bombarded with VHS copies of the film from associates imploring him to work with Anderson. "I have the largest single collection of *Bottle Rocket* videotapes in the world," Murray later claimed. Though he never watched them, the buzz was enough to persuade him to read Anderson's next script, *Rushmore*, and take the part that ushered in his late-'90s career renaissance.

BOY SCOUTS OF AMERICA

As a child, Murray was so unruly that he was kicked out of the Boy Scouts before even being issued a uniform.

BREAKFAST CLUB, THE

Murray is a big fan of director John Hughes's 1985 comedy about five high school misfits who spend a Saturday in detention together. He has called *The Breakfast Club* "an American gem, an amazing film, as important as any of Marty [Scorsese]'s movies. It's just a real fuckin' piece. And those kids were never better than that, and [Hughes] let 'em roll."

BROKEN FLOWERS

DIRECTED BY: Jim Jarmusch
WRITTEN BY: Jim Jarmusch
RELEASE DATE: August 5, 2005
FILM RATING: ★★
MURRAY RATING: ★★

PLOT: An aging lothario canvasses his ex-lovers in search of the son he never knew.

STARRING BILL MURRAY AS: Don Johnston, jaded rake

Completing the informal "sad middle-aged man" trilogy that began so promisingly with *Lost in Translation* and *The Life Aquatic with Steve Zissou*, Murray finally hit the wall with the torpid *Broken Flowers*. Playing an over-the-hill ladies' man named Don Johnston (Don Juan—get it?), Murray delivers an infuriatingly affectless performance. His impassive character makes Steve Zissou look like Sam Kinison. Directed by Jim Jarmusch, with his customary paint-drying languor, *Broken Flowers* is one of the most heartbreaking misfires in Murray's filmography—a movie that could have been great in the hands of a filmmaker more attuned to the importance of story and pacing.

Although an aspiring screenwriter would later claim in a lawsuit that

Broken Flowers, 2005

Jarmusch stole the idea for the film from him, the indie auteur maintained in interviews that he fashioned *Broken Flowers* as a showcase for the melancholic pole of Murray's personality. "I wanted to create a character where he wasn't reliant on things we expect or know or appreciate from Bill Murray," Jarmusch told *Movies Online*. "I wanted that other side." For his part, Murray was intrigued by the film's novel premise, which has Johnston setting out on a road trip to reconnect with four former flames. "Just the very thought of someone my age going to visit old girlfriends had instant appeal," Murray told the *Guardian*. "Even women think, 'That would be interesting.' Not comfortable, but interesting. It is not a comfortable film at any point."

Murray was entranced by the script but reluctant to commit to the project until Jarmusch promised him he could shoot the entire film within one hour of his house in New York's Hudson Valley. Since Jarmusch had a home in the Catskills, finding locations amenable to both men proved to be easy. Keeping the star on set at all times was not. One day, Murray wandered off and barged into a private home next door to the house where they were filming. He emerged ten minutes later with a plateful of cookies for the crew.

In an interview conducted for the Cinema.com website, Jarmusch compared working with Murray to capturing the attention of a small child: "If you sit down with some crayons and a coloring book and say, 'Look, Bill, I'm coloring. Isn't it fun?' he's not interested. But if you sit down and ignore him and you're coloring and he comes over and says, 'What are you doing?' And you say, 'Ehhh, I'm coloring.' He's like, 'Oh, can I color?' 'Yeah, let's color.'"

While *Broken Flowers* impressed **critics**—scoring the coveted Grand Prix at the 2005 Cannes Film Festival—even Murray seemed to sense that his days of playing fiftysomething sad sacks were coming to an end. Or perhaps he just felt he had left it all on the playing field. After *Broken Flowers* premiered, he considered retiring from show business entirely. "I thought that was as good as I could do and I should stop," he said. He would not play the lead in another live-action film until 2012. Fortunately for him, and the world, he reconsidered retirement in time to make *Garfield: A Tail of Two Kitties* barely a year later.

NEXT MOVIE: *The Lost City* (2006)

BUTLER, JENNIFER "JENNY"

Murray met his second wife, a Hollywood costume designer, on the set of *Scrooged* in 1988. At the time he was still married to his first wife. At Murray's insistence, Butler went on to work as a costumer on *Ghostbusters II* and *What about Bob?* and as a costume designer on *Groundhog Day*. Following the formal dissolution of Murray's first **marriage** in 1996, the couple married on July 1, 1997. Three days before their wedding, they signed a $7 million pre-nuptial agreement. Murray sired four sons by Butler between 1993 and 2001.

But the later years of their marriage were marked by rancor, attributed in press accounts to Murray's frequent travel. On May 12, 2008, Butler filed for divorce, citing her husband's "adultery, addiction to marijuana and alcohol, abusive behavior, physical abuse, sexual addictions and frequent abandonment." She alleged that he threatened to kill her, left menacing voicemail messages on her phone, and frequently left the country without notifying her for the purpose of engaging in "public and private altercations and sexual liaisons." While divorce proceedings wended their way through the court, a judge issued a restraining order barring Murray from the family home. The divorce was finalized on June 13. Butler was awarded custody of the children, and Murray was granted visitation rights and compelled to pay child support. Murray later called his split with his second wife "devastating" and "the worst thing that ever happened to me in my entire life."

> "I'VE HAD A GREAT DEAL OF SUCCESS IN LIFE. I'VE LEARNED HOW TO LIVE AND I THINK I'VE LEARNED THINGS ABOUT LIVING. IT'S ALMOST LIKE: 'OKAY, YOU LEARNED THAT MUCH, NOW LET'S TRY THIS. LET'S SEE HOW YOU CAN DO IF *THIS* HAPPENS TO YOU.'"
>
> —MURRAY, on the painful dissolution of his second marriage

TALES FROM
MURRAYLAND

№ 2

The Night He Crashed
the *Tommy* Premiere Party

Accompanied by his brother Brian, Murray crashed the lavish opening night party for the film version of the Who's rock opera, held on March 18, 1975, in the mezzanine of a New York City subway station. *Tommy* producer Robert Stigwood organized the bash, which cost $35,000 and attracted more than seven hundred A-list guests, including pallid pop artist Andy Warhol and twitchy *Psycho* actor Anthony Perkins. Mounted New York City police officers escorted partygoers via red carpet from the Ziegfeld Theater, where the movie premiered, to the dilapidated 57th Street station (best known to TV viewers for its appearance in the opening credits of the 1970s sitcom *Rhoda*). The Fellini-esque spread included fifty pounds of octopus flown up from the Bahamas, six hundred oysters, five thirty-pound lobsters, and several one-hundred-pound rounds of roast beef. On a buffet table near the subway entrance, the name Tommy was spelled out in three thousand cherry tomatoes. "We had no business being at this thing," Murray said later, "but we knew the guys in the kitchen. It was a party in the subway!"

CADDYING

As a teenager, Murray worked as a caddy at the upscale **Indian Hill Club** in Winnetka, Illinois. He made $3.50 for each "loop," or **golf** bag, carried. On a busy Saturday, he could usually do two eighteen-hole loops carrying two bags at a time, for a total take of $14. He received an extra 25 cents per loop if he got rained on. Golfers were discouraged from giving gratuities, although Murray often lobbied for tips by telling them he was paying his way through school—which he was. He used the money he made at Indian Hill to cover his tuition at **Loyola Academy**, a private Jesuit high school.

Murray first signed on at Indian Hill at age ten, following in the footsteps of his brothers Ed and Brian. (For years, he was known around the golf course as the "**New Murray**.") Before working his way up to caddy, he spent time as a "shag boy," retrieving practice drives for duffers for sixty cents an hour. "A guy would hit balls and you'd run out and collect them," he told *Sports Illustrated* magazine. "You were basically a human target."

Caddying, Murray told an interviewer, provided "my first glimpse of comedy. When you see grown men near to tears because they've missed hitting a little white ball into a hole from three feet, it makes you laugh." The experience also kindled his nascent class consciousness. "The kids who were members of the club were despicable," he once said. "You couldn't believe the attitude they had. I mean, you were literally walking barefoot in a T-shirt and jeans, carrying some privileged person's sports toys on your back for five miles." In a 2014 interview with radio host Howard Stern, Murray called his caddying days "a great education. . . . You learned a lot about how you wanted to be treated and you learned how to treat people by seeing how these people treated you."

> ## "WE DIDN'T HAVE COWS TO MILK SO YOU HAD TO GO CADDY."
>
> —MURRAY, on why he followed his older brothers into the family business

CADDYSHACK

DIRECTED BY: Harold Ramis

WRITTEN BY: Douglas Kenney, Harold Ramis, and Brian Doyle-Murray

RELEASE DATE: July 25, 1980

FILM RATING: ★ ★ ★ ⟩

MURRAY RATING: ★ ★ ★ ★

PLOT: Snobs take on slobs in a battle for the soul of a tony golf and country club.

STARRING BILL MURRAY AS: Carl Spackler, assistant greenskeeper and future Masters champion

Fresh off the set of *Where the Buffalo Roam* and about to start work on his final season of *Saturday Night Live*, Murray could spare only six days of his schedule to work on this anarchic golf comedy from the *Animal House* creative team of **Harold Ramis** and Doug Kenney. But what a week it was. Although critically derided on its release, *Caddyshack* became one of the defining films of Murray's career and a bona fide pop culture phenomenon. It wound up vastly outperforming the more ambitious *Buffalo* at the box office, setting the stage for far more lucrative Murray ventures in the 1980s.

As every sentient American moviegoer knows by now, *Caddyshack* transplants *Animal House*'s "snobs versus slobs" conflict to the tony environs of Bushwood Country Club. Murray plays **Carl Spackler**, the deranged assistant greenskeeper who wages a counterinsurgency campaign against a mischievous boogying gopher bent on destroying the club's golf course. Ramis directed, from a script he cowrote with Kenney and Murray's brother Brian. The screenplay drew heavily on the Murray siblings' experiences as caddies at the **Indian Hill Club** in Winnetka, Illinois. The character of Danny Noonan, the young looper who dreams of going to college on a caddy scholarship, was based on Murray's brother Ed, who did win such a scholarship. In fact, Murray has called *Caddyshack* "the gripping tale of the Murray brothers' first experiments with employment."

In early drafts, *Caddyshack* started out as a coming-of-age film centered on Danny Noonan and the other caddies, with a class warfare subtext inspired in part by British director Lindsay Anderson's *If....* The finished film deemphasized Noonan and tamped down the Marxist overtones,

Caddyshack, 1980

to Murray's chagrin. "The movie was knowledgeable about golf," he told the *New York Times Magazine* in 1988, "but it should have had more about the stratification of country club life."

To embody that stratification in the broadest possible way, Ramis cast two show business veterans: stand-up comedy legend Rodney Dangerfield (a late substitute for the director's first choice, Don Rickles) as vulgar condo developer Al Czervik; and *Mary Tyler Moore Show* stalwart Ted Knight (stepping in for Jason Robards) as pompous Judge Elihu Smails. Michael O'Keefe, a scratch golfer, played Noonan. (Fresh off an acclaimed performance in *The Great Santini*, O'Keefe was thought to be a safer choice than the other finalist, Mickey Rourke.) Murray's *Saturday Night Live* bête noire Chevy Chase rounded out the main cast as the Zen-spouting golf prodigy Ty Webb, with Doyle-Murray in a supporting role as caddymaster Lou Loomis, a character based on the Murray brothers' real-life loop whisperer, Lou Janis.

> ## "THEY GAVE ME THIS GREAT GREEN LINCOLN CONTINENTAL RENT-A-CAR WITH GREEN UPHOLSTERY, AND BACK THEN THERE WAS NO ONE LIVING IN FLORIDA SO YOU COULD DRIVE AT 90, AND GET REALLY HAMMERED. IT WAS A GOOD TIME TO BE AN AMERICAN."
> —MURRAY, on the experience of filming *Caddyshack* in 1979

Caddyshack was shot over eleven weeks during the late summer and early fall of 1979 at the Rolling Hills Golf and Tennis Club in Davie, Florida. The location was chosen principally for the lack of visible palm trees—the better to stand in for suburban Chicago. The budget was $6 million, the vast majority of which seems to have gone for drugs and alcohol. Cast and crew reportedly plowed through eighty grams of cocaine a week, part of a rolling orgy of overindulgence unseen since the days of Caligula. "Debauchery reigned every night," producer Jon Peters reported in his memoir.

Murray showed up in the midst of the bacchanal, at the last minute, reportedly after some haggling over the profit points in his contract. He immediately left an indelible mark on the production. On his first day on set, he filmed the legendary "Dalai Lama" speech, in which Carl waxes rhapsodic about the Tibetan holy man while menacing a caddy with a pitchfork. Other iconic scenes would follow: the classic "Cinderella Story" speech where Carl mock-narrates his miraculous victory at the Masters championship; and a bizarre encounter between Carl and Ty Webb in Carl's ramshackle greenskeeper's quarters. (Murray provided much of the decor for Carl's "apartment" himself.)

This last scene sprung from a note given by Peters to Ramis bemoaning the absence of a scene pairing Murray and Chase, two of the biggest comedy stars on the planet. Apparently Peters was unaware the two actors had recently come to blows backstage at *Saturday Night Live*. "I was never told that they shouldn't be on the set at the same time," said production executive Mark Canton, "but I think that they chose not to be on the set at the same time. They were not the best of friends. Everyone seemed to know it."

Somehow Murray and Chase were able to put aside their mutual antipathy and bulldog their way through the scene, which ended up being one of the film's most memorable. With Ramis's help, they sketched out a premise over lunch—Ty "plays through" Carl's place during a nighttime round of golf—and shot it later that afternoon. Like most of the best moments in

Caddyshack, the sequence was almost entirely improvised. "I just reacted to whatever he did," Chase remembered later. "I had no idea that Billy was going to go through the rap about being able to smoke the grass. Chinch bugs? I'd never heard of a chinch bug. The pond line. It all made sense. It took a lot to keep a straight face in that scene."

Today it is considered a minor classic, but *Caddyshack* received decidedly mixed reviews upon its July 1980 release. *New York* magazine's critic David Denby called it "a perfectly amiable mess, an undistinguished summer diversion." He slammed Murray in particular as "more of a nut brain solipsist than actor." The reviewer for the *Boston Globe* railed that "*Caddyshack* represents everything that is wrong with contemporary film comedy. It relies on stock television characters and a stale sitcom style. It is an unoriginal pastiche of other slapstick farces such as *Meatballs*, and it presupposes an audience with the collective intelligence of a lobotomized ape."

On the *Today* show, mustachioed movie maven Gene Shalit called Murray "wearisome" and the film "a sketchy bramble of golfers, caddies, and country clubs." *Newsweek*'s David Ansen predicted *Caddyshack* "will be of interest only to the actors' **agents**." The *New York Times*'s Vincent Canby was more charitable, writing of Murray's performance: "You don't for a minute believe him—you are always aware of the distance between the performer and the performance, but you appreciate the effort and the intelligence behind it."

Caddyshack's poor critical reception can be attributed in part to a disastrous press junket that Murray took part in the morning after the film's initial screening. Appearing on stage with his costars at Rodney Dangerfield's eponymous comedy club in **New York City**, an unshaven, surly, and apparently hungover Murray gave clipped answers to the assembled entertainment journalists. Even worse, screenwriter Doug Kenney loudly proclaimed his hatred for the film and told everyone in the audience—including his own parents—to "fuck off." "We were so poorly behaved," Harold Ramis said later. "We didn't create a popular rooting interest for the film. Someone wrote, 'If this is the New Hollywood, let's have the Old Hollywood back.'"

Although it failed to replicate the success of *Animal House*, *Caddyshack* did fare well at the box office, grossing nearly $40 million in the face of stiff competition from the likes of *The Blues Brothers*, *Airplane!*, and *Smokey and the Bandit II*. Over the ensuing decades, the film's reputation has only grown, fueled in part by its popularity among professional athletes and recreational golfers. For Murray, that has been something of a mixed blessing. "I can walk on a golf course, and some guy will be screaming entire scenes at me and expecting me to do it word for word with him," he said. "It's like: 'Fella, I did that once. I improvised that scene. I don't remember how it goes.' But I'm charmed by it. I'm not like, 'Hey, knock it off.' It's kind of cool."

One person who never shared the public's love for *Caddyshack* was its director, Harold Ramis. "I can barely watch it," he once said. "All I see are a bunch of compromises and things that could have been better. Like, it bothers me that nobody except Michael O'Keefe can swing a golf club. A movie about golf with the worst bunch of golf swings you've ever seen!"

NEXT MOVIE: *Loose Shoes* (1980)

CAINE MUTINY COURT MARTIAL, THE

As a high school senior, Murray played Lieutenant Thomas Keefer in the **Loyola Academy** Drama Club's production of this play based on Herman Wouk's Pulitzer Prize–winning 1952 novel. Keefer is an officer aboard the USS *Caine*, a U.S. Navy minesweeper whose crew revolts against the tyrannical Captain Queeg. In a 1984 interview, Murray described his character as "a sleaze guy who rats on everybody." "It wasn't much of a part," he recalled of his first dramatic acting experience. "The only great thing about it was that you got to get out of class for a few hours, and that was like getting a three-day leave in the army, because class was hell."

CANDY, JOHN

Larger-than-life comic actor who played Private Dewey "Ox" Oxberger in *Stripes*. Candy also appeared with Murray on a 1982 episode of *SCTV* and was offered the part of Louis Tully in *Ghostbusters*. The two **Second City** veterans remained close friends until Candy's **death** in 1994.

Candy and Murray joined the Chicago branch of Second City the same week in 1973. At the time, the troupe was known by the nickname the Seven Giant Goyim, because everyone in the cast was a gentile over six feet tall. The two neophytes often appeared together in scenes because, Murray claimed, no one else in the cast wanted to work with them. Murray later described their improv collaborations as "endless death, incredible death." A typical sketch, set in a delicatessen in India called the "New Deli" was, in Murray's words, "the dumbest thing I've ever been part of."

While they may not have clicked on stage, Murray and Candy became fast friends off it. The Chicago-area native took the Canadian-born Candy under his wing. "He was a wonderful tour guide," Candy once said. "He took me all over the city, showed me every landmark—we'd have a hamburger at the original McDonald's, a pancake at the first International House of Pancakes. We went to every weird, seedy area imaginable. He'd always say, 'This is my town, and this can be your town, too!' When we'd go to Wrigley Field, he knew every Cubs player that had ever lived."

In 1980, when Canadian diplomats gave safe harbor to six Americans trying to evade capture during the Iran hostage crisis—a rescue mission dramatized in the Oscar-winning film *Argo*—Murray called Candy at four o'clock in the morning to personally thank him for being a Canadian.

CAPE FEAR

Murray was director Steven Spielberg's first choice for the role of Max Cady, the vengeful ex-con, in his proposed early-1990s remake of the classic 1962 thriller. When Spielberg's friend Martin Scorsese took over the project, Robert De Niro won the role and with it an Oscar nomination for best actor.

CARAY, HARRY

Legendary **Chicago Cubs** play-by-play announcer, known for his predilection for Budweiser and his spaced-out affect. Caray welcomed Murray into the broadcast booth on many occasions, including the first night game at Wrigley Field, held on August 8, 1988. During their on-air conversations, Caray would invariably ask after the health of Murray's mother. According to Caray's broadcast partner Steve Stone in his book *Where's Harry?*, Caray kept on doing so even after **Lucille Murray** died. "Bill, how's your mom doing up there in Wilmette?" Caray asked Murray the very next time he came up to the booth. "Well, she's dead, Harry," Murray replied. "And don't ask me about my father, because he's dead too."

When Caray suffered a stroke in the spring of 1987, Murray was one of several **Chicago**-area natives—including Jim Belushi, George Wendt, and Tom Bosley—who filled in for him on WGN TV broadcasts. Murray's turn in the booth came on April 17, 1987. He prepared for the telecast by watching the other guest announcers and ignoring their example:

"I saw that these people were trying to be broadcasters. And I thought, 'What the hell?' That's not how I would do it. So I made the decision

> ## "THAT WAS A GREAT PIECE OF WORK. THAT WAS THE PEAK OF MY PERFORMING CAREER. THAT WAS THE PEAK—WHAT I WAS BORN FOR."
>
> —MURRAY, on the day he spent filling in for Harry Caray in the Chicago Cubs broadcast booth

to do it as a *fan*, calling it like a person would sitting in front of his TV. I was very fortunate. The Cubs had lost every game of the season so far, at the start of the season. I asked my friend if he had any suggestions for me, and he said, 'Well, you know what T. S. Eliot said. April is the cruelest month.' So that's how I started the broadcast. It's always true of the Cubs, they were always brutalized in the first month of the season. And a huge umpire named Eric Gregg—his equipment didn't show up. So they had to find some equipment for him, and what they found came from, like, a local high school. So this 220-pound guy comes out wearing a chest protector and shin guards of a high school kid. It looked hilarious. That was good for another fifteen, twenty minutes. I couldn't get enough of it. And then the Cubs won the game, on top of it. I also noticed under the desk, Harry Caray had a cooler there, his own refrigerator, and it was full of beer. So I started pulling out all this beer."

For the record, the Cubs defeated the Montreal Expos that day 7–0.

CATS

Murray is allergic to cats. During a 2014 appearance on *The Ellen DeGeneres Show*, he admitted that he once taught himself hypnosis in an effort to surmount his aversion to felines. "I read someplace that allergies are psychosomatic and you can actually hypnotize yourself and overcome the allergy," Murray said. "So I used to do that. I used to go to girls' houses and they had cats and all of a sudden I'd be looking at them crying and they'd be like, 'What did I say?' and I'd go, 'No, it's not you!' So I learned to hypnotize myself and get over it. But then I decided I didn't really like cats that much, so I stopped. I'm more of a dog guy." Murray only rarely interacted with cats on screen until 2014's *St. Vincent*, where his character cares for a cantankerous Persian named Felix. The two cats playing Felix, Teddy and Jagger, were kept meticulously groomed throughout the shoot to keep dander to a minimum.

CELTIC PRIDE

Murray claims this 1996 basketball comedy is the only Judd Apatow movie he's ever seen. Cowritten by Apatow and Colin Quinn, *Celtic Pride* stars **Dan Aykroyd** and Daniel Stern as a pair of rabid Boston Celtics fans who kidnap a star player for the Utah Jazz. Murray was not impressed by the film. "It's just brutal! Totally brutal," he once said. "And Danny's in it! Danny doesn't even know how many players are on a team in basketball. And he's in this movie? Oh my Jesus mercy."

CHAMPA TAMPA

Champagne and orange juice cocktail favored by Murray and roommate **John Belushi** during their time in the touring cast of *The National Lampoon Show*. The struggling performers saw the Champa Tampa as a less expensive alternative to hard drugs, which they couldn't afford. "We didn't have the money [for cocaine]," Murray told *Rolling Stone* magazine. Basically, we were juicers at the time." Murray has described the energizing libation as "a great drink to work on because it's got that sugar pump, and it's nice and cold."

See also **Montana Cooler.**

CHARIOTS OF FIRE

Oscar-winning 1981 historical drama about anti-Semitism and class conflict among British track-and-field athletes at the 1924 Olympics. The film is known for its majestic instrumental theme, composed by Greek synthesizer maestro Vangelis. On the set of *Nothing Lasts Forever* in 1982, Murray improvised his own lyrics to Vangelis's title theme:

They run by the ocean
They run by the shore
They run almost as fast as a chariot of fire!

CHARLIE AND THE CHOCOLATE FACTORY

Murray was among a who's who of A-list actors considered for the role of Willy Wonka in the second big-screen adaptation of Roald Dahl's classic children's novel. Nicolas Cage, Jim Carrey, and Christopher Walken were also in contention to play the mercurial candy magnate. Johnny Depp wound up with the part.

CHARLIE'S ANGELS

DIRECTED BY: McG

WRITTEN BY: Ryan Rowe, Ed Solomon, and John August

RELEASE DATE: November 3, 2000

FILM RATING: ★★

MURRAY RATING: ★★

PLOT: An elite crime-fighting team searches for a kidnapped software tycoon.

STARRING BILL MURRAY AS: John Bosley, Charlie's factotum

After several years in the indie wilderness, Murray returned to Popcornland with this slick, soulless big-screen reboot of the 1970s television series about three gorgeous female superagents. Directed by music video veteran Joseph McGinty Nichol, or "McG," as he prefers to style himself, *Charlie's Angels* is about as far from *Rushmore* as you can get without leaving Earth's orbit entirely. That Murray said yes to this cartoonish film speaks either to his boredom with lo-fi prestige projects or to his keen commercial instincts. Not surprisingly, an aggressively stupid action comedy headlined by the beautiful but talent-deficient trio of Drew Barrymore, Cameron Diaz, and Lucy Liu turned out to be a smash hit at the box office.

To its credit, *Charlie's Angels* doesn't pretend to be anything more than it is—a loud, leering smash-'em-up pitched at hormonal teenage boys with attention deficit disorder. Murray "plays" John Bosley, the buffoonish retainer originated by David Doyle in the TV version. While it is mildly amusing to

Charlie's Angels, 2000

watch him flounce around in loud clothes and a bad toupee, there is nothing distinctively "Bill Murray" about this thankless sidekick. Anyone could have played Bosley—a fact that became evident three years later when Bernie Mac replaced Murray in the sequel *Charlie's Angels: Full Throttle.*

In interviews, Murray has insisted his unwillingness to sign on to the follow-up had nothing to do with his legendary on-set clashes with McG and Lucy Liu. But given the ferocity of those dust-ups, that is hard to believe. In a 2009 article in the *Guardian,* McG revealed that Murray had head-butted him during a physical altercation on the set. "An inch later and my nose would have been obliterated," the director claimed. Murray later dismissed the charge. "That's bullshit! That's complete crap!" he railed. "I don't know why he made that story up. He has a very active imagination. . . . He deserves to die!" He went on to say that McG "should be pierced with a lance, not head-butted" for fabricating the incident.

As for Liu, the story goes that Murray stopped work midscene and pointed to Barrymore, Diaz, and Liu in turn, saying: "I get why you're here . . . and you've got talent . . . but what in the hell are you doing here? You can't act!" Liu reportedly flew into a rage and physically accosted Murray. The two had to be separated and sent to opposite ends of the set to cool off.

According to Murray, however, that's not quite how it happened. "We began rehearsing this scene and I said, 'Lucy, how can you want to say these lines? These are so crazy,'" he told *Access Hollywood*. "She got furious with me because she thought it was a personal assault, but the reality is she hated these lines as much as I did. But for fifteen or twenty minutes there, we went to our separate corners and threw hand grenades and sky rockets at each other. We made peace and I got to know her better from that day."

In Lucy Liu's version, the entire confrontation was blown out of proportion by the press, amounting to nothing more than "a creative difference about the script"—one of many that plagued the production. "They had a scene for me and they had written it in a certain way," she told an audience at San Diego Comic Con in 2002. "[Bill] came in and obviously he's a talented writer and he's very smart, and he had a writer that he was working with as well. . . . It wasn't that big of a deal. If I had punched him or anything, I would have remembered."

Whatever the truth of these encounters, by the time 2003 rolled around Murray wanted nothing to do with the *Charlie's Angels* sequel. He declined another go-round as Bosley, citing an unnamed enemy in the ranks. "That same person was going to be involved in the second one," he said, "so I wasn't going to show up again."

NEXT MOVIE: *Osmosis Jones* (2001)

CHARTREUSE

French liqueur favored by Murray in recent years. Made from a centuries-old recipe crafted by Carthusian monks, Chartreuse is distinguished by its high alcohol content and lime green color.

CHASE, CORNELIUS "CHEVY"

Glib comic writer and performer whose 1976 departure for Hollywood paved the way for Murray to join the cast of *Saturday Night Live*. Murray and Chase famously brawled backstage before the show's February 18, 1978, episode, Chase's first time back as guest host. According to multiple published reports, Murray personally called out Chase after learning how badly he had treated the other *SNL* cast members during his year and a half on the show. Chase responded by comparing Murray's acne scars to the craters of the moon. "Why don't you fuck your wife once in a while?" Murray taunted. "She needs it." A rolling fistfight ensued, which had to be broken up by Murray's brother Brian moments before Chase went on stage to start the show. "It was really a Hollywood fight," Murray later confessed to an interviewer for *Empire* magazine. "A 'Don't touch my face!' kind of thing. . . . So it was kind of a nonevent. It was just the significance of it. It was an oedipal thing, a rupture. Because we all felt mad he had left us, and somehow I was the

(CONTINUED ON PAGE 46)

TALES FROM
MURRAYLAND

Nº 3	The Day He Crashed Elvis's Funeral

On August 16, 1977, Elvis Presley died in his Memphis mansion. Two days later, he was laid to rest next to his mother at nearby Forest Hill Cemetery. A crowd of nearly eighty thousand fans gathered along the processional route in ninety-degree heat to pay their last respects to the King of Rock 'n' Roll. Numerous celebrities attended the funeral, including Caroline Kennedy, Ann-Margret, George Hamilton—and a junior member of the *Saturday Night Live* cast named Bill Murray. He had not been invited.

Murray was the twenty-seventh person on standby for the last flight out of New York to Memphis on the night of August 17. He made it onto the plane only because several celebrities who said they were going—including Sammy Davis Jr., Farrah Fawcett, Burt Reynolds, and John Wayne—failed to show up. When he embarked, he found a jet full of A-listers that was eerily silent. A couple hours later, the Elvis Funeral Express touched down in Tennessee.

The next morning, Murray took a cab to Graceland for the start of the service. He found Elvis's home jam-packed with mourners—more than thirty thousand of whom were allowed inside to view the King's body one last time. Paparazzi drifted in and out, desperately trying to snap pictures of Elvis lying in state. Security guards confiscated cameras as fast as the photographers could whip them out. After several hours, the gates were closed and the crowd escorted out so that the procession to the cemetery could begin.

Murray and the other celebrities were herded into a press bus that drove ahead of the slow-moving hearse. All along the road, Elvis fans held up homemade signs bidding goodbye to the fallen rock icon: "God Bless You, Elvis," they read. "The King Lives," "Long Live the King," "We Will Miss You." Murray believed he could feel the presence of Elvis's spirit all around. As he watched the hearse pass by the assembled throngs, "like a swan gliding down the road," he was moved to tears.

When the cortege arrived at the cemetery, the scene was more chaotic. A group of overzealous mourners tried to storm the rear gate. Murray jumped out of the press bus and started running toward the scene of the riot. He was greeted by the arriving hearse, flanked by a phalanx of two dozen motorcycle police officers. One cop turned to Murray and froze him in his tracks with a look that said, "If you move, I will shoot you right through the heart." As Murray stumbled backward, he realized he was standing on Elvis's mother's grave.

Dazed, Murray watched as the pallbearers lifted Elvis's enormous casket and carried it up the steps to the mausoleum. They staggered from the weight of it, nearly dropping it. The massive metal box was festooned with hundreds of roses, which shook loose with each uncertain step, drawing gasps from the crowds. Murray managed to grab one of the flowers to take with him on his trip back to New York. With the casket at last in place inside the crypt, Presley's widow, Priscilla, left the cemetery. So too, Murray felt, did Elvis's spirit.

After the burial, Murray returned to Graceland for one last look at Elvis's palatial home, which was soon to be turned into a museum. In a surreal coda to his funeral experience, a banged-up car with Michigan plates and a bad muffler rolled up beside him as he stood outside the mansion gates. The driver leaned out the window and asked, "Is there gonna be a reception?"

anointed avenging angel who had to speak for everyone." Murray and Chase later patched up their differences and worked together amicably on the set of *Caddyshack* in 1979.

CHEERS

Murray is not a fan of the classic 1980s sitcom about the denizens of a Boston bar. "I never really got it," he said.

CHICAGO

Murray grew up in **Wilmette, Illinois**, just outside Chicago. He once jokingly called his adopted hometown "the greatest city on Lake Michigan." In a 2008 interview with the *Chicago Tribune*, Murray listed a few must-see Chicago-area attractions he always recommends to tourists:

"I always tell them they have to get a cheeseburger over at the Billy Goat. I tell them, if they are downtown by Navy Pier, there's going to be fireworks. I tell them to see the Bean [*Cloud Gate*]; I love the spitting fountain. I tell them to go to the Original House of Pancakes in Wilmette. See the Baha'i Temple as well. Obviously Wrigley Field is on the trip, they have to see that. If there's a way they can just drive around in the Loop at sunset around the river and just see the light ricocheting off all those buildings, it's spectacular."

CHICAGO CUBS

Murray has been a passionate fan of **Chicago**'s North Side **baseball** team since he was a boy. "My passion for the Chicago Cubs is as deep as the green of the Chicago River on St. Patrick's Day," he once said. "It's a deep, deep color. Except that it's blue." Murray had the Cubs team logo painted on the floor of the swimming pool at his mansion in Palisades, New York.

Murray attended his first Cubs game when he was seven years old. Having seen Wrigley Field only on a black-and-white TV until then, he found the experience revelatory: "My brother Brian said, 'Wait, Billy,' and he put his hands over my eyes, and he walked me up the stairs. And then he took his hands away. And there was Wrigley Field, in green. There was this beautiful grass and this beautiful ivy. . . . It was like I was a blind man made to see. It was something." Around the same time, Cubs first baseman Dale Long bought a house a few doors down from the Murray home in **Wilmette, Illinois**.

Since achieving national celebrity in the late 1970s, Murray has been a fixture at Cubs games from coast to coast. He

> ## "THEY HAD THE PRETTIEST BALLPARK. AND THEY HAD ERNIE BANKS."
>
> —MURRAY, on why he became a Chicago Cubs fan

"I THROW A CHRISTMAS PARTY AT MY HOUSE. IT'S NOT REALLY A CHRISTMAS PARTY, BECAUSE I DON'T WANT TO CALL IT A CHRISTMAS PARTY. BUT LET'S JUST SAY I PUT A LOT OF CHRISTMAS TREES AROUND THE HOUSE, SO IT SMELLS GOOD."

—MURRAY, on his personal end-of-year holiday tradition

filled in for ailing play-by-play announcer **Harry Caray** in 1987 and led the Wrigley crowd through a spirited rendition of "Take Me Out to the Ballgame" at the club's home opener in 2012. In 1989, during a Cubs–Mets game at Shea Stadium in New York, Murray leaned over the edge of the visiting dugout and tried to hand a beer and some Cajun fries to pitcher Rick Sutcliffe. Sutcliffe declined the offer. "At least take the fries," Murray said, and then proceeded to eat them.

When he agreed to star in *The Life Aquatic with Steve Zissou* in 2003, Murray had it written into his contract that he would receive a live satellite feed of every Cubs game while on location in Italy.

CHRISTMAS

The yuletide season has always been fraught for Murray, whose parents couldn't afford to buy expensive Christmas presents for their nine children. "I never asked for toys," Murray admitted. "Asking for toys was out of the question; they were low priorities. It's not that we were denied anything so much as the fact that we knew not to make requests. For Christmas you got essentials: school clothes. Whenever toys surfaced at all, they were pretty much inherited."

Every December, Murray's parents gave him one dollar with orders to go to the dime store and buy something for each of his eight brothers and sisters. His siblings were issued the same instructions, resulting in a shambolic exchange of gifts on Christmas morning. Typical presents included a single battery (bestowed with the benediction "I hope you get something to put it in") or some paintbrushes and chalk (for the aspiring artist in the family). Often they were packaged so haphazardly they "resembled badly wrapped body parts," in Murray's words. **Brian Murray** once harvested scrap wood from his father's lumberyard, nailed it into blocks, and gave one to each of his siblings.

Bill Murray's own gift-giving nadir came on Christmas Day 1960. He purchased two pounds of peanuts, wrapped them in individual foil packets, and stashed them under the tree. "It was a terribly lazy move for a ten-year-old to pull," he remembered later. "I kept going in each day before Christmas and taking a few nuts from each package, so by the time the day rolled around the matter had grown disgraceful."

Three years later, Murray spent Christmas of his thirteenth year in a gloomy funk. "That was my 'unloved year,'" he told the *New York Times Magazine*. "I got everything I wanted, which was really only a clock radio, but I was in some sort of a state, going through a phase. They say the middle kid gets the least attention, but that can be accentuated in a house overrun with them. [My parents] gave me all these things, and I just sat there with a puppy dog's long face. Then I got even more attention because I wasn't happy. Then they got angry."

There were *some* happy times. Every Christmas Eve, the Murray kids clambered into the family car for a drive through Lincolnwood, a **Chicago** suburb known for its elaborate holiday light displays. But even after they grew up and moved away from home, the Murrays continued to keep some unusual holiday traditions alive. In a 2009 interview, Bill Murray revealed that his brother Brian has been buying him socks for Christmas for decades:

"He lived in a dry gulch where the world of socks and shoes became extremely fascinating, and he felt that everyone needs a good pair of socks, and why not limit his gift giving to something that everybody needs? He thought that there was something humorous about it. So he gives socks. The first year I had money, I really went shopping. I got really caught up in it. I bought all my brothers sets of luggage, and I bought 'em winter coats from Giorgio Armani— winter coats. And I got a pair of socks from this brother. I could tell by the look on his face that he was having a moment in front of himself, so I thought, Well, next year it'll change. But it didn't—he's continued to give socks."

See also **Christmas Tree**, "**Murray Christmas**."

CHRISTMAS TREE

In a 2014 interview with the *USA Today* website EntertainThis, comedian Chris Rock revealed that Murray maintains a "tricked out" Christmas tree outside his house year-round.

CIGARS

Murray is a longtime cigar smoker. He favored cheroots in the early 1990s and in recent years has become a devotee of Cuban cigars.

Murray smoked his first cigar at age thirteen while working as a caddy at **Indian Hill Club** in Winnetka, Illinois. "It was a broken cigar, thrown into a trash bin at the **golf** course," he told *Cigar Aficionado* magazine. "I remember seeing this cigar that hadn't been smoked, but it was broken in two pieces. And I thought, 'When I finish this round of **caddying**, I'm gonna walk back here and smoke it.' And I did. I don't remember the brand name, but I do remember it's hard to smoke a cigar that broken. And it was only when I got past the break that I found out what a cigar tastes like. But I liked that feeling."

That connection between golf and cigars persists to this day. The links remain one of Murray's favorite places to pass around the stogies. "People bring various levels of performance anxiety to the golf course," he says. "One of the things having smokes around

> ## "ONE OF THE PERKS OF BEING A MAN IS SMOKING A CIGAR."
>
> —MURRAY, on the pleasures of a good stogie

says is that, this experience is gonna be a lotta things, but not something so serious that you can't smoke a cigar."

As he's gotten older, Murray has cut back on his cigar consumption. But he still carries a few around, just in case he meets a fellow puffer. "I love just sharing cigars," he says. "I don't have to smoke 'em so much to enjoy 'em. . . . My favorite cigar is whichever one my friend is smoking, because I'll always say, 'I got some cigars. Which one would you like to smoke?' And he'll choose the one he'd like to smoke. And that's my thing—to me, it's something you do with someone. To me, it's not important that I smoke a cigar so long as someone does."

Another selling point for Murray is the lore and legend of cigar production. In 2010, he told the *New York Post* about his recent visit to the Padrón cigar factory in Miami, where he saw how some of his favorite hand-rolled Cuban-style cigars are made. "It's a family business, and their symbol is a hammer," Murray said. "Their grandfather came from Cuba—he was a refugee—and he went to another Cuban and said, 'Can you give me work? I gotta have a job.' And the guy said, 'I can't give you work, but I can give you a hammer.' And he gave him a hammer. And the guy went from house to house repairing and building. Within six months, he had somehow bought some tobacco and was rolling cigars out of the trunk of someone's car. Now they make a million cigars a year."

CINDERELLA STORY: MY LIFE IN GOLF

This 1999 book is the closest Murray has ever come to a proper autobiography. Written in collaboration with George Peper, then the editor-in-chief of *Golf* magazine, *Cinderella Story* combines reminiscences from Murray's **Wilmette, Illinois**, upbringing with anecdotes about his experiences on the pro-am **golf** circuit in the 1980s and '90s. Fittingly enough, Peper pitched the idea for the book to Murray on the driving range of the Sleepy Hollow Country Club near Murray's home in Palisades, New York. According to Murray's editor, Shawn Coyne, Murray sent in his chapters via fax, hastily—and often incorrectly—formatted: "They were written single-spaced and every letter was uppercase," Coyne said. "Somehow Bill had permanently locked the ALL CAPS button on his Pleistocene-age word processor."

CINNABON

Baked goods chain specializing in cinnamon rolls for which Murray has declared a predilection. "Everyone loves Cinnabons," he once told an interviewer.

CITY OF EMBER

DIRECTED BY: Gil Kenan

WRITTEN BY: Caroline Thompson

RELEASE DATE: October 10, 2008

FILM RATING: ★★⭒

MURRAY RATING: ★★★

PLOT: Two teenagers try to escape from a dystopian netherworld.

STARRING BILL MURRAY AS: Mayor Cole, gluttonous burgermeister of the city of Ember

In a rare villainous turn, Murray cranks his personal ham-o-meter up to eleven to play the venal, sardine-sucking ruler of an underground city in this postapocalyptic fantasy based on a popular young adult novel by Jeanne DuPrau. As Mayor Cole, Murray gets to wear a fat suit and cackle maniacally as he thwarts the efforts of the film's teenaged protagonists to save the citizens of Ember from encroaching darkness. In what is arguably his finest on-screen death scene, Murray's character is eaten alive by a giant mole.

Murray based his portrayal on a composite of all the corrupt politicians he encountered growing up in Illinois. "I'd hate to be selfish and pick just one," he told the *Chicago Tribune*. "There's no one that comes to mind.

City of Ember, 2008

They've all disappointed. They're like crack girls; no matter how attractive they are, they're going to break your heart." He also drew on his experience as a parent. "I think a mayor can be a father figure who can disappoint you," he said. "I'm a father figure and I've probably disappointed on occasion."

Murray was lured to the project by the prospect of working with screenwriter Caroline Thompson (*Edward Scissorhands*), with whom he partied in the early 1980s. "She works on a higher level than the rest," Murray told the *New York Daily News*. Murray's "gung-ho attitude" toward playing the heavy impressed director Gil Kenan, who foresaw Mayor Cole as heralding a turn toward new and more interesting character parts. "From my perspective, he's in a place where he's more open to things than he may have been in the past," said Kenan. "There's a lot in him. We've seen aspects of that on the screen now that he's had a career, but I actually feel like there's a lot more there that hasn't been seen."

Sadly, Murray's career as a big-screen baddie was to prove short-lived. Shot over sixteen weeks in the summer of 2007 in Belfast, Northern Island, *City of Ember* opened to considerable fanfare in the fall of 2008. But it failed to catch fire with audiences, grossing a paltry $3 million in its opening weekend. The film's grim steampunk mise-en-scène may have been slightly ahead of its time, while an inane online ad campaign featuring YouTube "celebrity" Lucas "Fred" Cruickshank appears to have driven away more moviegoers than it attracted.

NEXT MOVIE: *The Limits of Control* (2009)

CIVIC METROPOLITAN TRAUMA THEORY

Hypothesis developed by Murray that postulates that sports teams in cities that experience natural disasters are more likely to win championships.

CLOSE, DEL

Legendary improv teacher who coached Murray during his days at **Second City** in the mid-1970s. Murray has called Close's long-form improvisational techniques "the most important group work since they built the pyramids."

Born in Manhattan, Kansas, in 1934, Close spent much of his adult life in **Chicago**, where his improv students included **Dan Aykroyd**, **John Belushi**, Chris Farley, Mike Myers, Tina Fey, **Harold Ramis**, **John Candy**, and Stephen Colbert—as well as Murray's brothers Brian and Joel. "He was a guy who had great knowledge of the craft of improvisation," Murray told *Esquire* magazine. "And he lived life in a very rich manner, to excess sometimes. He had a whole lot of brain stuck inside of his skull. Beyond being gifted, he really engaged in life. He earned a lot. He made more of himself than he was given. . . . He was incredibly gracious to your talent and always tried to further it. He got people to perform beyond their expectations. He really believed that anyone could do it if they were present and showed respect. There was a whole lot of respect."

Hired by *Saturday Night Live* to serve as "house metaphysician," or improv coach, during the bleak 1980–81 season, Close battled ill health and substance abuse problems during the last two decades of his life. When he fell perilously behind on his taxes in the mid-1980s, Murray volunteered to pay his bill and refused Close's offers to reimburse him. "That guy is, and always will be, a friend and a gentleman," Close said. When Close was dying of emphysema in 1999, Murray was one of a select group of friends and former students to visit him in his hospital room to say goodbye. Close's decision to bequeath his skull to a Chicago theater for use in a production of *Hamlet* inspired Murray to muse publicly about doing the same with his own cranium after he dies.

In the mid-2000s, Harold Ramis wrote a screenplay for a proposed Del Close biopic, in which he hoped to convince Murray to star. The project never came to fruition.

CLUB PARADISE

Harold Ramis wrote the part of Jack Moniker, the lead in this 1986 comedy about a **Chicago** firefighter who retires to a Caribbean island, with Murray in mind. Monty Python's John Cleese was Ramis's choice for the role of Anthony Croyden Hayes, the British governor-general of the island. But both actors backed out of the project at the last minute. "When it came time to make it Murray said, 'Eh, it feels like I would be the guy from *Meatballs*, the camp counselor for grown-ups,'" said Ramis. "And John Cleese didn't want to leave home, didn't want to be in the West Indies for three or four months, which was what the film required." Robin Williams and Peter O'Toole stepped into the roles, resulting in a film that was, in Ramis's opinion, "not as interesting or as solid as it might have been if Bill and Cleese were there."

COFFEE AND CIGARETTES

DIRECTED BY: Jim Jarmusch

WRITTEN BY: Jim Jarmusch

RELEASE DATE: March 12, 2004

FILM RATING: ★ ★

MURRAY RATING: ★ ★

PLOT: A succession of eccentric diner patrons palaver over java and smokes.

STARRING BILL MURRAY AS: Himself

Murray enlivens this otherwise dreary anthology of short films from downtown New York auteur Jim Jarmusch. The eleven vignettes—nine of which are completely aimless—are loosely linked by the titular vices, which the characters all consume as if they are going out of style. In his segment, Murray plays "Bill Murray," a fictionalized version of himself who slings coffee in a diner. RZA and GZA of the hip-hop group Wu-Tang Clan are customers at his table. Their conversation revolves around alternative medicine and the interpretation of dreams. In one of several surreal scenes in this black-and-white indie, Murray drinks coffee straight from the pot and gargles with hydrogen peroxide.

Murray agreed to appear in the film after Jarmusch promised that shooting would take only one day. "Could you make it a half a day?" Murray asked. "No," replied Jarmusch. "I think it's going to take a whole day." "All right, I'll do it," Murray agreed. "Just leave a message on my machine the night before. Tell me where and what time and I'll be there." And he was.

In 2014, the **New York City** gastropub Sweetwater Social began serving a cocktail inspired by Murray's work in *Coffee and Cigarettes*. "For all of my smokers out there, this is right up your alley," said the drink's creator, Tim Cooper, who combined single malt scotch, bourbon, rum, coffee beans, and coffee-flavored demerara sugar to mimic the "flavors" of Murray's performance.

NEXT MOVIE: *Garfield: The Movie* (2004)

COLUCHE

Irreverent French comedian of the 1970s and '80s to whom Murray occasionally compares himself. Equal parts Red Skelton and Lenny Bruce, Coluche was known for his anarchic, politically charged brand of humor. He ran for president of France in 1981 and died in a motorcycle accident in 1986 at the age of forty-one. "He was really funny, and he was sharp—incredibly smart, savage wit," Murray once said. "He would say anything, and he wasn't mean, either. He was almost like a peasant in a way, but he was brilliant." When speaking to the French press in the '80s, Murray would often describe himself as "Coluche with cheekbones." "They used to think that was pretty good, except they didn't quite get what the 'with cheekbones' thing meant."

COMMUNALISM

Murray has likened the experience of making movies to life on a commune. "The movie business is the only place where communes still exist," he once said. "Maybe that system works because it's temporary and none of the political complications of communes come into play. And if everyone accepts that, that I'm gonna be taken care of by the state and also that I'm gonna take care of this movie when it needs me, then the movie becomes greater than the sum of its parts. . . . It sounds strange to say it, but I think communism—that is, communal living—starts at the top. That means if the person at the top— the stars, or the director—is willing to live with less and say, 'Whatever the movie needs, I'm gonna do,' then everyone benefits."

CON AIR

Murray has professed a fondness for this 1997 action movie from schlock-meister Jerry Bruckheimer. In one of his iconic roles, Nicolas Cage plays a recently paroled convict on board a hijacked prisoner transport plane. "Strangely, I thought *Con Air* was funny," Murray said. "I have no idea why, but that movie made me laugh."

COSELL, HOWARD

Toupéed, nasal-voiced sportscasting legend who gave Murray his first big television break. In 1975, while scouting for talent for his upcoming ABC variety series, Cosell saw Murray perform in the Off-Broadway revue *The National Lampoon Show*. Entranced, he offered him a spot in his repertory comedy troupe, the Prime Time Players. Although *Saturday Night Live with Howard Cosell* came and went in just eighteen weeks, it did put Murray on the national radar during a critical period in the history of television comedy. A year later, when **Chevy Chase** left the cast of *NBC's Saturday Night* (soon to appropriate the Cosell show's title and become *Saturday Night Live*), Murray was recruited to replace him.

CRADLE WILL ROCK

DIRECTED BY: Tim Robbins

WRITTEN BY: Tim Robbins

RELEASE DATE: December 10, 1999

FILM RATING: ★★

MURRAY RATING: ★★

PLOT: A loose dramatization of events surrounding the Federal Theater Project's controversial production of a pro-union musical in Depression-era New York City.

STARRING BILL MURRAY AS: Tommy Crickshaw, Commie-hating vaudeville ventriloquist

Fresh off his paradigm-shifting performance in *Rushmore*, Murray again put on his sad clown face for a featured turn in this politically charged period piece from director Tim Robbins. Playing a forlorn ventriloquist with a hatred of "Reds" and a weakness for the bottle, he is one of the only actors in the film unburdened with having to portray a historical character. Costars John Cusack, Rubén Blades, and Angus Macfadyen impersonate Nelson Rockefeller, Diego Rivera, and Orson Welles with varying degrees of success. Murray makes the most of his limited screen time, but his character turns out to be utterly tangential to the plot, and the overstuffed film creaks under the weight of its shrill left-wing didacticism. (In one unintentionally hilarious scene, Murray's dummy mysteriously turns into a Marxist in the middle of his act, warbling "The Internationale" to the consternation of stuffed-shirt nightclub patrons.) While *Cradle Will Rock*'s simple-minded politics polarized moviegoers, Tim Robbins's grandiose ambitions were what attracted Murray to the project in the first place. As he explained to *GQ* magazine: "I see the script, and he goes, 'Whaddya think?' And I said, 'It doesn't have a chance. It doesn't have a chance in hell, Tim! But you know what? I gotta like you for trying.' Those are my people, you know? The ones who are going to crash and burn."

For the record, Murray did not do his own ventriloquism in the film, although he did dub the dummy's voice and move his Adam's apple along with the recorded dialogue. Hollywood puppet master Alan Semok constructed six identical dummies for Murray's use and abuse, while ventriloquism coach Todd Stockman tutored Murray in the fine art of pretending to throw his voice.

NEXT MOVIE: *Hamlet* (2000)

CRITICS

Murray has no respect for film critics, whose opinions he does not value and whose physical deficiencies he once likened to the grotesque effects of medical experiments. "I really hate critics," he has said. "They're usually wrong, and when they're right, they're right for the wrong reasons. When they do like something, they like it for just *absurd* reasons. . . . They imply that they know everybody when there are all sorts of people who won't even talk to them and think of them as the sleaziest sort of person." In a 1998 interview for *Esquire*, Murray recounted the tale of a New York Film Critics Circle Awards ceremony he once attended:

"They called me up when somebody canceled two days before the thing and asked me to present some awards. So I went, and one of the funniest film moments I've ever had was when they introduced the New York film critics. They all stood up—motley isn't the word for that group. Everybody had some sort of vision problem, some sort of damage—I had to bury myself in my napkin. As they kept going, it just got funnier and funnier looking. By the time they were all up, it was like, 'You have been selected as the people who have been poisoned—you were the unfortunate people who were not in the control group that didn't receive the medication.'"

CROCKETT, DAVY

As a boy, Murray enjoyed reading children's biographies of Western heroes like Kit Carson, Wild Bill Hickok, and Davy Crockett. "I read them over and over, 'cause they were all poor kids when they started," he said. "The book that made the biggest impression was the one about Crockett, because he ran away from home as a kid, pulled it off, and his parents missed him when he came back. That's the kind of happy ending that sticks with me."

TALES FROM
MURRAYLAND

№ 4	The Vodka Luge

In a 2013 interview with *Esquire* magazine, Murray revealed that he had kicked his annual Christmas party "to a completely other level" by installing an alcohol-bearing ice luge in his home. The enormous ice sculpture, designed to resemble an Olympic ski jump course, was engineered to channel vodka to drunken revelers in the fastest and most efficient way possible. The spirit chills as it makes its way down the "mountain." "You can put your head underneath it, like you're guzzling gasoline, but we just fill shot glasses," Murray enthused. The actor credits the vodka luge for adding much-needed "octane" to his previously dull holiday get-togethers. "The year before, people would leave at, like, two or three in the morning. With the vodka luge, they didn't leave until five."

C-SPAN

Murray is a devoted viewer of this public affairs television channel, created and funded by America's cable companies. In a 2010 interview with *GQ*, he revealed that C-SPAN programs, along with sports and old movies, make up the bulk of his television viewing. One of his favorite C-SPAN moments occurred on November 4, 2008, when a candidate from Murray's adopted hometown was elected the nation's first African American president. "The night Obama won the election, C-SPAN was the greatest," Murray said. "There were no announcers, just **Chicago**. It was just that crowd in Grant Park, and it was just fuckin' jazz. You know, it was just, *wow*. And that's my town, you know? It was just: 'Oh, my God, it's gonna happen! It's gonna happen!' You just saw the pictures of it, like, oh, there's someone from the Northwest Side, there's someone from the South Side, someone from the suburbs. It was the most truly American thing you've ever seen. Oh God, I get jazzed just thinkin' about it. I don't know anyone that wasn't crying. It was just: Thank God this long national nightmare is *over*."

CUOMO, MARIO

Three-term governor of New York whose tenure in office coincided with Murray's rise to fame in the 1980s. Murray once appeared as a guest on the local **New York City** TV news program *Live at Five* on the same day as Cuomo and radio shock jock Howard Stern. The three men even posed for a photograph together. According to Murray, Cuomo insisted that Murray get in the middle of the picture so that he wouldn't have to stand next to Stern.

DALAI LAMA

Tibetan spiritual leader whose fictitious golfing prowess supplied the grist for one of Murray's most memorable speeches in *Caddyshack*. In reality, His Holiness does not play **golf**, has never seen *Caddyshack*, and claims to be ignorant of the rules of most competitive sports. In his youth, he did enjoy the occasional game of badminton and went through a brief but avid table tennis phase in the 1950s. In a 2014 interview, the Dalai Lama boasted that he had once defeated Chinese premier Zhou Enlai in a game of ping-pong.

DARJEELING LIMITED, THE

DIRECTED BY: Wes Anderson

WRITTEN BY: Wes Anderson, Roman Coppola, and Jason Schwartzman

RELEASE DATE: October 26, 2007

FILM RATING: ★★

MURRAY RATING: ★

PLOT: Three grieving brothers embark on a curry-scented journey of self-discovery.

STARRING BILL MURRAY AS: The Businessman, a passenger to India

Murray has a mostly silent cameo as a well-dressed train traveler in this self-indulgent fifth feature from director **Wes Anderson**. Anderson told *Rolling Stone* he modeled Murray's character on Karl Malden's traveller's check–wielding tourist in a series of American Express TV commercials from the 1970s. For his part, Murray was intrigued by the offer of an all-expenses-paid trip to India on the studio's dime. Scheduled for three days of filming, he completed his scenes in a day and a half and spent the next month visiting tourist sites. He later called the no-drama shoot "a great experience."

NEXT MOVIE: *Get Smart* (2008)

DEAD ZONE, THE

Murray was author Stephen King's first choice for the lead role of Johnny Smith, a small-town schoolteacher with clairvoyant powers, in this 1983 movie adaptation of King's novel. Producer Dino DeLaurentiis also wanted

The Darjeeling Limited, 2007

Murray to play the part, but Murray couldn't fit the film into his jam-packed early-'80s schedule. Christopher Walken eventually got the role.

DEATH

As a young man, Murray kept a large moose head on the wall of his **New York City** apartment as a reminder of his mortality. In 1984, he told an interviewer for *McCall's*: "I once read: Whenever you sit down for dinner, if you pull up a chair for Death, he will finally come and you'll be ready for him. That's what I'd like to teach my son. Be ready for death. Treat every day as if it is your last day."

In a 2008 interview with the *Chicago Tribune*, Murray revealed that he would like to have his skull put on display after his death: "If I felt myself getting ill, I'd like to have that paperwork sorted out before I went to the end. I love the idea of my skull being somewhere. It's not going to do anybody any good anywhere else. 'A fellow of infinite jest'—that would be a great thing to be known as."

DEMPSEY & CARROLL

High-end New York City stationery engravers whose products Murray has touted in interviews as the finest stationery in Manhattan.

DILAMUCA, TODD

Antic noogie-dispensing nerd played by Murray in thirteen *Saturday Night Live* sketches between 1978 and 1980. The character was originally called Todd LaBounta, after a high school classmate of *SNL* writer Al Franken. Murray was forced to change the name after the real-life LaBounta threatened to sue NBC. **John Belushi** was the first choice to play DiLaMuca but declined the part.

DiLaMuca is the boyfriend of Lisa Loopner, played by **Gilda Radner.** The Nerd sketches were often used as a vehicle for Murray and Radner to work out issues in their on-again, off-again romantic relationship. In an interview conducted for the book *American Nerd: The Story of My People,* writer Anne Beatts revealed that Murray would occasionally leave telephone messages for Radner, saying "Todd called." Beatts noted, "I think that mild sadism of Todd toward Lisa was a reflection of the dynamic of their relationship."

It was also a reflection of his suburban **Chicago** upbringing. Murray's sister Laura once revealed to an interviewer that Todd DiLaMuca's penchant for giving people noogies was based on her brother's own adolescent proclivities. "We just couldn't believe it," she said of her family's initial reaction to the sketches. "He was just in the kitchen giving us those, and now there he is suddenly doing it on national television and getting standing ovations. I actually felt sorry for those other cast members any time I saw him doing that, because they were painful."

DINNER FOR SCHMUCKS

Murray was one of several actors considered for the co-lead in this 2010 comedy. Steve Martin, Robin Williams, and Sacha Baron Cohen were also up for parts in the film, which gestated for more than a decade before finally being made with Steve Carell and Paul Rudd as the titular schmegeggies.

DIRECTING

Most actors aspire to direct at some point in their careers. Murray is no exception. "Directing is where the action is," he once observed. "It's like being the catcher in **baseball.** I was the catcher when I played, and you were in on every play. You called every play." To date, however, he has stepped behind the camera only one time, for 1990's *Quick Change,* and that was in collaboration with his good friend Howard Franklin. Murray's oft-stated aversion to hard **work** may have something to do with it. "It was like four times more work being the director," he told an interviewer on the eve of *Quick Change*'s release. "You can't even compare it. It's just ridiculous. It's the difference between being a child and being a parent." After his debut opened to mostly favorable reviews, Murray expected to direct again. "I thought I would do it all the time. I thought

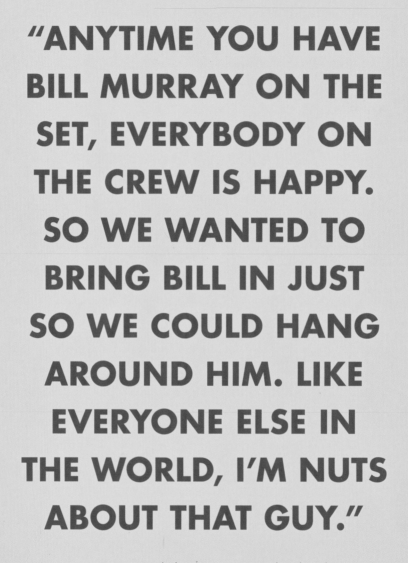

"ANYTIME YOU HAVE BILL MURRAY ON THE SET, EVERYBODY ON THE CREW IS HAPPY. SO WE WANTED TO BRING BILL IN JUST SO WE COULD HANG AROUND HIM. LIKE EVERYONE ELSE IN THE WORLD, I'M NUTS ABOUT THAT GUY."

—PETER FARRELLY, on why he cast Murray in *Dumb and Dumber To*

it would be a regular thing," he said. But he lost his yen to sit in the big chair after his proposed sophomore effort, *Beat*, went down in flames because of studio indifference. "I wrote a really funny script with my friend **Mitch Glazer**," Murray told the *Australian*. "Disney said, 'This is the greatest script we've seen in five years,' then, three days later, went, 'We don't want to make that movie.' It was such a low blow. It knocked the wind out of me."

DIRECTOR OF FUN

Murray's official title with the Charleston RiverDogs, the minor league **baseball** team in which he has had an ownership stake since the mid-1990s. Murray described his duties to the *Boston Globe*: "It means I have a portfolio. It means that if I'm arrested I'm to be taken to an embassy someplace. Like in a fun place. Monte Carlo or someplace where they have crimes of passion. I think then I have a chance of getting off."

DOGMA

Murray was one of the finalists for the role of Cardinal Ignatius Glick, a cynical Catholic prelate, in director Kevin Smith's 1999 comedy. Robin Williams and **Chevy Chase** were also considered for the part, which ultimately went to **stand-up comedy** legend George Carlin.

DOYLE-MURRAY, BRIAN

See **Murray, Brian**.

DUMB AND DUMBER TO

DIRECTED BY: Peter Farrelly, Bobby Farrelly

WRITTEN BY: Peter Farrelly, Bobby Farrelly, Sean Anders, John Morris, Bennett Yellin, and Mike Cerrone

RELEASE DATE: November 14, 2014

FILM RATING: ★

MURRAY RATING: ★

PLOT: Two imbeciles travel the country in search of a kidney donor.

STARRING BILL MURRAY AS: Icepick, a methamphetamine cook

Unrecognizable in a gas mask and yellow hazmat suit, Murray has a brief cameo as Harry Dunne's meth-making roommate in this sequel to the 1994 Farrelly brothers hit.

DUTCH MASTERS, THE

Murray's high school rock band, which specialized in cover versions of the hits of the 1950s and '60s.

EASTWOOD, CLINT

In the early 1980s, Murray briefly became fixated on making a film with Clint Eastwood. After seeing the 1974 heist thriller *Thunderbolt and Lightfoot,* Murray was particularly impressed with the way Eastwood allowed costar Jeff Bridges to steal so many scenes from him. "I could kill in one of those movies," Murray concluded. "I could be great in one of those. There's lots of fun action stuff to do. There's some funny repartee. You get some jokes. The sidekick gets all the funny stuff. And then you get killed so that Clint can avenge you. And you have a fantastic death scene. I thought 'This is brilliant. I want this gig.'" When Murray called Eastwood and volunteered his services, the *Dirty Harry* star offered him a role in a World War II comedy he was developing. But Murray, who had just made *Stripes,* feared being typecast as the "service comedy guy" and declined. The proposed Eastwood collaboration never came to fruition.

ED WOOD

DIRECTED BY: Tim Burton

WRITTEN BY: Scott Alexander and Larry Karaszewski

RELEASE DATE: September 30, 1994

FILM RATING: ★ ★ ★ ✦

MURRAY RATING: ★ ★ ★

PLOT: A chipper transvestite breaks into the movie business.

STARRING BILL MURRAY AS: John "Bunny" Breckinridge, actor and bon vivant

Murray lends panache to a somewhat nondescript supporting role in Tim Burton's twee black-and-white biopic about the cross-dressing auteur behind such Z-movies as *Glen or Glenda* and *Plan Nine from Outer Space.* Murray plays Bunny Breckinridge, a midcentury California socialite who became part of Ed Wood's entourage/repertory company. Murray later admitted that he accepted Burton's offer to play the very fey—and very gay—Breckinridge without reading the screenplay. "And then I saw the script and went, 'Oh, damn. This part is written nelly.' I said, 'The last thing I want is to be obvious, direct, and offensive.'"

NEXT MOVIE: *Kingpin* (1996)

800 NUMBER

Since dispatching his agents in 2000, Murray is notoriously difficult to contact. He owns a cell phone, an old Blackberry, which he uses primarily to text his immediate family. But he doesn't share the number with anyone outside his inner circle. Strangers wishing to get in touch with him are encouraged to contact one of those people and obtain his legendary 800 number, which terminates in an old-school voice mailbox that Murray checks only intermittently. The voice on Murray's outgoing message is not his own. It is an automated response that has been likened to "some kind of SkyTel voice mail: 'To leave a message, press five.'"

When Murray does review his messages, he quickly and unsentimentally deletes those he chooses to ignore. The overwhelming majority are pitches from filmmakers who want to work with him. "I just sort of *decide*," he told *GQ*. "I might listen and say, 'Okay, why don't you put it on a piece of paper? Put it on a piece of paper, and if it's interesting, I'll call you back, and if it's not, I won't.' It's exhausting otherwise. I don't want to have a relationship with someone if I'm not going to work with them. If you're talking about business, let's talk about business, but I don't want to hang out and bullshit."

Convincing Murray to pay attention to your message is only half the battle. Putting a script in his hands can be just as arduous. Some would-be auteurs report being instructed to leave their screenplays in a phone booth near Murray's home in New York's Hudson Valley. Others have been told to fax materials in care of his neighborhood office-supply store. Still others are directed to one of several post office boxes Murray maintains around the country. A production assistant working with Murray on one of his films was ordered to call his 800 number and leave contact information for a phone she wouldn't answer, so he could call back without having to talk to her.

The list of people who have Murray's 800 number is short. According to published reports, it includes directors Wes Anderson and Ted Melfi, long-

> **"I CAN'T ACCUMULATE MORE STUFF AND MORE RELATIONSHIPS. PEOPLE SAY, 'JUST GIVE ME YOUR NUMBER, I'LL GIVE YOU A CALL.' HA. NO. I'LL NEVER CALL YOU BACK AND I WON'T ANSWER THE PHONE EITHER."**
>
> —MURRAY, on why he uses an 800 number to communicate with the outside world

time Murray compadre **Mitch Glazer**, producer Fred Roos, Murray's attorney David Nochimson, and actors George Clooney, Woody Harrelson, and Naomi Watts. Murray's friend **Dan Aykroyd** undoubtedly has the digits, though he has described the process of getting written communications into Murray's hands as akin to serving someone a subpoena: "You gotta look him in the eye [and say], 'You *did* receive this.'" Rob Burnett, the executive producer of *Late Show with David Letterman*, has said the time frame for a response from Murray "can be anywhere from twenty-four hours to six months."

ELDINI, JERRY

Unctuous, cocaine-dispensing record company employee played by Murray in a series of *Saturday Night Live* sketches beginning in 1978. The satin-jacketed sleazebag, an A&R rep for the fictional Polysutra Records, routinely administers mood-elevating "tootskis" to his rock star clients. Murray has called Eldini "one of my favorite characters from the show." Murray's Tripper Harrison character briefly impersonates Eldini in the opening minutes of *Meatballs*.

E-MAIL

Murray is not an avid e-mailer. He prefers to exchange texts with his children whenever possible. "I have no interest in it," he once declared. "But the kids' school stuff is all e-mail, and they send thousands of e-mails. It's complete overload."

EVANSTON, ILLINOIS

Murray's place of birth. He was born in Evanston Hospital on September 21, 1950. He grew up in nearby Wilmette, Illinois.

TALES FROM
MURRAYLAND

Nº 5 | The Time He Came Up with
a Million-Dollar Invention

Anyone who has ever spent time behind a movie camera has experienced ocular fatigue—that special agony reserved for those who squint through the same lens all day. If Murray had had his way, he might have gotten rich off the cure. In the 1990s, he came up with the idea for a new kind of eyepiece that could be flipped from side to side, allowing cinematographers to toggle between their left and right eyes. "I knew a great cameraman and his eyes would become very fatigued," Murray told *Minnesota Business* magazine. "I said, 'Why don't they invent an eye piece that just flips over to the other side?'" When he tried pitching the invention to a camera manufacturer, however, he was laughed out of the office. "And damned if some guy didn't make this thing fifteen years later!"

FACT CHECKERS UNIT

Murray plays himself in this 2008 short film from director Dan Beers, who had previously worked as an associate producer on *The Life Aquatic with Steve Zissou*. Peter Karinen and Brian Sacca star as a pair of hypervigilant magazine fact checkers on a mission to verify whether Murray drinks warm milk at bedtime. (Spoiler alert: he does.) Murray donated eight hours of his time to the $12,000 production and reportedly helped the crew lug equipment around the set. In lieu of payment, he asked Beers to buy him a gun. When the director refused, Murray requested a knife instead—"a really big knife, like something I can tie around my leg." After shooting wrapped, Beers and the crew presented their star with a brand-new twelve-inch hunting knife. "Thanks for this," Murray said, and promptly vanished.

FANS

As much as he enjoys crashing the occasional kickball game or dropping in on someone's house party, Murray has little patience for fans who approach him in public. "Half the time they confuse me with someone else," he said. "'That one where you were in Vietnam? God, you were funny in that!'"

As for fan mail, don't bother sending any. He won't answer it. "I don't have time for that," he says. "It's like there are hundreds of thousands of people that think they're going to become millionaires getting **autographs** from movie actors. I don't have time for those idiots. I got stuff to do. Spelling my name? I did that a long time ago. When I run into someone on the street that's one thing, but answering mail for a living? Ay-ay-ay-ay-ay . . . I like a job where you sleep late, get kind of goofy and have some fun."

FANTASTIC FOUR RADIO SHOW, THE

Murray supplied the voice of Johnny Storm, the Human Torch, in this nationally syndicated 1975 radio series narrated by Marvel Comics editor-in-chief Stan Lee. Producer Bob Michelson recruited Murray for the part after working with him on *The National Lampoon Radio Hour*. **John Belushi** and **Gilda Radner** were also invited to join the cast, but both declined. Murray, who did not have a lot of voice-acting experience at this point, agreed to work for scale. Veteran performers Cynthia Adler, Bob Maxwell, and Jim Pappas played the other three members of the superhero team. "Bill was a relative rookie, a wild card and a risk," said *Fantastic Four* scriptwriter Peter B. Lewis. "At the time, he was not the strongest of actors." He often arrived late to recording sessions and routinely flubbed his line readings. He may have been hampered by his unfamiliarity with the Marvel milieu. "To my knowledge, Bill hadn't heard of the Fantastic Four" when he started work on the series, Lewis admits. Beset by budget problems, *The Fantastic Four Radio Show* was canceled after a brief thirteen-week run.

FANTASTIC MR. FOX

DIRECTED BY: Wes Anderson

WRITTEN BY: Wes Anderson and Noah Baumbach

RELEASE DATE: November 13, 2009

FILM RATING: ★ ★ ★

MURRAY RATING: ★ ★

PLOT: A vulpine rascal makes mischief for the local landed gentry.

STARRING BILL MURRAY AS: Clive Badger, attorney and demolitions expert

By all accounts, Murray had the time of his life lending his vocal talents to this endearing stop-motion adaptation of Roald Dahl's classic children's novel. "We really did have a chunky good time for the amount of work we did on this movie," he remarked of the less-than-arduous recording process, which saw the cast and crew decamp to a country estate in Connecticut to commune with the farm animals they were bringing to life. Much of the dialogue

for *Fantastic Mr. Fox* was recorded "live" on location, rather than in a studio. The actors spent their working hours galloping through fields and squatting in the dirt to simulate frantic digging while boom mike operators shadowed their every move. At night, the bacchanal began. "We recorded during the day and then at night we would have these magnificent meals and we would all tell stories," Murray told a gathering of

Reddit inquisitors in 2014 during an "Ask Me Anything" session. "We had a *lot* of great food, a lot of great wine, and great stories. It went on until people started literally falling from their chairs and being taken away."

(CONTINUED ON PAGE 72)

Fantastic Mr. Fox, 2009

Playing a more sympathetic lawyer than the sleazebags he portrayed in *Wild Things* and *Speaking of Sex*, Murray brought his trademark improvisational brio to his performance as Clive Badger—though the final characterization was somewhat muted by director **Wes Anderson**. Murray had intended to give Badger a "beatific" Wisconsin accent, but Anderson nixed it. "It was beautiful but no one really cared or noticed," Murray said. "They just went 'No, maybe not.' That was the most serious acting work I've done in a long time." One of Murray's contributions that did make the cut was the epic wolf impersonation he filmed for *Mr. Fox*'s denouement, where a lone wolf gives a Black Power salute to the assembled animals. "We didn't use his voice at all, but Bill ran up a hill and gave his best 'wolf stare' down on us," Anderson told *Rolling Stone*. "We filmed it and the artists used it for inspiration to what ended up on the screen."

Fantastic Mr. Fox also gave Murray a chance to work with George Clooney for the first time. The two men bonded during the Connecticut recording sessions and ended up taking an impromptu holiday together in northern Italy after the picture wrapped. They would reunite professionally five years later for Clooney's World War II adventure *The Monuments Men*. Cementing their unlikely friendship, Murray was one of the invited guests at Clooney's September 2014 wedding to Amal Alamuddin at the Ca' Farsetti palace in Venice.

NEXT MOVIE: *Ballhawks* (2010)

FATHERHOOD

Between 1982 and 1997, Murray sired six sons by two women. His public remarks on the subject of fatherhood often seem to echo the sentiments of Bob Harris from *Lost in Translation*. "People only talk about what a joyous experience it is, but there is terror," he said. "Your life, as you know it, is over. It's over the day that child is born. It's over, and something completely new starts." Murray has discussed the importance of ignoring your kids. "If you bite on everything they throw at you, they will grind you down," he told *Esquire* magazine. "When my kids ask what I want for my birthday or **Christmas** or whatever, I use the same answer my father did: 'Peace and quiet.' That was never a satisfactory answer to me as a kid—I wanted an answer like 'A pipe.' But now I see the wisdom of it: All I want is you at your best—you making this an easier home to live in, you thinking of others."

> ## "I HAVE TO LOVE YOU, BUT I HAVE THE RIGHT TO IGNORE YOU."
>
> —Murray's personal motto for raising children

FIELDS, TOTIE

Morbidly obese comedian and nightclub performer of the 1960s and '70s. Murray has called her the "benchmark" by which he

"IT TAKES A WHILE TO UNDERSTAND GEORGE BECAUSE HE'S A MOTOR-MOUTH.... YOU'VE GOT TO KIND OF WADE THROUGH A LOT OF IT BUT GEORGE IS A REAL FORCE, YOU KNOW? HE'S PROBABLY THE ONE PERSON WHO'S LIVING THE MOVIE STAR LIFE REALLY, REALLY WELL AND DOING GREAT AT IT."

—MURRAY, on his BFF George Clooney, whom he met on the set of *Fantastic Mr. Fox* measures show business professionalism. In 1976, Fields's left leg was amputated above the knee following unsuccessful surgery to remove a blood clot. Fitted with an artificial limb and confined to a wheelchair, she continued to perform her Las Vegas nightclub act. Murray attended one of her shows in the late 1970s and was blown away by her ability to persevere in spite of her disability. "Her act was rough," he recalled in a 2009 interview. "It was a blues act. Pickled with quarts of schmaltz. Her finale was, she'd sing this song, some piece of original material written for her. She was working on a stool: 'Any fields that Totie Fields can land on/Long as I've got a leg to stand on.' and she'd try to get up on her one leg and the one wooden one. Oh, she staggered. There was one more line, but it was designed to be drowned out in the applause. She had a wheelchair pusher, but when she's finished, he doesn't push her out. He backs her out. He's backing her into the wings, and she's waving thank you and goodnight. Kept me awake for hours."

FORREST GUMP

Murray was one of several A-list actors to turn down the title role in this 1994 best picture winner. **Chevy Chase** and John Travolta also passed on the part of the dim-witted eyewitness to history. Tom Hanks said yes and earned his second Academy Award for best actor. In a 2014 interview with radio host Howard Stern, Murray admitted that he still hasn't seen *Forrest Gump*.

FUNERALS

"I find funerals to be rewarding," Murray has said. He once described the family funerals he attended as a child as "times of great hilarity, even in times of deepest sadness." When Murray's father died in 1967, he and his siblings used the occasion as an opportunity to bust on their fellow mourners. "There were all of us, nine kids in a limousine, just laughing about all the cousins and relatives outside the window going, 'Get a load of that.' People are looking at the car going, 'Oh, it must be so sad in there,' and we're just roaring on the inside."

Murray has attended memorial services for such high-profile celebrities as **Elvis Presley**, John Lennon, **Hunter S. Thompson**, and *Saturday Night Live* costar **John Belushi**.

GARFIELD: THE MOVIE

DIRECTED BY: Peter Hewitt

WRITTEN BY: Joel Cohen and Alec Sokolow

RELEASE DATE: June 11, 2004

FILM RATING: ★ ★

MURRAY RATING: ★ ★

PLOT: A morbidly obese cat must cope with the arrival of his owner's new puppy.

STARRING BILL MURRAY AS: Garfield the Cat

Murray gives vocal life to the lasagna-loving feline in this enervating big-screen adaptation of Jim Davis's popular comic strip. (Oddly enough, the television voice of Garfield, Lorenzo Music, was also the voice of Peter Venkman in the *Ghostbusters* cartoon series.) Though savaged by **critics** and derided by most of Murray's **fans**, *Garfield: The Movie* was an enormous box office hit and spawned the superior 2006 sequel, *Garfield: A Tail of Two Kitties*. "I wasn't thinking clearly," Murray said of his participation in the Garfield enterprise. He once called *Garfield: The Movie* "more than I'd bargained for" and "sort of like *Fantastic Mr. Fox* without the joy or the fun."

In interviews conducted after *Garfield: The Movie*'s release, Murray admitted he accepted the role only because he was under the mistaken impression that Academy Award–winning screenwriter Joel Coen had written the script. The screenplay for *Garfield* was in fact written by Joel Cohen, a journeyman best known for his work on the family comedies *Cheaper by the Dozen* and *Daddy Day Camp*. "I thought it would be kind of fun, because doing a voice is challenging, and I'd never done that," Murray told *New York* magazine's Vulture blog (apparently forgetting about

his work in *Shame of the Jungle* and *B.C. Rock*). "Plus, I looked at the script, and it said, 'So-and-so and Joel Coen.' And I thought: 'Christ, well, I love those Coens! They're funny.' So I sorta read a few pages of it and thought, 'Yeah, I'd like to do that.'"

After some haggling, the price was right as well. "I had these agents at the time, and I said, 'What do they give you to do one of these things?' And they said, 'Oh, they give you $50,000.' So I said, 'Okay, well, I don't even leave the fuckin' *driveway* for that kind of money.' Then this studio guy calls me up out of nowhere, and I had a nice conversation with him. No bullshit, no schmooze, none of that stuff. We just talked for a long time about the movie. And my agents called on Monday and said, 'Well, they came back with another offer, and it was *nowhere near* $50,000.' And I said, 'That's more befitting of the work I expect to do!'"

G
H

Murray's enthusiasm for the project waned once he got in the recording studio. He spent several eight-hour days in a cramped booth guzzling coffee and perspiring through his shirt, desperately trying to ad-lib his way out of the hackneyed fat jokes that had been written for him. "I worked all day and kept going, '*That's* the line? Well, I can't say that.' And you sit there and go, 'What can I say that will make this funny? And make it make sense?' And I worked. I was exhausted, soaked with sweat, and the lines got worse and worse. And I said, 'Okay, you better show me the whole rest of the movie, so we can see what we're dealing with.' So I sat down and watched the whole thing, and I kept saying, 'Who the hell cut this thing? Who did this? What the fuck was Coen thinking?' And then they explained it to me: It wasn't written by *that* Joel Coen."

Retakes were ordered and continued in Italy, where Murray was on location shooting his next film, *The Life Aquatic with Steve Zissou*. He later credited his improvisations with salvaging the film: "We managed to fix it, sort of. It was a big financial success. And I said, 'Just promise me you'll never do that again.'" The promises must have been persuasive, because Murray signed on for the follow-up two years later.

NEXT MOVIE: *This Old Cub* (2004)

GARFIELD: A TAIL OF TWO KITTIES

DIRECTED BY: Tim Hill

WRITTEN BY: Joel Cohen and Alec Sokolow

RELEASE DATE: June 16, 2006

FILM RATING: ★ ★ ★

MURRAY RATING: ★ ★ ★

PLOT: The tubby tabby trades places with an English royal.

STARRING BILL MURRAY AS: Garfield, again

To the astonishment of the nation's critics (except Roger Ebert, who gave *Garfield: The Movie* three stars out of four), Murray returned for a second helping of lasagna in this inevitable sequel to the 2004 smash. If anything, he had an even worse experience. In interviews, he has all but disowned *A Tail of Two Kitties*, labeling it a "miscarriage" that was "beyond rescue" and "even more trouble" than the original. Having already played the "I thought it was a Coen Brothers movie" card, Murray pinned the blame for *Tail*'s creative deficiencies on meddling by the suits. "The first one had so much success," he said. "Success has many fathers—so by the time the second one rolled around there were, like, nine people having lots of input, including the studio head." Director Tim Hill was also singled out for Murray's ire. "There were too many crazy people involved with it," the actor told a group of Reddit "Ask Me Anything" inquisitors in 2014. "I thought I fixed the movie, but the insane director who had formerly done some *SpongeBob*, he would leave me and say 'I gotta go, I have a meeting' and he was going to the studio where someone was telling him what it should be, countermanding what I was doing."

Perhaps the voice of Garfield doth protest too much. While it will never be mistaken for *Fantasia*, *Garfield: A Tail of Two Kitties* is a vast improvement over its predecessor and represents Murray's finest vocal work to date. The plot, lifted from **Mark Twain**'s novel *The Prince and the Pauper*, relies less on the hackneyed dog-versus-cat humor that bogged down the first movie. Delightful verbal and visual jokes abound. Though his public utterances belie it, Murray seems to be having more fun despite having to share screen time with Tim Curry as the voice of Garfield's English "cousin." Best of all, the characters of Garfield's owner and his girlfriend (played by the insipid Breckin Meyer and Jennifer Love-Hewitt) are deemphasized in favor of a brilliant supporting cast headlined by Billy Connolly as the scheming Lord Dargis. If this was a "miscarriage," fewer animated movies should go to term.

NEXT MOVIE: *The Darjeeling Limited* (2007)

TALES FROM
MURRAYLAND

Nº 6	The Time He Got Busted for Pot

September 21, 1970, was Bill Murray's twentieth birthday. It was also one of the worst days of his life. After a family birthday celebration in Chicago, Murray was all set to fly back to Denver to resume his pre-med studies at Regis College. As he was waiting in line to board his flight at O'Hare International Airport, he made the mistake of telling one of his fellow passengers that he was carrying two bombs in his suitcase. A ticket agent overheard Murray's joke and immediately summoned a couple of U.S. marshals, who proceeded to root through Murray's luggage. They didn't find any explosives, but they did discover five two-pound "bricks" of marijuana. That much weed was worth $20,000 at the time (about six times as much today). In a panic, Murray tried to stash the pot-filled bags in a locker, but Chicago vice cops arrived on the scene and arrested him. He did manage to swallow a check from one of his "customers" before cops confiscated his suitcase. "That guy owes me his life and reputation," Murray said later.

Murray was charged with possession of marijuana and ordered to appear in narcotics court the next day. The bust made the front page of the *Chicago Tribune*. Because he was a first-time offender, Murray was spared jail time and placed on probation for five years. But his college career was over. After talking it over with his family, Murray opted to drop out of Regis before his criminal record got him kicked out.

GAROFALO, JANEANE

The stand-up comic, actress, and '90s icon considers Murray her personal hero. In 1982, she wrote an entire essay about her admiration for him as part of her application packet to Providence College. The two first met on November 12, 1994, during Garofalo's lone unhappy season on *Saturday Night Live*. Murray had dropped by to deliver a eulogy for the recently deceased *SNL* writer Michael O'Donoghue. "I saw him by the craft service table," Garofalo told the UCLA *Daily Bruin*. "I was dressed as Dorothy for a horrendously bad *Wizard of Oz* sketch, and I went and pretended that I had something to do by the coffee machine. . . . I went up and stood extra near him and then conjured up some question to ask someone near him and said, 'Hello,' and shook his hand." Four months later, in March 1995, Garofalo quit *SNL* midseason. "I think he was impressed when I quit," Garofalo said. "He was impressed with the balls it took to quit the show." In fact, Murray was so impressed that he lobbied hard for Garofalo to be cast opposite him as a kindly zookeeper in his 1996 film *Larger Than Life*.

GET LOW

DIRECTED BY: Aaron Schneider

WRITTEN BY: Chris Provenzano, C. Gaby Mitchell, and Scott Seeke

RELEASE DATE: July 30, 2010

FILM RATING: ★ ★ ★

MURRAY RATING: ★ ★

PLOT: A cantankerous old hermit plans his funeral.

STARRING BILL MURRAY AS: Frank Quinn, Depression-era funeral director

Refining a character he created for the classic 1998 *Saturday Night Live* sketch "Who's More Grizzled?" Robert Duvall plays a backwoods curmudgeon harboring a dark secret in this Faulknerian period piece loosely based on a true story. Murray provides able support as the undertaker who helps Duvall's character choreograph his own elaborate funeral service. A showcase for the performances of its two stars, *Get Low* was somewhat surprisingly snubbed by all the major award-granting entities.

Murray came to the project via the usual circuitous route: entreaties to his attorney, scripts sent to mysterious post office boxes, weeks of radio silence followed by an out-of-the-blue phone call expressing his interest in joining the production. In the end, it took a personal plea from director Aaron Schneider to seal the deal. "I sat down and I wrote a letter," Schneider told an interviewer. "Took me like two or three days to write it because it's like, how do you write a letter to Bill Murray? Dear Bill, then what? I finally just decided to tell him, kind of put my heart on the page and said here's why we want you and here's what I think this could be." Whatever Schneider wrote, it must have impressed Murray, who was recovering from the heartbreak of his second divorce at the time and thought he might never work again. He immediately said yes, though his superstitious insistence on not signing a contract nearly jeopardized the film's tenuous financing.

The opportunity to work with one of his acting idols may have also factored into Murray's decision to accept the part. "I've always liked [Duvall's] stuff," he told *Entertainment Weekly*. "I think he's incredibly real and a certain kind of actor that all actors go, 'Okay, I give. That guy, he's better than I am.' You can't really pass up that opportunity to work with someone who has more stuff than you, because it's part of your education. It was amazing to see how accessible all his emotions are and how he was able to touch all these things in an instant. You realize you have a long ways to go." The chance to observe Duvall in his natural thespian habitat, playing a crusty old hermit who might as well be Boo Radley's grandfather, was too good to pass up. Or, as Murray put it in another interview: "[Duvall] can coot with the best of them."

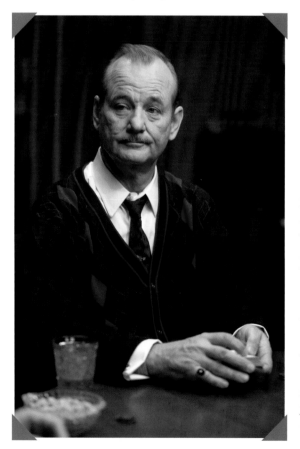

For his own part, which Murray somewhat unfairly described as "a bozo on the side," the actor drew on the experience of his grandfather, who once worked as a greeter in a funeral home. "He was such an amazing person," Murray told the *New York Post*. "He would just be there as if he were a friend to the deceased, and people would talk to him about the deceased. When he died himself, there was an enormous turnout for him, because all these people had become friends with him at their own family's **funerals**." On the challenge of holding his own on-screen alongside Duvall, he said: "You're playing behind the beat, because he's set in this crazy rhythm, and you're sort of chasing a meat wagon that's rolling down the street. It's either challenging or nervous, but you know that he can do anything you can do, so you don't wanna aim low. You don't wanna throw a softball out there. You gotta just open a can of beans on him every time, because that's your job. I'm gonna push him as hard as I can to get the best out of him. It's like testing spaghetti. You throw it on the wall and see what happens."

Financial backing for *Get Low* came, in part, from investors in Poland. That compelled Murray and the rest of the cast and crew to spend Thanksgiving 2009 promoting the film at the International Film Festival of the Art of Cinematography in Lodz, Poland. Murray described the junket as "a total blast . . . much cooler than Cannes." Asked to present an award at the festival, Murray regaled the crowd by opening with "I love you, may I borrow some money?" in fluent Polish. He and producer Dean Zanuck followed that up with a road trip to Warsaw, where they crashed a stranger's house party and sat in the front row at a Polish fashion show. "With Bill, you never know where you are going to end up," Zanuck later confided. "You come to expect the unexpected."

NEXT MOVIE: *Passion Play* (2010)

GET SMART

DIRECTED BY: Peter Segal

WRITTEN BY: Tom J. Astle and Matt Ember

RELEASE DATE: June 20, 2008

FILM RATING: ★★

MURRAY RATING: ★

PLOT: After being passed over for a promotion, an aspiring spy infiltrates a terrorist organization to prove his mettle.

STARRING BILL MURRAY AS: Agent 13

Murray has a brief cameo in this ghastly unnecessary reboot of the classic TV sitcom about an inept secret agent. In a scene that seems to have no relation to the rest of the film, he plays Agent 13, an operative for CONTROL who inexplicably plies his trade from inside a hollowed-out tree on the National Mall in Washington, D.C.

NEXT MOVIE: *City of Ember* (2008)

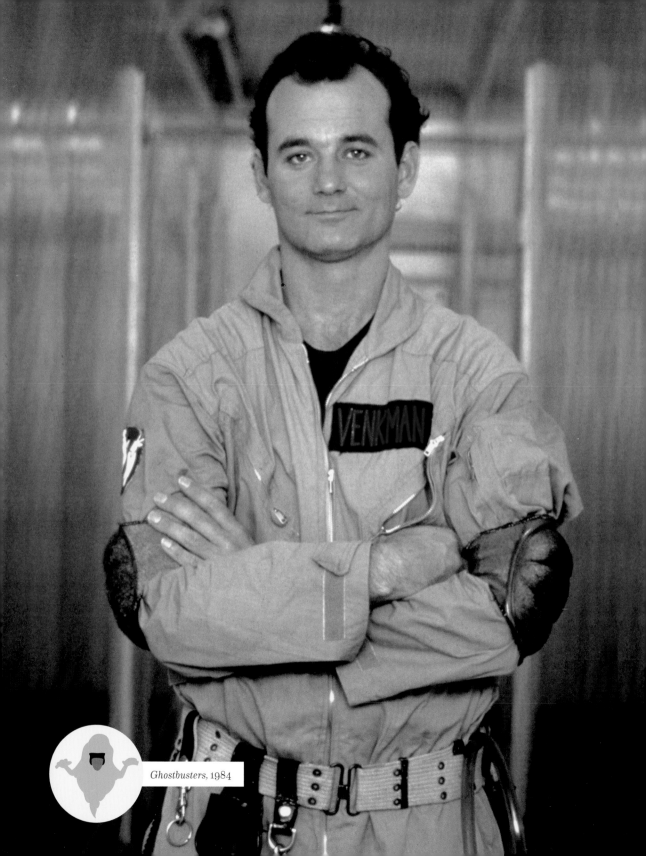

Ghostbusters, 1984

GHOSTBUSTERS

DIRECTED BY: Ivan Reitman

WRITTEN BY: Dan Aykroyd and Harold Ramis

RELEASE DATE: June 7, 1984

FILM RATING: ★ ★ ★

MURRAY RATING: ★ ★ ★ ★

PLOT: A trio of paranormal investigators (plus Ernie Hudson) thwarts a ghost invasion of New York City.

STARRING BILL MURRAY AS: Peter Venkman, leader of the Ghostbusters

In the summer of 1984, three goliaths bestrode the American cultural landscape: Bruce Springsteen, Ronald Reagan, and Bill Murray—star of the season's highest-grossing film, *Ghostbusters*. *Saturday Night Live* may have made Murray a household name, but this crowd-pleasing, special-effects-driven supernatural action comedy put his smirking puss on every school lunchbox from coast to coast. Depending on your taste—and the age you were when you first saw it—*Ghostbusters* may not be the best film of Bill Murray's career, but it's unquestionably the most important.

An evolutionary leap forward in the chain of comedy blockbusters that began with *The Blues Brothers*, *Ghostbusters* likewise sprang from the fertile mind of one man: **Dan Aykroyd**. Murray's former *SNL* cast mate and a lifelong believer in the supernatural (several of his relatives were professed spiritual mediums), Aykroyd modeled his script on the ghost-hunting comedies of Bob Hope and Abbott and Costello. He wrote it for himself and **John Belushi**, but Belushi's tragic death in March 1982 compelled him to rethink the entire project. Aykroyd showed his screenplay-in-progress to director **Ivan Reitman**, who suggested a repeat of the successful *Stripes* formula: entice **Harold Ramis** to join the cast and then have him do a rewrite tailored to the strengths of Murray in the Belushi role. Thus Dr. Peter Venkman, libidinous parapsychologist and nominal leader of the Ghostbusters team, was born. Aykroyd and Ramis rounded out the trio as Raymond Stantz and Egon Spengler, "the Lion and the Tin Man" to Murray's Scarecrow. Or as Murray put it: "They figured out that I would be the mouth, Dan would be the heart, and Harold would be the brains."

When Aykroyd sent him the finished screenplay, Murray was impressed. In fact, he saw no need to improve it with his trademark improvisations. "I'd never worked on a movie where the script was good," he said later. "*Stripes* and *Meatballs*, we rewrote the script every single day." There was just one hang-up. Murray was gung-ho to get his passion project, *The Razor's Edge*, green-lit by a major studio. Dan Aykroyd counseled him to say yes to *Ghostbusters* on the condition that Columbia Pictures bankroll *The Razor's*

Edge as well. "Forty-five minutes later, we had a caterer and a producer and a director for *The Razor's Edge*," Murray said.

Filming of *Ghostbusters* was scheduled to begin in the fall of 1983, immediately after Murray finished work on the exhausting *Razor's Edge* shoot in India. With Aykroyd and Ramis all set to go before the camera, studio executives went into a full-blown panic over Murray's whereabouts. They bombarded him with international telegrams demanding that he show up on the *Ghostbusters* set in New York in time for the first day of shooting. At one point, Murray made the mistake of calling in from a phone booth at the Taj Mahal, only to be ordered home by a Columbia suit with little regard for the difficulties involved in adapting Somerset Maugham's classic novel.

After a brief stopover in London, Murray finally made it home on the Concorde. Ramis and Reitman personally met him at John F. Kennedy International Airport for an impromptu "story conference." Murray "came through the terminal with a stadium horn—one of those bullhorns that plays eighty different fight songs," Ramis later recalled. "He was addressing everyone in sight with this thing and then playing a song. We dragged him out of there and went to a restaurant in Queens. I've never seen him in higher spirits. We spent an hour together, and he said maybe two words about the whole script. Then he took off again."

The boisterous behavior continued on the location set in midtown Manhattan. On the first day of shooting, Reitman squired the dazed and jet-lagged Murray over to the wardrobe department. ("I still had no idea if he'd actually

read the script," the director said later.) After trying on his costume, Murray realized he'd lost a significant amount of weight in India. "So I started eating right away. A production assistant said, 'Do you want a cup of coffee?' And I said, 'Yeah, and I want a couple of doughnuts, too.'" On being introduced to costar Sigourney Weaver for the first time, outside the New York Public Library, Murray greeted her with a hearty "Hello, Susan." Then he picked her up, threw her over his shoulder, and carried her down the street. "It was a great metaphor for what happened to me in the movie," Weaver said later. "I was just turned upside down and I think I became a much better actress for it."

Once the initial adrenaline rush wore off, Murray found the first month of the *Ghostbusters* shoot an enervating slog. "For the first few weeks, I was getting beaten to go to work," he said. "It was like, 'Where's Bill?' 'Oh, he's asleep.' Then they'd send three sets of people to knock on the door and say, 'They really want you.' I'd stumble out and do something and then go back to sleep. I kept thinking to myself: 'Ten days ago I was up there working with the high lamas in a gompa, and here I am removing ghosts from drugstores and painting slime on my body.'" As autumn wore on, however, he caught his second wind. The cast's spirits were buoyed by the tremendous response they received from ordinary New Yorkers, who quickly learned to identify the 'Busters by their distinctive beige jumpsuits. "It was tremendous fun running around **New York City** in those suits," Harold Ramis said. "People would cheer; restaurants would stay open after hours for us. And even if they couldn't see who we were, they were seeing this ambulance with the logo on it."

That "no ghost" logo became one of the most recognizable icons in movie history. When *Ghostbusters* opened in June 1984 it burned through box office records, disproving the prevailing wisdom that a big-budget comedy headlined by television actors could not compete with the likes of *Indiana Jones and the Temple of Doom*. The film went on to gross more than $230 million in the United States alone, easily earning back its $30 million budget. When summer turned to fall, the film continued to pick up steam as millions of American children donned *Ghostbusters* costumes for **Halloween**. By **Christmas**, Venkman-, Stantz-, and Spengler-themed toys were all the rage—much to the delight of the stars' accountants. "I remember during *The Blues Brothers* Dan had been down on doing a lot of merchandising," Harold Ramis later remarked. "He would say, 'I don't want to be on every lunchbox in America.' Well, when it came time for *Ghostbusters* his tune had changed, and he said, 'Now I *do* want to be on every lunchbox in America.' And we were."

For Murray, the phantasmagoric success of *Ghostbusters* was a somewhat mixed blessing. He was now the most popular comic actor in Hollywood (at least until *Beverly Hills Cop* dropped later that year). But the film's box office prowess did little to boost the fortunes of his true labor of love, *The Razor's Edge*. It opened to harshly negative reviews and a mostly puzzled audience reaction in the fall of 1984. And while Murray the performer was now at peak demand, Murray the private citizen found himself melting under the glare of an exponentially higher level of fame. Tired of being stopped on the street by **fans**, he holed up in his New York apartment, didn't cut his fingernails for ten weeks, and grew a salt-and-pepper beard that made him "look

"THIS *GHOSTBUSTERS* THING IS NOT GOING TO GO AWAY UNTIL SOMEONE KILLS THEMSELVES WITH ONE OF THE TOYS."

—MURRAY, on fans constantly intruding on his privacy
in the wake of *Ghostbusters'* success

like a malamute/husky cross." The mountain man look lasted only about a month, but by the end of the year Murray had fled to France to escape the spotlight and consider the next phase of his career. He would not star in another film for four years.

NEXT MOVIE: *Nothing Lasts Forever* (1984)

GHOSTBUSTERS II

DIRECTED BY: Ivan Reitman

WRITTEN BY: Dan Aykroyd and Harold Ramis

RELEASE DATE: June 16, 1989

FILM RATING: ★★

MURRAY RATING: ★★

PLOT: The Ghostbusters reunite to stop a seventeenth-century sorcerer from returning to life and resuming his reign of evil.

STARRING BILL MURRAY AS: Peter Venkman, 'Busters frontman

"Why did I make that movie?" Murray wondered aloud just seven months after the release of this unnecessary sequel to the 1984 hit. After five years of saying no to *Ghostbusters II* ("I don't think there's enough money to make me do it," he declared in a 1984 interview), he finally acquiesced after a two-hour powwow with director **Ivan Reitman**, costars **Dan Aykroyd** and **Harold Ramis**—and their representation.

"The clever **agents** got us all together in a room," Murray said afterward, "and we really are funny together. I mean they are funny people—Harold and Danny and myself. . . . And we were just blindingly funny for about an hour or so. And the agents, there was just foam coming off of them. And so they had this pitch and Danny and Harold had already concocted some sort of story idea, and it was a story, it was a good story. I think I had even already read one or two that Danny rolled out before that, but this one was a good one. I said, 'Okay, we can do that one.' It was just kind of fun to have all of us together."

At first, that sense of fun seemed to translate to the screenplay, which Aykroyd and Ramis once again cowrote. "It returns the story to a human scale," Murray told an interviewer before shooting began, "with subtlety and no silly explosions at the end. Like *Scrooged*, it's a story about innocence restored, and good values, and the power of faith in ordinary people." Like *Scrooged*, however, *Ghostbusters II* was fatally undermined by a director—Reitman—who preferred "silly explosions" and special effects to the character-driven comedy that attracted Murray to the project.

"It didn't end up the way it was presented," Murray explained after *Ghostbusters II* opened to decidedly mixed reviews. "The special effects guys took over. I had something like two scenes—and they're the only funny ones

Ghostbusters II, 1989

in the movie." To be fair, Murray's Peter Venkman character has more than two scenes, although he doesn't dominate the action the way he did in the original. The attempt to give more screen time to Aykroyd, Ramis, and Rick Moranis did prove somewhat successful. *Ghostbusters II* is more an ensemble piece and less a showcase for Murray's talents. But the long, loud, enervating sequel doesn't do nearly enough to distinguish itself from the first movie. For that, Murray placed the blame squarely on Reitman's shoulders.

"It's hard, it's really hard to make a sequel, no matter how sincere you are," Murray mused. "Somehow the directors take over from the writers and the comedians, and the thing ends up being a lot more action than comedy. Action is a lot easier to direct than comedy." For his part, Reitman faulted the deficiencies of the script. "It didn't all come together," he told *Vanity Fair* in 2014. "We just sort of got off on the wrong foot story-wise on that film." Rick Moranis cited unrealistic public expectations: "To have something as offbeat, unusual, and unpredictable [as] the first *Ghostbusters*, it's next to impossible to create something better," he said. "With sequels, it's not that the audience wants more of something; they want better."

Ghostbusters II was definitely not better, although it's not nearly so bad as its creators remember. It grossed more than $215 million and raised hopes for a third installment that have so far gone unrealized, thanks largely to Murray's distaste for repeating himself—unless he's making a *Garfield* sequel, in which case, all bets are off.

NEXT MOVIE: *Quick Change* (1990)

GHOSTBUSTERS III

Over the decades, Murray has made it clear he has no interest in appearing in a proposed third *Ghostbusters* movie. He has gone out of his way to belittle the efforts of **Harold Ramis** and others to revive the franchise, dismissing various rumored storylines as "ridiculous," "a crock," and "not the way I would have gone." He reportedly put down one *Ghostbusters III* script after reading just twenty pages. "It didn't touch our stuff," Murray groused. During a 2010 appearance on *Late Show with David Letterman*, Murray called the prospect of starring in a third *Ghostbusters* "my nightmare." When Letterman asked if he'd participate in the film at all, Murray replied, "I told them if they killed me off in a first reel, I'd do it." In 2014, Murray gave his

> ## "NO ONE WANTS TO PAY MONEY TO SEE FAT, OLD MEN CHASING GHOSTS!"
>
> —MURRAY, in a handwritten note to Dan Aykroyd and Harold Ramis that accompanied a shredded copy of their latest *Ghostbusters III* script, according to a 2011 report in the *National Enquirer*

blessing to a possible all-female reboot of the franchise, to be directed by *Freaks and Geeks* creator Paul Feig. "I'm fine with it," he said. "I would go to that movie, and they'd probably have better outfits, too."

GHOSTBUSTERS: HELLBENT

See Ghostbusters III.

GHOSTBUSTERS: THE VIDEO GAME

Along with the other three original *Ghostbusters*, Murray did vocal work for this 2009 Atari video game based on the 1980s film franchise. Atari promoted the game as if it were the second sequel to the original film, hyping the supposed creative contributions of **Dan Aykroyd** and **Harold Ramis**. But Ramis told the *New York Times* their input was minimal. "They were happy to have our involvement at all," Ramis said. "The crassest way I can put it is that they couldn't have paid us enough to give it the time and attention required to make it as funny as a feature film." Murray reportedly had a ball donning the figurative jumpsuit for the first time in twenty years. "That was fun," he said afterward. "I'm not really a game guy, but I enjoyed recording it. It was funny. I liked being the guy [Peter Venkman] again." He had such a good time, in fact, that he admitted to sauntering out of the New York recording studio singing Ray Parker Jr.'s *Ghostbusters* theme song. According to Murray, one of the locals "gave me this really pathetic look and shouts over at me: 'Hey man, get over it will you? That was a long time ago, okay?'"

GILLIAM, TERRY

Murray is an admirer of the brilliant, mercurial director of *Time Bandits* and *Brazil*. He was reportedly offered a part in Gilliam's 2013 sci-fi dystopia *The Zero Theorem* but turned it down in order to finish work on *The Grand Budapest Hotel*. "Terry's a fun guy to hang out with," Murray told the *Sunday Times*. "His stuff doesn't always work for me, but it's not for lack of trying. He really throws it out there."

> ## "IF I HAD A PINT OF TERRY'S BLOOD, I WOULD GET SOME SHIT DONE."
>
> —MURRAY, on the cinematic brio of director Terry Gilliam

GLAZER, MITCH

Screenwriter and producer who has collaborated with Murray on numerous films, including *Mr. Mike's Mondo Video*, *Scrooged*, and *Passion Play*. A onetime music journalist, Glazer first met Murray in 1977 on the introduction of **John Belushi**, whom he'd recently profiled in *Crawdaddy* magazine. Glazer and Murray have remained friends ever since. Since the early 2000s, when Murray fired his **agents** and cut off most communication with the Hollywood film community, Glazer has also served as one of the actor's informal conduits to the outside world. Producers often pester Glazer with calls to his home phone, asking him to pitch their projects to Murray. "I'm like an unpaid manager," Glazer told *Entertainment Weekly*.

GLIMPSE INSIDE THE MIND OF CHARLES SWAN III, A

DIRECTED BY: Roman Coppola

WRITTEN BY: Roman Coppola

RELEASE DATE: February 8, 2013

FILM RATING: ★★

MURRAY RATING: ★

PLOT: Fantasy sequences illuminate the inner life of a loathsome graphic designer.

STARRING BILL MURRAY AS: Saul, business manager and would-be libertine

Murray has a small, underwritten supporting role as the boon companion of a scuzzy 1970s album cover designer in this self-indulgent admixture of *Boogie Nights* and *All That Jazz*. If Federico Fellini and **Wes Anderson** had a baby, and that baby had no talent, the movie he produced might have been *A Glimpse inside the Mind of Charles Swan III*.

A vile, misogynistic car wreck of a film "directed" (it might be more accurate to say "perpetrated") by Francis Ford scion and frequent Anderson collaborator Roman Coppola, *Swan* was constructed as a showcase for a post-meltdown Charlie Sheen. But all it does is showcase how far he has fallen. Outfitted in tinted aviator glasses and a shaggy '70s toupee, Sheen gives an abysmal performance as a character so irredeemably dickish he can only have been painted from real life. The rest of the cast consists of called-in favors by the well-connected writer/director. Anderson regular Jason Schwartzman debases his personal brand as Swan's reprehensible Jewfro'd best friend. Murray, who worked with Coppola on *Moonrise Kingdom* and *The Darjeeling Limited*, showed his passionate commitment to the screenwriter's sophomore directorial effort by arriving on set at the last possible minute. "Bill gave me the impression he was interested," Coppola told the *Times* of London. "So I thought it was going to work out, but there was no sign of him and we needed to get him a costume and a hotel. Then he just showed up the day before."

NEXT MOVIE: *The Grand Budapest Hotel* (2014)

GOLF

"Golf has been really kind to me," Murray once said. "I've met a lot of extraordinary people through golf." He has described the sport's appeal as rooted in the unwritten rules by which players score themselves. Golf, he said, is "a game of self-report [with] codes of behavior and honor about it."

> ## "EVERY YEAR I SAY I'M GONNA PLAY MORE. BUT THEN A MOVIE COMES ALONG, AND I CAN'T GET SERIOUS ABOUT GOLF."
>
> —MURRAY, on his links obsession

Murray developed his love of golf as a child on the streets of Wilmette, Illinois. He and his brothers fashioned a makeshift golf course along a twenty-foot-wide parkway near their house. The "holes" were trees and telephone poles. When the boys' shots went awry, they could count on the nuns at the nearby Sisters of Christian Charity convent to retrieve them. "They would just show up at the door every once in a while with a bag of golf balls," said Murray's brother Ed.

In interviews, Murray has blamed his poor performance in school on his passion for golf. "I was on the golf course rather than being in lessons," he once admitted. "I couldn't really think of anything that interested me." When he was fourteen, Murray worked as a standard-bearer—a scoreboard carrier—at the Western Open, held at the Tam O'Shanter Golf Course, just outside Chicago. He had an up-close view of a thrilling fight to the finish between Arnold Palmer and the eventual tournament winner, Chi-Chi Rodriguez.

GOODBYE POP 1952–1976

National Lampoon comedy album from 1975 on which Murray appears. The record features

TALES FROM
MURRAYLAND

№ 7	The Stockholm Golf Cart Joyride

In August 2007, Murray was pulled over by Swedish police for driving a golf cart through the streets of Stockholm while under the influence of alcohol. The actor was in town attending the Scandinavian Masters golf tournament when he commandeered the cart, which was parked outside his hotel, and drove it to the Café Opera nightclub about a mile away. "I don't hold any grudge against Bill Murray for borrowing our cart for a while," said tournament organizer Fredrik Nilsmark. Although he refused to take a Breathalyzer test, Murray allowed police to draw a blood sample and signed a document admitting that he was driving under the influence. He later paid a fine and avoided jail time.

musical parodies of such pop and rock artists as Elton John, the Beatles, Helen Reddy, and Neil Young. Performers on the vinyl LP include Christopher Guest, Paul Shaffer, and **Gilda Radner**. Murray's most memorable contribution is the soul spoof "Kung Fu Christmas."

GRAND BUDAPEST HOTEL, THE

DIRECTED BY: Wes Anderson
WRITTEN BY: Wes Anderson
RELEASE DATE: February 6, 2014
FILM RATING: ★ ★ ★
MURRAY RATING: ★ ★ ★

PLOT: A fey concierge maintains his dignity while contesting a bogus murder charge in a fictitious Alpine country.

STARRING BILL MURRAY AS: Monsieur Ivan, crisply efficient hotel concierge

"I didn't have much to do with it," Murray declared of his seventh feature for director **Wes Anderson**. "I just showed up and did what I was told." An elegy to a vanished age of Old World refinement, *The Grand Budapest Hotel* is chock full of cameos from Anderson regulars, including Owen Wilson, Jason Schwartzman, and Bob Balaban. Although Murray appears in only a couple short scenes, he manages to leave a mark nonetheless. Playing the hirsute leader of the Society of the Crossed Keys, a secret intelligence-gathering agency made up of fastidious European hotel concierges, he takes the concept of customer service to a whole new level.

"Bill's role is a small part—but it's very important," Anderson told *Rolling Stone*. "He's the head man of this secret society that is immensely important to the story. It was one of those moments that I decided I wanted to save Bill for this very quick but critical secret mission at the climax of the story. Even with just a few minutes of screen time, he truly steps right up to it and is someone that I can always rely on."

As usual, it was Anderson's idiosyncratic writing that attracted Murray to the project. "When I first read the script, I went 'Holy cow, this is crazy!'" the actor told the *Independent*. Elsewhere, he likened *The Grand Budapest Hotel* to "a Times Square billboard dropped on your head. It's amazing." While perhaps not quite as mind-altering as Murray made it seem, this dapper little jewel box of a movie is one of Anderson's more engaging efforts. That is thanks largely to the winning performance of Ralph Fiennes in the lead role and the lavish production design, including some of the most formidable facial hair committed to film since the 1970s.

Murray sports an elegant walrus mustache in the film, a far cry from the bushy look he showed up with to the set. "[Wes] wanted me to ask everybody in the cast who could to grow anything they could," said hair and **makeup**

The Grand Budapest Hotel, 2014

designer Frances Hannon, Murray's personal stylist dating back to 1997's *The Man Who Knew Too Little*. "So I asked them to grow full beards and moustaches so that I could cut the shape in that Wes would want. Then Wes and I would get together with the actor—usually the night before they were to be on camera—and the three of us would discuss the references and inspirations and then we'd start cutting it and adjusting it. Bill, for example, came in and he had grown a full beard and this wonderful mustache that didn't look anything like he did in the film. We went for the biggest one—you have to start big and then scale back."

NEXT MOVIE: *The Monuments Men* (2014)

GRAND HOTEL ET DE MILAN

This five-star luxury hotel in **Milan**, Italy, is one of Murray's favorite hotels in the world.

GRANT, CARY

Murray is a big fan of this effortlessly elegant Old Hollywood leading man, whom he impersonated in a 1977 *Saturday Night Live* sketch. "He was able to make being suave and debonair seem so natural," Murray once said. "He moved so elegantly. He moved so gracefully. Everything he did. He gets a suit out of the closet in *North by Northwest*, you're like 'Wow, look at that man get that suit out of the closet.' It's breathtaking."

Murray had a brief encounter with Grant while having dinner with his agent in the 1980s. "I was a movie star, a big shot, in my mind," Murray remembered later. "There across the restaurant was Cary Grant. I was gobsmacked. It was everything I could do to not get up and walk over to his table. But I didn't. I just held it together. And as he left the restaurant, he gave me a look that said, 'That was cool. I know what you were doing. I know what you felt. And you sat here and didn't do it. And that was cool.' I thought, 'I did the right thing.' Later I met someone who told me, 'Yeah, he knew you and he liked you. He thought your movies were good.'"

GROUNDHOG DAY

DIRECTED BY: Harold Ramis

WRITTEN BY: Danny Rubin and Harold Ramis

RELEASE DATE: February 12, 1993

FILM RATING: ★ ★ ★ ★

MURRAY RATING: ★ ★ ★ ★

PLOT: A misanthropic TV weatherman must relive the same day over and over until he learns how to cultivate benevolence toward others.

STARRING BILL MURRAY AS: Phil Connors, meteorologist for WPBH-TV 9 in Pittsburgh

In the annals of high-concept cinema, *Groundhog Day* stands alone. Its very title has entered the popular lexicon, invoked by hack writers everywhere as universal shorthand for "that thing that repeats itself over and over." It is also one of the principal rune texts in the Murray canon. Murray has called his performance in this movie "probably the best work I've done" and Danny Rubin's original screenplay "one of the greatest conceptual scripts I've ever seen." Although the film was denied a single major award nomination, it is now regularly included on lists of the best fantasy and romantic comedy films of all time. *Groundhog Day* is "romantic without being nauseating," Murray once said, "which is what we're all looking for—romance without nausea."

Yet it almost never came to be—at least, not with Bill Murray in the lead role. Director **Harold Ramis** was reluctant to cast his old friend after an unpleasant experience working with him on their previous film together. "Bill Murray was not at the top of my list," Ramis told *GQ*. "He'd been getting crankier and crankier. By the end of *Ghostbusters II*, he was pretty cranky. I thought: Do I want to put up with this for twelve weeks?" The part of Phil Connors was originally offered to Michael Keaton, who turned it down because he "didn't get it." Tom Hanks was also considered, but he considered himself too nice for

the role of the glib, womanizing weatherman. In retrospect, it seems almost blasphemous to imagine anyone else playing Connors, so fully committed was Murray to what would be a career-defining performance.

Before shooting began, Murray and Danny Rubin collaborated closely on improvements to the latter's screenplay. They spent several weeks holed up in an office in **New York City** fine-tuning story elements between pick-up basketball games. At one point, at the insistence of the studio, a gypsy curse sequence was inserted at the beginning of the film to set the time loop plot in motion. But Murray preferred Rubin's original scenario, which offered no explanation for the supernatural premise.

The star and the screenwriter also made a Groundhog Day 1992 road trip to Punxsutawney, Pennsylvania, the setting of the film, where they sought inspiration from the locals. "We got to the only hotel in the town," Murray told the *Guardian.* "I woke up at five a.m. and took a shower. The water was freezing cold. I went downstairs and said that there was no hot water. And the woman behind the counter said, 'Oh, of course, there wouldn't be any hot water today. Today is the only day in the year that the hotel is even close to full.'" That scene wound up going in the finished film.

In the end, Punxsutawney was abandoned as a location in favor of Woodstock, Illinois, a town close to the **Chicago** homes of Ramis and Murray. The shoot took place during one of the coldest winters anyone there could remember. On his first day on the set, Murray bought coffee and danish for the freezing crew. From then on, Murray prepared for his performance by watching **the Weather Channel** and trying to predict the bone-chilling climatic conditions on the set. "I went outside every day and guessed what was going to happen when I got there," he said.

Complicating the already arduous winter shoot was Ramis's insistence on shooting and reshooting the same scenes in different weather conditions, so that he could assemble the footage in the proper sequence in the editing room. This led to some inspired moments of improvisation, as in the scene where Murray's character bear-hugs his nemesis, Ned Ryerson, played by Stephen Tobolowksy. Reshoots were also a consequence of nearly continuous rewrites. According to Tobolowksy, Ramis and Rubin threw out nearly half of Rubin's original script while on the set: "We were getting pages just hot off the press while we were shooting this," Tobolowsky told the website Epoch Times. "The way the movie was originally . . . Bill had a series of odd events, and then at

> ## "I'M NOT JUST GONNA LOSE WEIGHT AND FLOSS, I'M GONNA LIVE."
>
> —MURRAY, when asked what he would do if he had one day of his life to live over and over

the end he got bored and killed himself and then woke up and time started again. [Instead] they cut out the last third of the movie, moved the suicide up, and added the whole last part of the movie where he's taking piano lessons, and he saves the woman with the flat tire and saves the boy from the tree." Excised from the movie at various points were a scene in which Phil Connors destroys his hotel room with a chainsaw and several scenes involving the groundhog (which reportedly bit Murray a couple times during filming). As a result of the changes, *Groundhog Day* went from being what Tobolowsky called "a mediocre Bill Murray movie . . . a rowdy comedy with Bill being rowdy" to "a great film . . . about healing and making the choice to survive and to heal."

Not all the tweaks met with Murray's approval. "I thought there was a lot of overwriting," he declared in 2014. "And I held Harold responsible for that." By all accounts, Murray was at his absolute surliest during the making of this film. "Bill was not easy to work with," Tobolowksy admitted. "If I had been on my first movie, he would have brought me to tears more than once." Most famously, Murray refused to shoot the film's climactic scene—in which Phil Connors wakes up in bed with Andie MacDowell's Rita Hanson, having escaped the time loop—until somebody told him whether he was still wearing the same clothes from the night before. When Ramis refused to take the bait, an assistant set decorator was forced to make the call on this crucial plot point.

Adding to the bad vibes was the fact that Murray's first **marriage** was disintegrating around the time *Groundhog Day* was being shot. Part of the reason Danny Rubin was dispatched to babysit Murray during preproduction was to get him away from Ramis, who was sick of dealing with Murray's temper tantrums. "They were like two brothers who weren't getting along," Rubin told the *New Yorker*. "And they were pretty far apart on what the movie was about." In classic passive-aggressive fashion, Murray took out his anger at Ramis by showing up late to the set, berating members of the crew, and engaging in occasional outbursts of autodestruction. "Whoever was around had to take it from him," Ramis later said. "Or he'd go back and trash his motor home. I'd say, 'Well, now you've trashed your motor home. Good idea.'" After weeks of being "irrationally mean and unavailable," in Ramis's view, Murray finally stopped speaking to the director altogether. They would remain estranged for more than twenty years.

Although **critics** responded positively, *Groundhog Day* was not exactly a commercial triumph on its original release. Shortly after the film opened, a colossal blizzard buried much of the eastern half of the United States under a blanket of snow. "How could anyone go to the movies when they couldn't even get out of their driveway?" Murray complained. "Two weeks later there

6 00

Groundhog Day, 1993

was another ten inches of snow—same thing. So it wasn't the box-office success it should have been." Still, despite the agony he had gone through to get the picture made, Murray was proud of the work he had done and encouraged by the favorable notices he received for his performance. "That was sort of the turning point," he later said. "That was the first time the New York press went, 'Hey, wait a minute—this is a real movie here, not just that broad thing.'" One day that spring, Murray saw a caricature of himself in the *New Yorker*, depicting him emerging from the soil like the proverbial groundhog. "It was so cute and it was so great," he said. "That felt good. It wasn't an Academy Award, but it was somethin' I liked a lot. It was more significant."

NEXT MOVIE: *Mad Dog and Glory* (1993)

GUNG HO

During his mid-1980s **sabbatical** from Hollywood, Murray passed on the lead role in this 1986 comedy directed by **Ron Howard**. Michael Keaton ended up playing the part of Hunt Stevenson, the cocksure American foreman of a Japanese-owned auto plant.

GURDJIEFF, GEORGE IVANOVITCH

Mid-twentieth-century Greco-Armenian spiritual guru whose teachings Murray began to study in the 1980s. Gurdjieff's quasimystical philosophical system, commonly called "the Work," "the Fourth Way," or "the Way of the Sly Man," is based on the idea that human beings live their lives in a state of perpetual sleep, ruled by forces beyond their control. Only by "waking up" through the practice of Gurdjieff-approved awareness exercises can they achieve a state of true enlightenment and free will. In his Jazz Age heyday, Gurdjieff ran an institute near Paris where he would unexpectedly create unorthodox events designed to startle his disciples into consciousness in the same way that Zen masters whack meditating students over the back with a stick.

Dismissed by some as a crackpot, Gurdjieff developed a cult following among artists, intellectuals, and wealthy socialites. His esoteric teachings are still followed by a small and secretive coterie of adherents. Murray first began studying Gurdjieff in earnest during his Parisian **sabbatical** from filmmaking in the mid-1980s. Every January 13, Gurdjieff's followers gather to commemorate his birthday with elaborate vodka toasts and performances of the *Epic of Gilgamesh*. According to eyewitness accounts, Murray has attended at least one such celebration. He has also taken part in so-called ideas meetings, during which passages from Gurdjieff's masterpiece *Beelzebub's Tales to His Grandson* are read and discussed.

In a 2009 interview with *GQ* magazine, **Harold Ramis** attributed some aspects of Murray's notoriously surly personality to his study of the spiritual figure. "Gurdjieff used to act really irrationally to his students, almost as

The Connected Wisdom of Bill Murray and G. I. Gurdjieff

"Only by beginning to remember himself
does a man really awaken."

—Gurdjieff, from his essay "Awakened Consciousness"

"Whatever the best part of my life has been,
has been as a result of that remembering."

—Murray, in an interview with the *New York Times*

"Only he who can take care of what
belongs to others may have his own."

—Gurdjieff's Aphorism #20

"I think if you can take care of yourself and
then maybe try to take care of someone else,
that's sort of how you're supposed to live."

—Murray, during a 2009 appearance on CNBC's *Squawk Box*

"A man may be born, but in order to be born he must
first die, and in order to die he must first awake."

—Gurdjieff, *In Search of the Miraculous*

"It's not easy to really engage all the time. It's so
much easier to zone, to get distracted, to daydream."

—Murray, to interviewer Charlie Rose in 2014

"I love him who loves work."

—Gurdjieff's Aphorism #15

"I don't want to have a relationship with someone
if I'm not going to work with them."

—Murray, to *GQ* magazine in 2010

"He who has freed himself of the disease of tomorrow
has a chance to attain what he came here for."

—Gurdjieff's Aphorism #28

"What if there is no tomorrow?
There wasn't one today!"

—Murray, as weatherman Phil Connors in *Groundhog Day*

"All that men say and do, they say
and do in sleep. All this can have no
value whatsoever. Only awakening and what
leads to awakening has a value in reality."

—Gurdjieff, from "Awakened Consciousness"

"You're unconscious most of the time. Not out cold,
but you're unconscious. Lights on, nobody home. If
you come back, 'Oh, there I am again.' All of a
sudden, you're looking at yourself, like, 'Where am
I now? What was I thinking? What am I feeling?
What's my body doing?' Usually, I have a pang of
remorse or a reminding, like, 'Oh, here I am again.
How was it I wanted to be living?'"

—Murray, in an interview with the *Detroit Free Press*

"One of the best means for arousing the
wish to work on yourself is to realize that
you may die at any moment."

—Gurdjieff's Aphorism #33

"I've got a moose head on the wall. The
biggest moose head I've ever seen. It's a sobering
thought that something that big can die."

—Murray, describing the decor in his
New York City apartment, in 1981

if trying to teach them object lessons," Ramis observed. "Bill was always teaching people lessons like that. If he perceived someone as being too self-important or corrupt in some way that he couldn't stomach, it was his job to straighten them out." According to *Nothing Lasts Forever* director Tom Schiller, also a Gurdjieff devotee, Murray's connection to the Mediterranean mystic also accounts for his party-crashing and photo-bombing antics of recent years. "Bill fits Gurdjieff's description exactly," Schiller says. "At any moment, anywhere, he can engage perfect strangers in hilarious and spontaneous acts of humor that a mere mortal could never get away with."

GUYS, THE

In one of his rare forays onto the dramatic stage, Murray played a **New York City** firefighter haunted by his memories of September 11 in this 2001 play by Anne Nelson. Sigourney Weaver starred as the newspaper editor who helps him compose eulogies for his fallen comrades. *The Guys* opened at the Flea Theater, just a few blocks from Ground Zero, in December 2001. In an interview, Murray described the experience as cathartic and credited his costar with giving him the strength to get through it. "It was just something that had to be done," he said. "It was so hard going out there night after night with a situation that was so raw. She never lost sight of the moment onstage, because she kept focus, and that kept things going right. It helped me keep on track, too." Although Murray left the production shortly after opening night, replaced by Bill Irwin, it was not because of poor notices. *Variety* found the play "dramatically a bit on the dull side" but praised Murray's performance as "utterly artless and unactorly, and very touching in its honesty."

TALES FROM
MURRAYLAND

Nº 8	## The Day He Played Kickball with Strangers

On a brisk fall day in 2012, Murray visited New York City to check out the recently completed Franklin Delano Roosevelt Four Freedoms Park, located at the southern tip of Roosevelt Island. After getting a sneak peek at the FDR memorial, which was not yet open to the public, he found himself inexorably drawn to a beer-league kickball game being played on a nearby stretch of grass. Kickballers were surprised by the apparition of a slightly disheveled older man, wearing blue cutoffs and a loose-fitting flannel shirt, who suddenly and without warning jumped into their game. "We just figured he was someone's dad on the other team and kept playing," one of the players said later. Taking a turn at the plate, Murray launched a booming single but was chased back to first when he attempted to go for two. It was at that point that the other players realized who he was. After getting erased on an ensuing double play, Murray jogged around the bases high-fiving everyone, bear-hugged a player's mother, posed for a team photo, and then went home.

HACKMAN, GENE

When he first arrived in New York City in 1974 to work on *The National Lampoon Show*, Murray sublet an apartment in a building that was once home to Academy Award–winning actor Gene Hackman. According to Murray, the woman from whom he was subletting "hadn't paid her gas or electric bill in eight years. She told me Gene Hackman had lived in this building. There were millions of cockroaches, but I thought, 'Well, Gene put up with it, I can put up with it.'" The two men later worked together on *The Royal Tenenbaums*.

HALLOWEEN

When dressing up for Halloween, young Murray stuck with the classics: hobos and ghosts. "I didn't have any costumes when I was a kid," he told the *New York Daily News*. "We were basically working with a sheet most of the time or I went as a bum, which is basically cork smeared on my face and some bad clothes."

HAMLET

DIRECTED BY: Michael Almereyda
WRITTEN BY: Michael Almereyda
RELEASE DATE: May 12, 2000
FILM RATING: ★★
MURRAY RATING: ★★

PLOT: A brooding slacker plots the hostile takeover of his uncle's company.

STARRING BILL MURRAY AS: Polonius, prattling corporate toady

Following in the footsteps of such distinguished actors as Hume Cronyn, Ian Holm, and Michael Redgrave, Murray essayed the role of Polonius, the pompous royal retainer who gets plugged in his arras, in this modern-day reimagining of Shakespeare's tragedy.

The challenge of taking on a classic appealed to the scrapper in Murray. "A lot of people act like they're destined to play Shakespeare, and that pisses me off," he told an audience at a retrospective of his films in 2004. Finding the humor amid all the gloom and gore was also part of the project's allure. "Polonius is a guy who's spying for the king on the prince to the throne which was usurped by the brother who killed the actual king and then stole his wife. Shakespeare knows there are laughs there, but where the hell are they? You've got to find those laughs and at the same time make the drama work. That's why comedy is harder to do than straight drama."

Although Murray seems somewhat ill at ease mouthing Shakespeare's dialogue—he comes off more like a fey imbecile than the tedious old windbag called for in the text—he fares better than some of the other actors in this intriguing but uneven film. As Hamlet, Ethan Hawke is practically catatonic. He mumbles his way through soliloquies he doesn't seem to understand, repeatedly putting the stresses on the wrong words and syllables. Still, if you've always wondered what it would be like to see Hamlet faxing, riding a motorcycle, or renting videos at Blockbuster, this is the adaptation for you.

For Murray completists, *Hamlet* is also noteworthy for the scene in which Hawke's vengeful prince shoots Polonius in the eye with a handgun. It marked the first time Murray had ever died on-screen—unless you consider *The Man Who Knew Too Little* a prolonged suicide attempt.

NEXT MOVIE: *Charlie's Angels* (2000)

HEISS, CAROL

Murray has named this mid-twentieth-century Olympic figure skater as the one sports figure in the world he would most like to be. Heiss won a gold medal at the 1960 Winter Olympics in Squaw Valley, California, and went on to star in the 1961 film *Snow White and the Three Stooges*. "I always had a thing for Carol Heiss," Murray said. "I just thought she was kind of special."

HERKIMAN, RICHARD

See "Shower Mike."

HITCHHIKER'S GUIDE TO THE GALAXY, THE

Murray was briefly under consideration for the role of Ford Prefect in a proposed early 1980s big-screen adaptation of Douglas Adams's novel. The film, which would have reunited Murray with *Stripes* director **Ivan Reitman**, was shelved in favor *Ghostbusters*.

HOLDEN, WILLIAM

The Academy Award–winning star of *Stalag 17*, *The Bridge on the River Kwai*, and *Sunset Boulevard* is one of Murray's all-time favorite actors. In a 2004 interview with film critic Elvis Mitchell, Murray lauded Holden for his chiseled physique, admiring his ability to work without a shirt on for long stretches of the 1955 film *Picnic*. He described Holden as "a total stud" and called his Oscar-nominated turn in 1976's *Network* "a totally stud performance."

HOME ALONE

Murray was one of many actors considered for the role of Peter McCallister, Macaulay Culkin's absent-minded father, in this 1990 film about a mischievous eight-year-old who outwits a pair of idiotic burglars. Jack Nicholson and Harrison Ford were also considered for the part, which went to John Heard.

HONKER, THE

Mush-mouthed, possibly schizophrenic drunk played by Murray in numerous *Saturday Night Live* sketches, as well as the short film *Perchance to Dream*. The Honker is one of Murray's oldest characters, dating back to his **Second City** days. He performed a brief monologue as the Honker for his *Saturday Night Live* audition. A scene of Murray as the Honker was cut from *Ghostbusters*. **Carl Spackler**, the deranged assistant greenskeeper Murray played in *Caddyshack*, shares some DNA with this woozy character.

HOOSIERS

Murray has called this heart-tugging 1986 film about a small-town Indiana high school basketball team "a movie I cannot turn off" whenever it is on television. "[*Hoosiers*] makes me cry and laugh at the same time," he said in a 2008 interview. "It's corn, but corn's okay. Indiana basketball is a corn tradition." On the general subject of schmaltz in films, Murray believes it all depends on how it's ladled out. "It's only how it's executed that makes it sappy or sentimental. It's emotional and you have to have emotion. But it's only when you execute it poorly and you arrive at sentimentality, then you have to take those people out and shoot them. You have to take them out in the cornfield and bury them like Joe Pesci in *Casino*."

> **"I CAN CRY AT HOOSIERS. I USED TO CRY AT BURGER KING COMMERCIALS. I CAN GO."**
>
> —MURRAY, on his weakness for mawkish entertainment

HORNY DEVIL

Unproduced screenplay commissioned by Murray in the mid-1980s from the screenwriting team of Tom Schiller and Lauren Versel Bresnan. The script had Murray's character traveling back in time to review the events of his life in a manner reminiscent of the Frank Capra classic *It's a Wonderful Life*. Murray lost interest in the project following the disappointment of *The Razor's Edge* and his subsequent **sabbatical** from Hollywood.

HOWARD, RON

Murray has had a somewhat fraught relationship with the former child star turned Hollywood director. In the 1980s, he turned down chances to play the lead roles in Howard's films *Splash* and *Gung Ho*. Then, in 1990, when Murray was looking for a director for *Quick Change*, Howard returned the favor in a particularly irksome manner. Impressed by Howard's work behind the camera on the 1977 car chase comedy *Grand Theft Auto*, Murray sent him the script for *Quick Change* and asked him to consider taking it on. "I don't get it," said Howard after reading it. "There's no one to root for." "He lost me at that moment," Murray remembered later. "I've never gone back to him since." He has called Howard's rationale for passing on the project "the craziest Hollywood jive" he ever heard.

HOW DO YOU KNOW?

Murray verbally agreed to play wealthy businessman Charles Madison in this 2013 comedy from director James L. Brooks. He started rehearsals with the rest of the cast and then mysteriously disappeared two weeks before shooting was scheduled to begin. Jack Nicholson ended up replacing him.

HUGHES, JOHN

Although the beloved director of *The Breakfast Club* and *Sixteen Candles* was born the same year as Murray and spent part of his childhood living in the suburbs of **Chicago**, Murray claimed in a 2010 interview that they never met—despite his having done a cameo in Hughes's 1988 film *She's Having a Baby*. "Steve Martin said to me once, 'You'd *hate* him,'" Murray told *GQ*. "'He'd say, 'Do this, where you stick something in your nose!' That kind of stuff drives me nuts." And though Murray has professed his admiration for *The Breakfast Club*, he was shocked by the over-the-top memorial tribute Hughes received at the 2010 **Academy Awards** ceremony. "I was kind of surprised they gave him a big thing at the Oscars," Murray said. "I mean, I remember Hal Ashby barely got mentioned, and this guy made half a dozen *unbelievable* movies."

HYDE PARK ON HUDSON

DIRECTED BY: Roger Michell
WRITTEN BY: Richard Nelson
RELEASE DATE: February 1, 2013
FILM RATING: ★★
MURRAY RATING: ★★

PLOT: As clouds of war gather overseas, a randy Franklin Delano Roosevelt consoles himself with hand jobs from his cousin Daisy.

STARRING BILL MURRAY AS: Franklin Delano Roosevelt

"Can this guy be serious?" Murray thought when director Roger Michell offered him the chance to play America's thirty-second president in a big-screen biopic based on the private journals of FDR's sixth cousin, Daisy Suckley. "I wouldn't have cast myself," he confessed to the *New York Times*. Although Murray may have been an unconventional choice, he proved to be an inspired one. Although he struggles a bit to capture FDR's high-toned Mid-Atlantic accent, Murray won plaudits for his empathetic portrayal of the historical icon he called "the most formidable character" he'd ever played. "Murray, who has a wider range than we sometimes realize, finds the human core of this FDR and presents it tenderly," wrote Roger Ebert in a review that was representative of the critical consensus.

After securing the part in the spring of 2011, Murray spent the next several months reading biographies of Roosevelt and listening to recordings of his speeches. But he drew the most direct inspiration for his performance from the experience of his sister Laura, who had contracted polio as a girl. "That shaped the state I was in while I worked," Murray explained to the *Los Angeles Times*. "Because I realized she didn't complain about anything." By the time shooting was under way in the summer of 2011, Murray had overcome his initial reservations and convinced himself he was the perfect man for the role. "Not to compare myself, but certain personality things were similar, like the way [FDR] tried to leaven things and move attention around a room, get everyone their little slice of the sun."

Unfortunately, though Murray acquits himself favorably, his efforts are undermined by a screenplay that depicts the polio-stricken president as a pervy creep. The decision to center the film on a purported sexual relationship between Roosevelt and his naive female cousin ensured that it would generate controversy, but the plot was historically and dramatically dubious. Directed with the gauzy stateliness of an episode of *Downton Abbey*, *Hyde Park on Hudson* is much too charitable to its lecherous protagonist. But Murray had made it clear from the beginning that he wanted no part of a movie that called FDR's character into question. "The story that we're going to tell, is it going to be a tearing down of an icon?" he told the *New York Times* of his mind-set in accepting the part. "I don't know if I want to be part of that kind of action, where you trash someone. What was the John Travolta movie, *Primary Colors*? I didn't want to do something where you were really just napalming someone."

NEXT MOVIE: *A Glimpse inside the Mind of Charles Swan III* (2013)

TALES FROM
MURRAYLAND

Nº 9	The Deaf-Mute Assistant

Murray was at his absolute prickliest during the making of *Groundhog Day* in 1992. Relations between him and the studio got so bad that producers asked him to hire a personal assistant to serve as a go-between. Murray responded by hiring a deaf-mute who could communicate only in Native American sign language—which Murray promised to learn. (As it turned out, the only sign he mastered was the one for "tractor trailer.") The passive-aggressive move angered director Harold Ramis, who denounced it as "anticommunication" and added it to the list of reasons why he would soon stop talking to Murray in any language.

In his 2014 "Ask Me Anything" session on Reddit, Murray revealed that things ended badly for him and the assistant too: "I was sort of ambitious thinking that I could hire someone that had the intelligence to do a job but didn't have necessarily speech or couldn't quite hear or spoke [*sic*] in sign language. She was a bright person and witty but she had never been away from her home before and even though I tried to accommodate more than I understood when I first hired her, she was very young in her emotional self and the emotional component of being away from her home was lacking.... She was like one of your own kids that never had a job, and then they get a job and realize that certain things are expected, and you can't react to everything you don't like or care about. So the first time you have a job and someone says 'you have to do this'—it was more complicated than she imagined. We were both optimistic, but it was harder than either of us expected to make it work."

IMPRESSIONS

During his years on *Saturday Night Live*, Murray did impressions of celebrities and public figures, including Robert Duvall, **Cary Grant**, David Susskind, Walter Cronkite, Robert F. Kennedy, Ted Kennedy, Ralph Lauren, Richard Dawson, Paul McCartney, and the shah of Iran. He also performed a convincing impersonation of an over-the-hill Joe DiMaggio on a 1982 episode of *SCTV* and attempted a brief Richard Burton impression in *Scrooged*. Although he has a knack for mimicry, he has rarely performed the same impression twice. He does not consider them to be his strong suit. "Impressions really aren't a higher form of life," he once said. "There aren't too many people who make their career by them, and those who do end up hanging by a noose doing eight different characters as they swing."

INDIAN HILL CLUB

Winnetka, Illinois, **golf** and country club where the Murray brothers worked as caddies in the 1960s. During the time the Murrays lugged bags at Indian Hill, club membership was restricted to wealthy Protestants. Caddies were mostly Irish American and Italian American Catholics. The club's eighteen-hole golf course was built in 1920 to the specifications of master course designer Donald Ross. The bushy area behind the ninth green was where Bill Murray "learned to curse, smoke, and play cards for money," according to his autobiography.

IN-N-OUT BURGER

Murray is a passionate devotee of this regional fast food chain beloved by southern Californians since 1948. "It's a great burger," he has said. "They do a great job with it. The french fries are real potatoes. The burger's great. You can get it all kinds of ways. It's definitely the best franchise burger by a million miles." In a 2014 interview with radio host Howard Stern, Murray revealed that he once ordered his chauffeur to take him through the drive-through at a Las Vegas In-N-Out Burger and then tipped the driver with In-N-Out Burger coupons. According to published reports, Murray sealed the deal to appear in 2014's *St. Vincent* during a visit to a **Los Angeles** In-N-Out Burger with the film's director, Ted Melfi.

INSIDE THE ACTORS STUDIO

Popular basic cable interview series hosted by composer and soap opera actor James Lipton. Murray has declined numerous invitations to appear on the program, out of disgust at the prospect of being "trumpeted and fellated" by the unctuous Lipton. "I met that guy a while ago," he told *Esquire* magazine in 2004. "He said, 'You're never gonna do the show, are you?' I guess I've been invited before, but I always had a problem with it being called *Inside the Actors Studio*. When I was at **Second City**, we always had a bit of an attitude about the Actors Studio. The Actors Studio—yeah, they had a couple of good actors. So? Do we all have to get down and worship 'em? It always bothered me. And when he called the show *Inside the Actors Studio*—well, what're you talkin' to Meg Ryan for, or any number of these people they've got now who couldn't find the Actors Studio with a phone book?"

IRELAND

Murray has a special fondness for the Emerald Isle, largely because of his Irish heritage. His paternal grandfather emigrated from Cork, and his mother's people are from Galway. Murray has visited Ireland many times to play **golf**. "It's the most beautiful country to play golf in," he once declared. "When you come as a guest to play golf you are treated like a king." Murray's favorite place is the Tralee Golf Club in County Kerry. He has called the par-72 course, designed by Arnold Palmer, the prettiest he has ever played.

ISLEY, RUDOLPH

Founding member of the 1960s R & B group the Isley Brothers whose mansion overlooking the Hudson River Murray purchased at auction for $7 million in 1990.

I
J
K

JANIS, LOU

Legendary caddy master at the Indian Hill Club in Winnetka, Illinois, in the late 1950s and early 1960s. Janis introduced the Murray brothers to the world of caddying and was the real-life model for the Lou Loomis character in *Caddyshack*.

Ed Murray, Bill's oldest brother, was the first of the Murray boys to work under Janis's tutelage. "I was an altar boy at the church, and me and four boys serving Mass saw this man standing off to the side of the sacristy," Ed recalled in a 2005 interview with *Chicago* magazine. "After Mass he told us he was the caddy master for the Indian Hill Club. If we wanted to make some money, he said, he would take us up that day and show us how to do it." Brian, Bill, and Andy Murray soon followed in Ed's footsteps.

Janis was a rough-hewn but neatly dressed man who drove a Ford Falcon. Bill Murray once dubbed him the "prince of polyester." A compulsive gambler, he was known to bet heavily on NCAA football games. While working at the Indian Hill Club in the mid-1960s, Bill Murray helped Janis make his weekly college football picks.

JERK, THE

Murray filmed a cameo as a gay Jewish interior decorator that was cut from the final version of this 1979 comedy starring Steve Martin as the titular wanker.

JUNGLE BURGER

See Shame of the Jungle.

KELLY, MARGARET "MICKEY"

Murray met his first wife while they were teenagers growing up in Wilmette, Illinois. They dated off and on for more than a decade before tying the knot on January 24, 1981—Super Bowl Sunday, which Murray considers a national holiday.

The wedding took place in Las Vegas. Murray was taking a break from filming *Stripes* and told Kelly he was taking her out for dinner to a Mexican restaurant in the San Fernando Valley. They ended up driving to Vegas to elope, a matrimonial method Murray once called "efficient, fast, and binding." A mysterious officiant in dark sunglasses performed the ceremony, which got under way at four thirty in the morning. For musical accompaniment, Murray selected "Ave Maria" as sung by Luciano Pavarotti, but by the time the bride and groom were in place, "Pagliacci" was playing instead. "It was grim," Murray later recalled.

A second, more traditional ceremony was staged two months later, on March 25, in front of family and friends at the Catholic church in Wilmette where Murray was baptized. Murray's sister Nancy planned the event. His brother Brian served as best man. "We did the whole thing," Murray recalled. "Church, priest, reception. All those Irish people drinking heavily. It was great."

A onetime talent coordinator for *The Tonight Show* and *The Dick Cavett Show*, Mickey Kelly later ran a custom furniture shop near the couple's home in New York's Hudson Valley. In a 1984 interview, Murray admitted he "ruined" his first wife's career. "She used to be in TV. At one time, she was the head of comedy development at HBO. She was fired for telling them what she thought of them. It was the best way out. If both of you have careers, then *nobody's* there when you get home." In another interview, Murray expressed his displeasure with Kelly's constant nagging: "I probably take more grief than anybody in the world who earns enough to buy his wife jewelry. Some people would call it keeping him in line, some people would call it maintaining communication, others would say it's having your chops busted."

Murray's marriage to Mickey Kelly lasted fifteen years, officially, during which time she bore him two sons. When they separated in 1994, it was revealed that Murray had been in an extramarital relationship with his costume designer **Jennifer Butler** for several years. The divorce was finalized in 1996.

KINDERGARTEN COP

Director **Ivan Reitman** offered Murray the part of classroom lawman John Kimble in this family-friendly 1990 comedy. When Murray passed, the role went to Arnold Schwarzenegger.

KINGPIN

DIRECTED BY: Peter and Robert Farrelly

WRITTEN BY: Barry Fanaro and Mort Nathan

RELEASE DATE: July 4, 1996

FILM RATING: ★★⸝

MURRAY RATING: ★★★

PLOT: A crippled bowler confronts the man who ruined his once-promising career.

STARRING BILL MURRAY AS: Ernie "Big Ern" McCracken, the Muhammad Ali of bowling

Before returning to lead roles with *Larger Than Life*, Murray gifted the world with one last indelible character turn, playing an obnoxious professional bowler with a gravity-defying comb-over in this lowbrow sports comedy from the then red-hot Farrelly brothers. Although it bombed at the box office on its initial release, *Kingpin* has gained a cult following over the decades. It would be Murray's last watchable film until he reinvented himself as a serious character actor in 1998's *Rushmore*.

> "STRIKE, STRIKE, STRIKE—THE FIRST THREE HE THROWS. THE PLACE WENT BALLISTIC. THEY COULDN'T BELIEVE WHAT HE DID."
>
> —PETER FARRELLY, on Murray's amazing exhibition of bowling prowess in *Kingpin*

Jim Carrey was the Farrellys' first choice for the role of "Big Ern" McCracken, the sleazy grifter whose machinations lead to Woody Harrelson's permanent disfigurement. Once he won the part, Murray put his own unique stamp on the character. He ad-libbed nearly all of his lines, discarding much of the scripted dialogue. He also managed to out-bowl the other actors, rolling a "turkey"—bowling argot for three strikes in a row—in one take for the film's climactic showdown sequence. "He was just the consummate pro," Bobby Farrelly told *USA Today*. "When we shot the big tournament in Reno, we had about 2,000 extras. And over three, four days, they could get bored. But

I J K

Bill was in the stands playing with the people. No one wanted to leave."
NEXT MOVIE: *Larger Than Life* (1996)

KING RALPH

The part of Ralph Jones, the titular monarch in this 1991 comedy about
a slovenly American lounge singer who inherits the British throne, was
written with Murray in mind. Producers ultimately opted to go with John
Goodman, who was riding a wave of TV fame spawned by the hit sitcom
Roseanne.

KUNG FU HUSTLE

Murray has called this cartoonish 2004 homage to Hong Kong action movies
"the supreme achievement of the modern age in terms of comedy." In a 2010
interview with *GQ* magazine, he described the experience of watching
his 1990 comedy **Quick Change** on a double bill with *Kung Fu Hustle*. *Quick
Change* "looked like a home movie" compared to Stephen Chow's film, Murray contended. "It looked like a fucking high school film. . . . There should
have been a day of mourning for American comedy the day that movie came
out." In a 2015 *New Yorker* profile, Murray asserted that, next to *Kung Fu
Hustle*, "pretty much anything is Cream of Wheat."

I
J
K

Kingpin, 1996

TALES FROM
MURRAYLAND

№ 10	The Time He Photobombed a Couple's Engagement Photos

In June 2014, lovebirds Ashley Donald and Erik Rogers of Charleston, South Carolina, were posing for photos to commemorate their recent engagement when Murray snuck up behind the photographer, lifted his shirt, and started rubbing his distended belly in a clownish manner. Photographer Raheel Gauba initially pegged him for a crazed vagrant and tried to go on with the shoot, but the actor's frenzied mugging quickly became a distraction. When Gauba finally realized whom he was dealing with, he invited Murray to pose for a photograph with the happy couple. "I took the shot and off he goes," Gauba said afterward.

№ 11	The Night He Danced to Lil John

Capping off an eventful summer of 2014, Murray spent the Saturday before his sixty-fourth birthday partying down at the home of Marvin "Larry" Reynolds in Jedburg, South Carolina. According to eyewitness reports and a widely circulated YouTube video, Murray ended the evening feverishly boogying to Tommy Tutone's "867-5309/Jenny" and DJ Snake and Lil Jon's "Turn Down for What." He also took moose-call lessons from some of the "old country people" in attendance.

LABOUNTA, TODD

See DiLaMuca, Todd.

LA CROIX

Faux French sparkling water brand preferred by Murray until the early 1990s because it was bottled in La Crosse, Wisconsin. According to a 1990 magazine profile, Murray "will drink anything made in Wisconsin."

LANSON

Murray's preferred brand of French Champagne.

LARGER THAN LIFE

DIRECTED BY: Howard Franklin

WRITTEN BY: Roy Blount Jr.

RELEASE DATE: November 1, 1996

FILM RATING: ★★

MURRAY RATING: ★★

PLOT: A motivational speaker travels across America with an 8,000-pound elephant.

STARRING BILL MURRAY AS: Jack Corcoran, self-help author turned elephant companion

By 1996, Murray had not played the lead in a film since *Groundhog Day* three years earlier. "I really have to get more active," he confessed to *USA Today*. "I've been lazy. . . . I don't work as much as other people do." His agent, Mike Ovitz, thought he had the perfect starring vehicle to lift Murray out of the doldrums. "You know, you and an elephant would be funny," Ovitz told his client. Murray immediately smelled a rat. "When he says stuff, I always know there's an agenda. Somebody he knows has got an elephant script."

That "elephant script" turned out to be *Larger Than Life*, an innocuous road movie about a Tony Robbins–type motivational guru who inherits custody of a four-ton pachyderm from his late father. Originally called *Nickel & Dime*, the project was briefly redubbed *Elephant Man 2* before an on-set contest was launched to come up with a final title. *Larger Than Life* was selected, with *Elephant Men* and *The Wackyderm* among the runners-up. Humorist Roy Blount Jr. was brought in to revise the script to fit Murray's comic persona.

Howard Franklin, Murray's erstwhile *Quick Change* collaborator, was hired to direct. Tai, an Asian elephant best known for her performance in the previous year's *Operation Dumbo Drop*, took on the challenging role of Vera, the orphaned circus animal who teaches Murray how to care.

From the first day of filming, Murray formed a deep and lasting bond with his elephantine leading lady. "She has probably spoiled me for all other elephants," he declared on the eve of *Larger Than Life*'s release. "This was the only time I cried when I said goodbye to a costar." Having worked opposite Andie MacDowell, Geena Davis, and Sigourney Weaver, among others, Murray boldly placed Tai in the top ranks of actresses with whom he'd shared the screen. "She's the best," he gushed. "She's definitely the most talented—except for Gilda [Radner]."

When he wasn't cavorting with Tai, Murray was his usual Jekyll and Hyde self on the set. According to a published report, he demanded that a member of the crew be fired because he objected to the man's cologne. During filming of a scene in which Murray and the elephant trek through the Rocky Mountains, traffic became so snarled that Murray had the entire cast and crew line the highway and perform the "YMCA" dance for the entertainment of enraged motorists.

That wasn't the only snafu that bedeviled the production. When studio executives were given a look at a rough cut, they were appalled. Murray

appeared to be sleepwalking through his performance. Reshoots were ordered, with new scenes added for Matthew McConaughey as a methed-out truck driver who gives Murray and the elephant a ride. *Larger Than Life*'s opening was delayed and then hidden from the eyes of **critics**. When reviewers did get a look at it, they were not impressed. The *Boston Globe* called it "a thin, disjointed road comedy," while *Variety*'s Todd McCarthy rated it "entirely mirthless" and railed: "Some talented people step in a rather large pile of elephant droppings."

Sensing that he had a turkey on his hands, Murray embarked on a frenetic one-man publicity campaign. He appeared on Larry King's CNN talk show, submitted to several newspaper and magazine interviews, and even filmed a promotional featurette—in drag—as a Mary Hart–like entertainment reporter. *USA Today* described Murray in lipstick and a wig as resembling "RuPaul after a nuclear accident." But the promo tour failed to have much of an effect. *Larger Than Life* came and went quickly, leaving Murray fans to console themselves with his two-scene cameo in *Space Jam*, which opened two weeks later.

NEXT MOVIE: *Space Jam* (1996)

> ## "THEY SAY AN ELEPHANT NEVER FORGETS, BUT WHAT THEY DON'T TELL YOU IS THAT YOU NEVER FORGET AN ELEPHANT."
>
> —MURRAY, uttering perhaps the most wince-inducing line of his career, in 1996's *Larger Than Life*

LATE NIGHT WITH DAVID LETTERMAN

Murray was the first guest on the first episode of this iconic late-night comedy series on February 1, 1982. Adopting a mock combative tone throughout his conversation with Letterman, Murray played with the lint in his pockets, showed a video of a family of pandas purportedly living in his backyard, and performed an impromptu aerobics routine to Olivia Newton-John's hit single "Physical." Unbeknownst to the audience, Murray almost didn't make the appearance. According to the recollections of crewmembers recounted in Brian Abrams's Amazon Kindle Single *AND NOW . . . An Oral History of "Late Night with David Letterman," 1982–1993*, Murray disappeared from the building shortly before taping began. A frantic search ensued. At the last minute, Murray returned to the studio, claiming he had gone home to feed his cat.

LEGAL EAGLES

Debra Winger supplanted Murray in the lead role of this 1986 romantic comedy from director **Ivan Reitman**. *Legal Eagles* was originally written as a buddy picture, with Murray and Dustin Hoffman slated to costar as bickering attorneys. The plot was based on the protracted lawsuit over the estate of Mark Rothko, the celebrated abstract expressionist painter who committed suicide in 1970. "The movie was supposed to be about the marriage of art and commerce," Murray mused in an interview. "And the more I learned about Rothko, the more I wanted to make the movie." Indeed, Murray was jazzed enough about *Legal Eagles* to cut short his Parisian sabbatical and return to the United States. When Hoffman backed out to make *Ishtar* with Warren Beatty, Murray lost interest in the project. Robert Redford stepped in, demanding that the script be retooled around a Tracy/Hepburn–style couple.

L
M

LIFE AQUATIC WITH STEVE ZISSOU, THE

DIRECTED BY: Wes Anderson

WRITTEN BY: Wes Anderson and Noah Baumbach

RELEASE DATE: December 25, 2004

FILM RATING: ★ ★ ★

MURRAY RATING: ★ ★ ★

PLOT: A washed-up marine explorer pursues the man-eating "jaguar shark" that devoured his friend.

STARRING BILL MURRAY AS: Steve Zissou, lugubrious pot-smoking oceanographer

Murray had a miserable time making this, his third film for director **Wes Anderson**. Shot on location in Italy during the harsh winter of 2003–2004, *The Life Aquatic with Steve Zissou* was "by far the hardest job I've ever had," according to the actor. He called the five-month location shoot "absolute hell" and claimed he never would have taken the part had he known it would drag on that long—or that the weather would be so cold. "I got a bone chill so bad that Anjelica [Huston] came in and was rubbing my body trying to keep my blood moving," Murray said. "They were covering me with cashmeres and all these kinds of crazy things they were getting from town. My bones got so cold. They were cold for months afterwards." Adding insult to Murray's agony was the fact that retakes for *Garfield: The Movie* forced him into an Italian recording studio to redub tiresome cat jokes during breaks in the *Zissou* shooting schedule.

In the end, Murray's loyalty to Wes Anderson won out over his desire for comfort. Despite the tsouris that attended the film's making, he has called *The Life Aquatic* "the best film Wes has ever made" and placed it in the top ranks of his own work. "I'm proud of everything that's on the screen," he told an audience at a 2004 retrospective of his career at the Brooklyn Academy of Music. Whatever one thinks of the film's mannered style and hipper-than-thou deadpan humor, the part of Steve Zissou—an over-the-hill undersea explorer modeled on Jacques Cousteau—seems tailor-made for his mid-2000s persona. As a grown-up leading man role, it makes a worthy follow-up to *Lost in Translation* and rates as one of Murray's most quietly commanding performances.

"Every single scene of that movie was funny," Murray told *GQ*. "But when Wes assembled it, he streamlined and excised the detonation point of the laughter. The idea is you keep it bouncing and never skim the energy off of it. You keep it building in the name of a big emotional payoff—which comes when they're all in the submarine together and they see the jaguar shark."

NEXT MOVIE: *Broken Flowers* (2005)

The Life Aquatic, 2004

LIMITS OF CONTROL, THE

DIRECTED BY: Jim Jarmusch

WRITTEN BY: Jim Jarmusch

RELEASE DATE: May 1, 2009

FILM RATING: ★

MURRAY RATING: ★

PLOT: A contract killer exchanges matchboxes with people at various Spanish cafés.

STARRING BILL MURRAY AS: The American, reclusive target of assassination

"Sometimes I like it in films when people just sit there, not saying anything," says a character in *The Limits of Control*. So does director Jim Jarmusch, who once again subjects his audience to two hours of characters sipping coffee, gazing blankly into the distance, and occasionally engaging in inane conversations. If that's your cup of espresso, you will be mesmerized by this "thriller" starring Isaach De Bankolé as the world's most inert hitman. Murray, in an instantly forgettable cameo, plays his latest victim, a mysterious American who lives in a heavily fortified compound in the Spanish countryside. In the film's climactic scene, De Bankolé garrotes Murray with a guitar string.

The Limits of Control was Murray's third collaboration with Jarmusch and the last film he made before his rancorous divorce from second wife **Jennifer Butler**. If he seems to be phoning in his performance, it may be because he had personal matters on his mind. It took several months for Murray to emerge from the torpor of his broken **marriage**. In an interview conducted in October 2008, after shooting had concluded on *The Limits of Control*, Murray reflected on this unhappy period of his life and declared himself rejuvenated: "I've just come out of a sort of doldrums and I feel like I want to go," he said. "I want to **work**. I want to get going. I want to do a few things at once. I really want to connect with other people that are going that way and 'Let's go'. . . I want to bounce off like a pinball. Like a pinball, I want to bounce off bumpers that are positive. I want to bounce off people that are positive and hope that'll make me more positive and give me momentum." A few months later, he pinballed his way to a much more successful cameo in the comedy-horror romp *Zombieland*.

NEXT MOVIE: *Zombieland* (2009)

LITTLE CAESARS

After he dropped out of college in 1970, Murray worked part-time as a pizza maker in the **Evanston, Illinois**, branch of this national pizza chain. In 2014, during a speech at a charity event, Murray revealed that he was so poor at the time that he often ate raw pizza dough when no one was looking: "It has active yeast inside of it, so when you're full of the raw dough, the yeast con-

TALES FROM
MURRAYLAND

Nº 12	The Texas Tequila Bar Takeover

In March 2010, while attending the weeklong SXSW festival in Austin, Texas, Murray rolled into the Shangri-La bar accompanied by RZA and GZA of the hip-hop group the Wu-Tang Clan. Taking over the bartending duties, Murray insisted on serving shots of tequila—and only shots of tequila—for the remainder of the evening. Over the course of the week, Murray was also spotted at various house parties in the Texas capital.

Nº 13	The New York City Karaoke Party

In December 2010, a group of revelers at the New York City karaoke bar Karaoke One 7 were shocked when Murray accepted their half-joking invitation to join them in their private karaoke room. Murray rolled into the room with an entourage of female companions and proceeded to treat everyone to a round of "weird green drinks" made with Chartreuse liqueur. He stayed for four hours, performed a duet of the 1961 Elvis Presley hit "(Marie's the Name) His Latest Flame," posed for photos with the partygoers, and then left.

tinues to expand until your body begins to explode. But those are the early days, when we went through some stuff, didn't we all? Huh? So. Anyway."

LITTLE MISS SUNSHINE

Oscar-nominated 2005 comedy about a dysfunctional family on a road trip to a beauty pageant. Screenwriter Michael Arndt wrote the part of Frank Ginsberg, the suicidal Marcel Proust scholar, with Murray in mind. The studio preferred Robin Williams. In the end, the two sides agreed to offer the part to Steve Carell. Murray later said he regretted missing out on the role.

LITTLE SHOP OF HORRORS

DIRECTED BY: Frank Oz

WRITTEN BY: Howard Ashman

RELEASE DATE: December 19, 1986

FILM RATING: ★ ★ ★

MURRAY RATING: ★ ★ ★

PLOT: A nebbish adopts a man-eating plant.

STARRING BILL MURRAY AS: Arthur Denton, masochistic dental patient

After two years of self-imposed exile from Hollywood, Murray returned to do a cameo in this musical adaptation of Roger Corman's camp horror classic. In a brief scene that marks his first and only big-screen collaboration with Steve Martin, Murray plays Arthur Denton, a masochistic dental patient who flummoxes Martin's best efforts to torture him. While Martin's performance is showier—he wears a fright wig and huffs nitrous oxide in a madcap attempt to live up to Muppeteer Frank Oz's stylized direction—

Murray plays it low-key and ends up stealing the scene, much as Jack Nicholson did as an analogous loon in Corman's original.

NEXT MOVIE: *She's Having a Baby* (1988)

L
M

Little Shop of Horrors, 1986

LOOSE SHOES

DIRECTED BY: Ira Miller

WRITTEN BY: Royce D. Applegate, Ira Miller, Dan Praiser, and Charley Smith

RELEASE DATE: August 1, 1980

FILM RATING: ★

MURRAY RATING: ★

PLOT: A collection of mock trailers for coming movie attractions.

STARRING BILL MURRAY AS: Lefty Schwartz, condemned prisoner and gastronome

Murray has a small role in this agonizingly unfunny film spoofing movie trailers in the manner of the then-popular satirical anthologies *The Groove Tube* and *The Kentucky Fried Movie*. Also known as *Coming Attractions* and *Quackers, Loose Shoes* was shot in 1977 but released in 1980 to capitalize on Murray's *Saturday Night Live* fame. (The film's puzzling title is a riff on an infamous, now forgotten quote from former U.S. Secretary of Agriculture Earl Butz: "The only thing the coloreds are looking for in life are tight pussy, loose shoes, and a warm place to shit.") Of the eighteen sketches that make up the 84-minute feature—many of which trade in crude racist, sexist, and anti-Semitic stereotypes—Murray's segment is by far the funniest. In "Three Chairs for Lefty!" he plays the title character, Lefty Schwartz, a death row inmate who starts a riot in the prison mess after he is served insufficiently flavorful quiche. Wearing a bald cap and mascara, Murray does what he can with the sophomoric material—the punch line involves Lefty "cooking" a roast for the warden in the electric chair—but the skit sinks under the weight of its own stupidity. Although Murray is on-screen for all of five minutes, he was featured prominently in promotional materials for the film.

NEXT MOVIE: *Stripes*

LOS ANGELES

Like most successful movie actors, Murray has spent a considerable amount of time in southern California. But he remains largely immune to its charms. Of his periodic residencies in L.A., he once remarked: "It just never took. It's like the first day you check into a hotel in L.A. there's a message under your door. The second day, there's eleven messages under your door. The third day, there's thirty, forty, fifty, sixty, seventy messages. And I realized that they just want fresh blood. They. Just. Want. Fresh. Blood. You gotta get the hell out of there. And you really feel, if you live in New York, that you're three hours ahead of them—I mean that literally. It's like, *Oh man, we gotta help these people!* And the longer you stay there, the less ahead of them you get, and then you're one of them. No way, man. Not for me."

Murray spent much of 1976 living full-time in Los Angeles following the

"CALIFORNIA BEFUDDLES ME. THEY HAVE FLOWERS THAT BLOOM AT NIGHT, WHICH IS VERY BEAUTIFUL, AND THERE'S SOME NICE PLACES ALONG THE OCEAN AND THEY HAVE IN-N-OUT BURGER, WHICH IS A GREAT HAMBURGER."

—MURRAY, on his love/hate relationship with the Golden State demise of the New York–based *Saturday Night Live with Howard Cosell*. It was not a happy sojourn. In a 1984 interview, Murray described his rented home in L.A. as "the most disgusting house in California. It was like a den of evil. There were statues of embracing nudes all over, the library was *The Joy of Sex, Good Sex, Better Sex*, that kind of thing. There was an electronic bed. It was basically built to spend seventy-two hours in with a runaway teenage girl. Or boy, if that's your taste. Scampering from the sauna to the Jacuzzi to the pool to the mechanical bed. The walls were velour, the rocks were velour, it was sleazy and amazing."

LOST CITY, THE

DIRECTED BY: Andy Garcia
WRITTEN BY: Guillermo Cabrera Infante
RELEASE DATE: April 28, 2006
FILM RATING: ★ ★
MURRAY RATING: ★ ★

PLOT: A Havana nightclub owner is caught up in the tumult of the Cuban Revolution.

STARRING BILL MURRAY AS: "The Writer," mysterious unnamed wag

Fittingly, for a deal that was sealed on the golf course, Murray delivers a workmanlike supporting performance in this ponderous period piece from actor/director Andy Garcia. A sweeping family drama set in the last days before Castro took power in Cuba, *The Lost City* was Garcia's passion project, sixteen years in the making. He first pitched the film to Murray on the back nine at the 2004 Pebble Beach Pro-Am and then pestered him with phone calls begging him to join the cast. Fresh off the grueling shoot for *The Life Aquatic with Steve Zissou*, Murray was not sure he ever wanted to work again. But his wife convinced him to give in to Garcia's entreaties. "What made the Andy movie happen is my wife likes Andy," Murray told *Cigar Aficionado* magazine. "'That's okay. Go work with him. He's a gentleman.'"

Murray called the script for *The Lost City*, by legendary Cuban novelist Guillermo Cabrera Infante, "one of the most extraordinary pieces of material I've ever read"—a considerable overstatement if true. "No one's gonna see this movie," he told Garcia, "but I want to be in it." According to the director, Murray faxed over his signature without ever reading his contract. When Garcia informed him he could only pay him scale, Murray paused, said "What's that?" and never mentioned salary again.

Playing an ambiguously gay gag writer loosely based on Cabrera Infante, Murray supplies much-needed comic relief. He does a brief Jack Benny impression, rocks the short-pants-and-suit look made famous by Angus Young of AC/DC, and comments mordantly on the revolutionary goings-on. Much of his dialogue was improvised, including a scene in which Murray and Dustin Hoffman discuss the proper way to make an egg cream. In an interview conducted for the DVD release of *The Lost City*, Garcia likened Murray's character to a "Cuban Groucho Marx" and "a satirical Greek chorus."

NEXT MOVIE: *Garfield: A Tail of Two Kitties* (2006)

LOST IN AMERICA

Director Albert Brooks offered Murray the male lead in this 1985 comedy about a married couple who quit their jobs to drive across America in a Winnebago. Murray was living in Paris at the time, in the midst of his four-year sabbatical from Hollywood, and explained to Brooks that he wouldn't be available for another two and a half years. Brooks ended up playing the part himself.

LOST IN TRANSLATION

DIRECTED BY: Sofia Coppola
WRITTEN BY: Sofia Coppola
RELEASE DATE: October 3, 2003
FILM RATING: ★ ★ ★ ★
MURRAY RATING: ★ ★ ★ ★

PLOT: A pair of unhappy hotel guests runs through the streets of Tokyo together.

STARRING BILL MURRAY AS: Bob Harris, melancholic whiskey pitchman

"I had a wish that I could do a movie that was sort of romantic," Murray said of his state of mind in 2003, when he accepted the lead role in writer/director Sofia Coppola's bittersweet paean to emotional dislocation. *Lost in Translation* wound up being the crowning achievement of Murray's career to that point, earning him multiple industry **awards** and his first Oscar nomination for best actor. "I knew I was going to nail that character," he said of Bob Harris, the melancholy movie star who forges an intense bond with a sullen young woman in a Tokyo hotel. In fact, the project called out to him the first time he read Coppola's 90-page screenplay. "It wasn't overwritten, it wasn't sentimental, it wasn't maudlin," he told PBS gabber Charlie Rose. "It was clean. It was really spare."

Getting Murray interested in the script was easy. Getting him to take a look at it in the first place was the hard part. After writing the role of Bob Harris with Murray in mind (reportedly because she liked the idea of seeing him in a kimono), Coppola spent the better part of a year calling him on the phone and begging him to do the film. "I left him a lot of messages," she said. "He probably got sick of it. I sent him pages, and then I would leave him messages about what I was thinking about it." To seal the deal, she enlisted two Murrayland insiders: producer **Mitch Glazer** and director **Wes Anderson**.

Glazer arranged a lunch with Murray in New York, where Coppola made her pitch. Anderson wooed him over dinner the following night. "It was one of those patented Bill evenings," the *Rushmore* director told the *New York Times*. "He was driving. He went through a red light, reversed the car, and then ducked into this Japanese place that only he could see. By the time the sake came, I knew he would do the movie."

Even after all that, Murray's participation was far from assured. He wavered on committing to the project until the last possible moment. After a week of filming at Tokyo's Park Hyatt Hotel, Murray still had not shown up on the set. In a panic, Coppola called Glazer looking for her wayward star. When Murray finally arrived, he was jet-lagged and grumpy—conditions he ended up incorporating into his performance. The four-week Tokyo shoot was arduous, and elements of Bob Harris's plight hit uncomfortably close to home for a husband and father all too used to being separated from his family. "You are always away from home, as a film actor," Murray told the *Guardian* after the film's release. "You can be stuck in a hotel, several thousand miles away in a whole different time zone, and it is never glamorous. You can't sleep, you put on the television in the middle of the night when you can't understand a word, and you make phone calls back home which don't really give you the comfort they should. I know what it's like to be that stranger's voice calling in." For the record, Murray modeled Harris's weary affect on Harrison Ford, whose glowering visage loomed over Tokyo in billboard ads for Asahi beer.

Murray took home nearly every major acting award for *Lost in Translation*, although the most coveted prize of all—the Oscar for best actor—eluded him. Few people remember *Mystic River* today, or Sean Penn's rather pedestrian performance in it, whereas Murray's portrayal of the morose Suntory whiskey spokesman has only grown in stature as the years have passed. In part that's due to the enduring mystery of *Lost in Translation*'s final scene. The question of what Bob Harris whispers to Scarlett Johansson's Charlotte comes up nearly every time Murray discusses the film. Digital enhancement of the soundtrack has narrowed the field to two possibilities ("I have to be leaving, but I won't let that come between us, okay?" or "Go to that man and tell him the truth, okay?"), but Murray is characteristically cagey about what he actually said. "I told the truth once and they didn't believe me," he told Charlie Rose in 2014. "So I just said, 'To hell with it, I'm not telling anyone.' I whispered in her ear, but the moment happened, and I was wired—they had microphones—and Sofia and Ava Cabrera, the script supervisor, had this moment where they just looked at her and said, 'He doesn't have to say anything. You don't have to hear anything.' And I had the same feeling from sixty yards away. I went, 'It doesn't matter what the hell I say in her ear. This will be a wonderful mystery.'"

Elsewhere, Murray told a story about a time he was getting on a ferry at Martha's Vineyard when someone in the line asked him to reveal the secret. Murray waited a beat before he started to speak, letting the sound of a bellowing foghorn drown out his answer. "I acted it out like I was saying something really sincere, and the crowd laughed so hard," he said. "It was great. I couldn't have bought that moment."

NEXT MOVIE: *Coffee and Cigarettes* (2003)

> ## "THE MOVIE IS THE PRIZE. IN TIME, NOBODY REMEMBERS WHO WON THE DAMN OSCAR. THEY JUST REMEMBER THE MOVIE IF IT WAS GOOD. IF YOU HAD SAID TO ME, 'YOU COULD BE IN *MYSTIC RIVER* AND WIN THE OSCAR OR YOU COULD BE IN YOUR MOVIE AND NOT WIN'—NOT A FUCKIN' CHANCE. NO CONTEST. I LOVED THE WHOLE EXPERIENCE. IT'S A GREAT, GREAT MOVIE."
>
> —MURRAY, on not winning the best actor Oscar for *Lost in Translation*

LOVE

"I had girlfriends from the time I was in kindergarten," Murray once confessed. He fell in love for the first time at the age of twelve but was devastated when he discovered that the object of his affection didn't share his feelings. "She was in love with another guy at school," he said. "It baffled me that you could love someone so much and not get it back. That changed me in certain ways, which I've never been able to plumb. I stopped reading, and I used to read all day long. I just stopped and something changed in me, and I don't know how, but it's affected what I've become."

Since then, Murray has been through two marriages, at least one extramarital affair, and two bitter divorces—as well as a tempestuous relationship with his *Saturday Night Live* cast mate **Gilda Radner**. But he remains a proponent of old-fashioned romance, which, he says, "basically starts with respect." In an interview, Murray claimed that he took romantic inspiration from Stephen Stills's 1970 free-love anthem "Love the One You're With":

Lost in Translation, 2003

"There is something to that. It's not just make love to whomever you're with, it's just love whomever you're with. And love can be seeing that here we are and there's this world here. If I go to my room and I watch TV, I didn't really live. If I stay in my hotel room and watch TV, I didn't live today."

LOYOLA ACADEMY

Murray attended this private Jesuit high school in **Wilmette, Illinois**, from 1964 to 1968. He paid his own tuition with money saved up from **caddying**. Murray has described Loyola Academy as a "preppie Catholic school" and dubbed it his "caddy money repository." Murray caught the acting bug at Loyola, appearing in school productions of *The Music Man* and *The Caine Mutiny Court Martial*.

Although the arts intrigued him, Murray was not nearly as committed to his studies. He was notorious for his indifference to classwork. In a 1984 interview with *Rolling Stone*, he referred to himself as "an underachiever and a screw-off" as a high school student. "I just didn't care for school much," he said. "Studying was boring. I was lazy . . . and I had no interest in getting good grades." He was bright enough to score highly on the National Merit Scholarship test but was disqualified because of his poor grades. He later called the rejection "devastating, really bad news, 'cause my father would have loved to have heard somebody was going to come up with the money for college."

Murray often misbehaved in class. "He was always a rebel," said one of his high school friends, Lena Zanzucchi. "If there was one thing you knew, it's that he was going to do what he wanted." Another student remembered him as "a kid who liked to sit and observe people in the hallways. He'd select a spot where he could avoid the wrath of the Jesuit priests for loitering, then just sit and take it all in. If someone stared back at him, he just made a face at them, a consummate goof-off." Around campus, Murray was known as "the man least likely to succeed." His high school English teacher, Father Lawrence Reuter, called him "brilliant, but a terrible student." Instead of making Murray sit at the head of the class with the other unruly pupils, Reuter often put him in the back so he would not act out in front of his classmates.

Shortly after arriving at Loyola, Murray fell under the influence of a group of nonconformist "troublemakers." "These guys were really smart—with 148 IQs," he told *Rolling Stone*, "and really nuts, the first guys that got kicked out of our school for grass." Although long hair was officially banned at the school, "these guys would let their hair grow long and grease it down so it looked like it was short, and you'd see them on the weekends, and you couldn't believe how much hair they had, 'cause they'd washed it. They put up with all the grief that the preppie crowd gave them for being greasers, and they didn't care. Because come the weekend, they were doing a completely different thing than the guys from Wilmette who were trying to drink beer and get high. They didn't have any interest in being part of the social scene.... They were downtown, stoned, listening to blues."

Murray would have liked to join them, but he lacked the necessary funds—and, more important, the means of transportation—to do so. "I didn't have enough money to really have a lot of fun," he said. "I didn't have a car; I didn't have a driver's license until God knows when. So I basically relied on friends; they were my wheels. Or I'd take a bus or hitchhike. And in the suburbs, that's really lowballing it. Everybody else's parents drove them, or they had their own car. My parents just looked at me: 'Your brother hitchhiked to school, and *you'll* hitchhike to school.'"

When Murray graduated from Loyola Academy in 1968, as a final kiss-off to the school he made a point of wearing a Nehru jacket and tennis shoes to the graduation ceremony.

L
M

TALES FROM
MURRAYLAND

Nº 14 | The Halloween Hipster Dance Party

On Halloween night in 2008, Murray attended a concert by the Brooklyn-based electro-pop duo MGMT at the Music Hall of Williamsburg. After the show, he went party-hopping with the band and eventually ended up in the apartment of twenty-nine-year-old graduate student Dave Summers at three thirty in the morning. Summers's costume party was just winding down, but the unexpected arrival of Murray immediately energized the remaining revelers—one of whom was dressed as Carl Spackler from *Caddyshack*. Murray guzzled Modelo Especial beer, boogied down on the dance floor, and rhapsodized about his fondness for sweet potato casserole with marshmallows before departing into the Billburg night. The prevailing good vibes were interrupted only briefly when a party guest brought down the room by informing Murray—who had just gone through an acrimonious divorce—that he was "making bad life choices."

MAD DOG AND GLORY

DIRECTED BY: John McNaughton
WRITTEN BY: Richard Price
RELEASE DATE: March 5, 1993
FILM RATING: ★★⸙
MURRAY RATING: ★★★

PLOT: A ruthless mobster gives a timid CSI photographer a week of Uma Thurman's services as a reward for saving his life.

STARRING BILL MURRAY AS: Frank "the Money Store" Milo, loan shark and stand-up comic

After successfully playing against type in *What about Bob?*, Murray took another chance with this dark comedy written by acclaimed crime novelist Richard Price. It was the first of his three collaborations with Chicago-based independent filmmaker John McNaughton, director of the cult hit *Henry: Portrait of a Serial Killer*.

Robert De Niro was the original choice to play Murray's character, Frank Milo, a sinister loan shark with a sideline in stand-up comedy. But De Niro passed on that role in favor of the lead, Wayne "Mad Dog" Dobie, a milquetoast Chicagoland crime scene photographer. That left an opening for Murray to do some of his finest character work since *Tootsie*, in a performance he credits with forcing Hollywood to take a second look at him as a dramatic actor. Uma Thurman rounds out the main cast as Glory, the beautiful barmaid who comes between Frank and Mad Dog.

Shot on location in Chicago over the summer of 1991, *Mad Dog and Glory* was scheduled to come out in the spring of 1992. But it remained in limbo for nearly a year as Universal Studios demanded reshoots. "We had an agreement with the writer, Richard Price, to shoot every single word as it was written," said producer Steven A. Jones. "We delivered the movie to Universal. They watched it and said: 'You did exactly what he wrote. You did exactly what we expected you to do. Now let's figure out how to fix it.'" Test screenings revealed that audiences were not buying the film's ending, a fight scene in which Murray's character beats De Niro to a pulp. Studio executives refused to release the film until the scene was reshot to show Mad Dog landing a few haymakers on his rival. In the interim, De Niro had his hair buzz cut for *This Boy's Life* and Murray put on twenty-five pounds. Continuity

demanded the filmmakers wait until De Niro's hair grew back and Murray got himself into reasonable shape to resume filming.

When the climactic fight scene was finally restaged in July 1992, De Niro got his licks in. But it was Murray who landed the killing blow. According to legend, he broke De Niro's nose with one of his punches. But Murray disputes that claim. "No, I actually shattered his pancreas with a blow to the body," he told a British newspaper. "I don't think I broke his nose but I did hit him on the nose. If you see it, it's a very realistic looking fight but all I could think was 'This is the Raging Bull.'"

After a year's worth of bad press about the reshoots, *Mad Dog and Glory* finally opened in March 1993, just a few weeks after **Groundhog Day** hit theaters. Audiences were misled by the film's marketing—posters inexplicably positioned it as a zany comedy—and most moviegoers elected to go see Murray chase Andie MacDowell around a time loop rather than pummel Robert De Niro on a Chicago sidewalk. *Mad Dog* bombed at the box office, although **critics** were more favorably disposed. Kenneth Turan of the *Los Angeles Times* called it "a small gem of deadpan humor and yearning hearts." Writing in the *Chicago Tribune*, Dave Kehr raved that "there are moments [in *Mad Dog and Glory*] as gripping and inventive as anything American movies have offered in years." He singled out Murray for achieving "a striking, immediate menace" reminiscent of Jackie Gleason in *The Hustler*.

NEXT MOVIE: *Ed Wood* (1994)

MAGNETS

In the 2000s, Murray lost a sizable chunk of money investing in a failed magnet business. "I helped a fellow who was making beautiful magnets," he explained to *Minnesota Business* magazine. "Instead of cutting the magnets by hand, he wanted to get a [water cutter]. He said if he had one he could do some crazy numbers more. I was in New York and he was in California, but I liked what he was making so I said okay. It was a fair amount of money, and the inventor had to get a new place for the machine because it took up a lot of room. I went to visit and when I walked in there was the machine, but there were also thirteen carpenters building a monument to the executive in charge. I said, 'Oh no!'"

MAKEUP

Murray is wary of stage makeup, believing it causes melanoma. "They put plastic on your face, and then they put stuff on that dissolves the plastic," he once told an interviewer. "All entertainers end up with skin cancer. That's how Emmett Kelly died. Did you know that?" In fact, Kelly—the midcentury hobo clown best known for his sad-sack "Weary Willie" character—died of a heart attack at age eighty.

MAKING OUT IN JAPANESE

Phrasebook, published in 1988, that Murray used to teach himself how to speak Japanese. The 104-page paperback promises to instruct English speakers in the "language of **love**" by supplying Japanese equivalents for such common English phrases as "I'm crazy about you," "You have a beautiful body," and "Are you on the pill?" When he visited Japan in the early 1990s, Murray would take the book into sushi bars, where he would pepper the staff with rude questions. "I would say to the sushi chef, 'Do you have a curfew? Do your parents know about us? And can we get into the back seat?' And I would always have a lot of fun with that."

MAME

Broadway musical, based on the best-selling novel *Auntie Mame* by Patrick Dennis, about the zany adventures of a devil-may-care bohemian. Murray intensely dislikes the show, considering it the worst musical ever made.

A MAN'S A MAN

Still on hiatus from Hollywood, Murray starred as Galy Gay, a guileless Irish dockworker dragooned into the British army, in a 1986 production of this Bertolt Brecht play. *A Man's a Man* was staged at the Hyde Park Festival Theater in upstate New York, near Murray's Hudson Valley home. Stockard Channing costarred as the conniving Widow Begbick. Reviewers were unimpressed by Murray's performance. "It cannot be said that he convincingly becomes a warrior," carped Melvin Gussow in the *New York Times*. "Remembering Mr. Murray's *Saturday Night Live* impersonation of a tuneless lounge singer, one is pleased to note that he refrains from singing." The critic for the Associated Press wrote: "Murray has a comfortable stage manner, but **fans** of the former star of *Saturday Night Live* may be bewildered by their hero's performance."

L
M

MAN WHO KNEW TOO LITTLE, THE

DIRECTED BY: Jon Amiel

WRITTEN BY: Robert Farrar and Howard Franklin

RELEASE DATE: November 14, 1997

FILM RATING: ★

MURRAY RATING: ★

PLOT: While visiting his brother in London, a dullard is mistaken for a secret agent.

STARRING BILL MURRAY AS: Wallace Ritchie, dim-witted American tourist

"I've never made any horrible, horrible movies," Murray once declared. Apparently he never saw *The Man Who Knew Too Little*. Though not as mind-meltingly aggravating as *Scrooged*, this witless 1997 comedy is one of the lowlights of his career. It's hard to believe the same man who stole scenes in *Kingpin* just a year earlier said yes to this misbegotten mélange of Hitchcock and Maxwell Smart.

Based on Robert Farrar's unpublished 1989 novella *Watch That Man*, *The Man Who Knew Too Little* follows the misadventures of a Des Moines video store clerk who stumbles into a web of intrigue during a trip to London. The feeble one-joke premise hinges on a series of misunderstandings straight out of the *Three's Company* playbook. Murray had successfully portrayed mentally damaged characters before, most notably in *Caddyshack* and *What about Bob?*, but his talents are wasted here. As dull-witted patsy Wallace Ritchie, he is essentially playing the Dean Jones role in one of those live-action Disney movies from the 1970s.

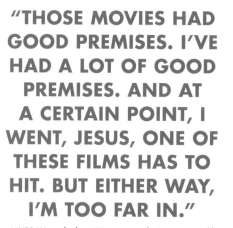

"THOSE MOVIES HAD GOOD PREMISES. I'VE HAD A LOT OF GOOD PREMISES. AND AT A CERTAIN POINT, I WENT, JESUS, ONE OF THESE FILMS HAS TO HIT. BUT EITHER WAY, I'M TOO FAR IN."

—MURRAY, on the late-'90s career tailspin epitomized by *Larger Than Life* and *The Man Who Knew Too Little*

It is unclear why Murray decided to make this film, though a free trip to London may have had something to do with it. During breaks in filming, he played some **golf**, rode a tour boat down the Thames, and "walked over to Big Ben one night and saw where Danger Mouse lives." Murray's need to maintain viability as a leading man may have been a factor as well. If so, the one-two punch of *Larger Than Life* and *The Man Who Knew Too Little* effectively killed that dream, forcing him to concentrate on high-impact character parts for the rest of the decade.

The Man Who Knew Too Little opened in the fall of 1997 to widespread public indifference. Murray dutifully plugged the film in numerous talk show appearances, offering moviegoers a money-back guarantee if they didn't like what they saw. No one took him up on his offer.

NEXT MOVIE: *Wild Things* (1998)

MARCHING CABBAGE

Murray once told an interviewer for *McCall's* that this Tibetan dish was his culinary specialty. "You make it cold, and it's red—spicy," he said. "It's good. It makes you want to cross a mountain range and attack another country."

MARIJUANA

In 1970, Murray was busted by **Chicago** police for marijuana possession while boarding a plane to Denver on his way back to college. By all indications, it was not his first—or last—attempt to transport a little "product" to market. In a 1981 interview with *Playgirl* magazine, Murray admitted that he dropped out of school "to deal drugs and travel around."

In his 2014 "Ask Me Anything" session on Reddit, Murray addressed the issue of marijuana legalization:

"Well that's a large question, isn't it? Because you're talking about recreation, which everyone is in favor of. You are also talking about something that has been illegal for so many years, and marijuana is responsible for such a large part of the prison population, for the crime of self-medication. And it takes millions and billions of dollars by incarcerating people for this crime against oneself as best can be determined. People are realizing that the war on drugs is a failure, that the amount of money spent, you could have bought all the drugs with that much money rather than create this army of people and incarcerated people. I think the terror of marijuana was probably overstated. I don't think people are really concerned about it the way they once were. Now that we have crack and crystal and whatnot, people don't even think about marijuana anymore, it's like someone watching too many video games in comparison. The fact that states are passing laws allowing it means that its threat has been overexaggerated. Psychologists recommend smoking marijuana rather than drinking if you are in a stressful situation. These are ancient remedies, alcohol and smoking, and they only started passing laws against them 100 years ago."

MARRIAGE

Murray has been married twice—to **Margaret "Mickey" Kelly** from 1981 to 1996 and to **Jennifer Butler** from 1997 to 2008. His comments on the subject of marriage are rarely positive. "There's such a finality about marriage," he once said. "What you're doing is saying you have to change the way you are, now, as of a Saturday in June, and most people are incapable of change on short notice. Or even on long notice." Of wives, Murray has complained that "at moments they demand regular, socially acceptable behavior." The institution of marriage "has to adapt to the culture if we're going to take it seriously again," he once opined. "I think people's conception of it comes from romance magazines. People make mistakes in marriage, they make mistakes all the time, and then other people won't let them slide on a mistake. They say he or she screwed up, and that's it. They break friendships over an act which could be forgiven, and won't be, because they take themselves too seriously. I guess that's what's happening with marriage, too, the lack of forgiveness that makes people less open."

Two bitter divorces may have colored Murray's thinking on long-term relationships. His first marriage reportedly ended because of his affair with Butler, and his second disintegrated amid charges of abandonment and spousal abuse. Of the breakup of a marriage, Murray once observed: "It's like your faith in people is destroyed because the person you trusted the most you can no longer trust at all. . . . The person you know isn't there anymore." When counseling others about the pitfalls of matrimony, Murray has been known to quote his friend John Heller: "Would you buy a product that fails one out of three times?"

MARX BROTHERS, THE

Sibling comedy team from the first half of the twentieth century whose anarchic brand of humor touched a chord with Murray. He has called the Marx Brothers "comedy assassins . . . killers" and cited the aggressively physical style of Groucho Marx as a particular inspiration. "He really did go to the body on people. He was like a boxer. He'd zip in, he had that crazy duck walk he'd do. And he'd go right at people, he'd go right at their body and get right in their space and just sort of shake their jelly. . . . I figured out a long time ago that the only way for me to go was through the body to get it done. That's what I need to do. That's how I work."

MASERATI

Murray is an aficionado of this Italian luxury auto brand. He has called Maserati "the best car" in the world.

MAY, ELAINE

This actress, screenwriter, and improv legend—one half of the comedy team of Nichols and May—did uncredited last-minute revisions on the scripts for *Tootsie* and *Scrooged*. Murray has praised May in interviews, saying she has "a great coconut when it comes to throwing dead flesh off a rotting script." He once called her "the most attractive woman in the world" and cited her as the archetype of the "funny female" he has always been drawn to. "If I'd come up when Elaine May was coming up, I would have chained her to a typewriter and made love to her every four hours just to keep her going," Murray told movie critic Elvis Mitchell in a 2008 interview. He also claimed to have once seen May eat an entire pound of cherries in one sitting. "She's crazy about cherries."

MEATBALLS

DIRECTED BY: Ivan Reitman

WRITTEN BY: Len Blum, Dan Goldberg, Janis Allen, and Harold Ramis

RELEASE DATE: June 29, 1979

FILM RATING: ★ ★ ★

MURRAY RATING: ★ ★ ★ ★

PLOT: Hijinks abound at a low-rent Canadian summer camp populated by misfits and slackers.

STARRING BILL MURRAY AS: Tripper Harrison, wisecracking camp counselor

In his first starring role, Murray scored a huge box office hit with this raunchy Canadian-made summer camp comedy that spawned three sequels and a slew of imitative teen sex romps in the 1980s. The delightfully plotless *Meatballs* was originally conceived as an ensemble piece, but Murray steals the show as Tripper Harrison, the libidinous counselor-in-training at Camp North Star.

Meatballs was the brainchild of *National Lampoon's Animal House* producer **Ivan Reitman**, who was eager to cash in on the success of that film and establish himself as a director. To entice Murray to join the cast of what was then called *Summer Camp*, Reitman hired Murray's old friend **Harold Ramis** to doctor the script, tailoring it to the actor's strengths (and reducing the screen time of everybody except Murray and child actor Chris Makepeace). But not even Ramis's involvement could ensure Murray's participation in the project—or even his attendance.

When shooting began in the summer of 1978, during the break in production following Murray's first full season on *Saturday Night Live*, he still hadn't formally committed to do the movie. "I want to play **baseball** and **golf** all summer," he announced at one point, then initiated radio silence. "We couldn't reach him," production chief Don Carmody recalled in a 2014 interview. "It was very worrying, but Ivan always believed he would show up."

Reitman shot around Murray's scenes with the rest of the cast at the real-life Camp White Pine near Haliburton, Ontario. At last the star ambled onto the set, disheveled and sporting the Hawaiian shirt and red short shorts Tripper wears in the finished film. Three days into his work on the film, Murray finally signed his contract.

"We worked like dogs," Murray said of the arduous *Meatballs* shoot. On his first day on the set, the makeup artist burned his face with a cigarette. "So I wasn't going to have my hair done," he kvetched. "I was gonna do it with my fingers and get a suntan and that was gonna be that." As the summer wore on, the camp, which was located deep in the Canadian wilderness, was besieged by deerflies. To escape them, Murray took to sleeping in his car. He spent most of his downtime doing rewrites of the screenplay, which he considered "a mess." It was then, he recalled in a 2004 interview, that he first realized he could improve a script by ad-libbing his own dialogue. "That's when I knew that I was better than the material," he said.

Full of antic Bugs Bunny energy, Murray's performance enlivens the entire film. It marked the first flowering of what would become his 1980s persona: the brash outsider full of snarky bravado. "He was funny and bold and said things no one else would say," Harold Ramis later observed. "The prevailing Woody Allen–type heroes at the time were losers, nebbishes,

Meatballs, 1979

schlemiels. Bill's character wasn't a loser; he was a rebel. He was an outcast by choice. He had confidence and power."

Audiences responded, making *Meatballs* the sleeper hit of the summer of 1979— and a landmark in the history of Canadian cinema. Made for a mere $1.6 million, the film pulled in an impressive $43 million at the box office, setting a record for the highest-grossing Canadian film ever (until *Porky's* came along in 1982). At the first-ever

Genie Awards ceremony—the Canadian equivalent of the Oscars—held in Toronto on March 20, 1980, *Meatballs* snagged three **awards**, including best actress (Kate Lynch) and best original screenplay. It also won the coveted Golden Reel—presented annually to the Canadian film with the biggest box office gross—but was beaten out for best picture by the haunted house thriller *The Changeling*. George C. Scott, the star of that film, bested Murray for best foreign actor in a Canadian film. For Murray, the loss established a pattern for future awards-ceremony disappointments. "I got nominated for a Canadian Oscar—for *Meatballs*. For *MEATBALLS*!" he railed. "And who am I up against? George C. Scott. So he wins the award and I stand up and go, 'That's it—let's get the hell outta here.'"

In the end, Murray preferred to get his validation in the form of the instant gratification to be found at the local cineplex: "There's nothing more exciting than sneaking into the back of a theater to watch your movie and hearing people laughing out loud. I remember the first time that happened, when I was at a screening of *Meatballs*. You get an electric charge through your whole body. It's great to hear the waves of laughter, because you never get a laugh while you're shooting a movie. If anyone laughs on a movie set, it ruins the take. But seven or eight months later, you go to a theater and get this huge laugh for a comic bit that you'd forgotten all about. It's like finding lots of money in a big bank account that you didn't know you had."

NEXT MOVIE: *Shame of the Jungle* (1979)

MEDICINE

As a young man, Murray aspired to become a doctor. "I wanted to do something hard," he once explained. "I figured to be a doctor you had to know

TALES FROM
MURRAYLAND

Nº 15	Driving Lorne's Car

In the summer of 1979, after completing work on *Where the Buffalo Roam* in Hollywood, Murray volunteered to drive *Saturday Night Live* producer Lorne Michaels's Volkswagen Super Beetle cross-country from Los Angeles to New York. It turned out to be a very circuitous journey. Accompanied by his brother John, Murray drove from southern California to Aspen, Colorado, and then nonstop going ninety-five miles an hour through Texas to Mobile, Alabama. "Remember, I was his boss," Michaels recalled. "Occasionally, I would hear from Bill on the road. He'd be in Florida, and I'd say, 'But Bill—is Florida on the way?'" It is if you're stopping off in Broward County to shoot a few scenes in *Caddyshack* before returning to New York. Finally, in September, just before the start of the new *SNL* season, Murray returned the car to its owner—with one slight enhancement for his trouble. "It took all summer to get the Beetle," Michaels said, "but Bill had installed a stereo."

something, you had to have some humanity." But his idealized vision of a medical practice may have been somewhat unrealistic. "I wanted to be some kind of emergency surgeon who would be down in the Caribbean going from island to island in paradise where I would be the only doctor for a hundred miles, and everyone would really need me in these life-or-death situations." When he entered **Regis College** in 1968, he briefly enrolled in the premed program. However, he was dismayed at the amount of study involved. "Besides, most of the people in med school are no fun." After Murray was busted for **marijuana** possession in 1970, he was forced to drop out of college, and his medical dreams went up in smoke.

MENDEL, GREGOR

In a 2014 "Ask Me Anything" session on Reddit, Murray identified this nineteenth-century geneticist as the historical figure he would most like to go back in time to meet. "He was a monk who just sort of figured this stuff out on his own," the actor opined. "That's a higher mind, that's a mind that's connected. They have a vision, and they just sort of see it because they are so connected intellectually and mechanically and spiritually, they can access a higher mind. Mendel was a guy so long ago that I don't necessarily know very much about him, but I know that Einstein did his work in the **mountains** in Switzerland. I think the altitude had an effect on the way they spoke and thought. But I would like to know about Mendel, because I remember going to the Philippines and thinking, 'This is like Mendel's garden' because it had been invaded by so many different countries over the years, and you could see the children shared the genetic traits of all their invaders over the years, and it made for this beautiful varietal garden."

MEXICAN COKE

When he's in the mood for a soft drink, Murray insists on Coca-Cola imported from Mexico, where it is sweetened with cane sugar rather than corn syrup.

MICHAELS, LORNE

Legendary television producer who rescued Murray from the ruins of *Saturday Night Live with Howard Cosell* and installed him in the Not Ready for Prime Time Players. Murray had nothing but praise for Michaels during a 2011 appearance on Howard Stern's radio show: "He's a complicated character and he really has gotten really, really good at that job. He's a million times better at it now. He really is good at the job. . . . He keeps the people together, which is really a hard part. I mean, there are infamous people in the comedy world that had all the talent and alienated them and they went away. But he's managed to keep good people, good writers, good actors, and good technicians—I mean good cameramen, good lighting guys. That's a tough building to keep all the best guys in one room."

MILAN

This densely populated Italian city and international fashion capital is one of Murray's favorite cities to visit. "I like Milan a lot," he once said. "It reminds me of **Chicago**, where I come from, because it's tough; it's a working city, but it's beautiful. It's like a hard-working industrial city, but it's also got this crazy fashion thing. So all the women are dressed like crazy. And they're riding around on motor scooters, smoking cigarettes and doing their makeup at the same time. It's hilarious. It's my kind of fun."

MONSTERS, INC.

Murray tested for the role of James P. "Sulley" Sullivan, the genial horned beast who frightens children for a living, in this 2001 comedy from Pixar Animation Studios. But when studio executives tried to contact him to offer the part, he was nowhere to be found. Calls to the actor's vaunted **800 number** went unanswered. "We took that to mean 'No,'" said director Peter Docter. Murray would have to wait three years before taking on another voice-acting role, in 2004's *Garfield: The Movie*.

MONTANA COOLER

In 2013, Murray told an interviewer from *Dazed and Confused* magazine his preferred method for drinking champagne, a proprietary iced drink he calls a Montana Cooler:

"You buy a case of champagne and you take all the bottles out, and you take all the cardboard out, and you put a garbage bag inside of it, then you put all the bottles back in and then you cover it with ice, and then you wrap it up and you close it. And that will keep it all cold for a weekend and you can drink every single bottle. And the way I like to drink it in a big pint glass with ice. I fill it with ice and I pour the champagne in it, because champagne can never be too cold. And the problem people have with champagne is they drink it and they crash with it, because the sugar content is so high and you get really dehydrated. But if you can get the ice in it, you can drink it supremely cold and at the same time you're getting the melting ice, so it's like a hydration level, and you can stay at this great level for a whole weekend. You don't want to crash. You want to keep that buzz, that bling, that smile."

See also **Champa Tampa.**

MONUMENTS MEN, THE

DIRECTED BY: George Clooney

WRITTEN BY: George Clooney and Grant Heslov

RELEASE DATE: February 7, 2014

FILM RATING: ★★

MURRAY RATING: ★★

PLOT: It's *Ocean's Eleven* with Nazis as an all-star team of scholars scours war-torn Europe for purloined art treasures.

STARRING BILL MURRAY AS: Richard Campbell, laconic Chicago architect

Murray's late-life BFF George Clooney pitched him on this well-intentioned World War II drama over pasta and salad one day in 2012. "I thought, 'Oh, God, this sounds so good,'" Murray told PBS's Charlie Rose. "But then, I thought, 'I wish George would have asked me to be in that movie, it sounds so good.' And then, nine months later, he said, 'Are you busy?' And I said, 'I'm busy, but I'm not that busy!'" *The Monuments Men* reunited Murray with

The Monuments Men, 2014

his *Moonrise Kingdom* costar Bob Balaban, with whom he shares most of his scenes. But while the company was congenial, the German location shoot was arduous, providing Murray with a reminder of why he hadn't made an army movie since *Stripes* in 1981. "They're hard," he said. "You have to get in and out of vehicles that are made for the 1930s, you know? So you are fitting into a small space, and we're huge people now compared to what they were then. So it's physically uncomfortable. We were outdoors all the time and it was a long movie. Long."

Murray called the true-life tale of a hardy band of museum curators who recover masterpieces looted by the Nazis "a great script and a fascinating story that no one has ever heard before." But audiences were not nearly as intrigued. Although the film's all-star cast did its best to promote *The Monuments Men* on the international festival and junket circuit, the ponderous, old-fashioned prestige picture fizzled like an unexploded land mine at the box office. Confidential e-mails leaked in 2014 portray Clooney as wracked with guilt over the movie's failure to ignite. "I fear I've let you all down," he confesses at one point to Sony Pictures Entertainment honcho Amy Pascal. "Not my intention. I apologize . . . I won't do it again."

NEXT MOVIE: *St. Vincent*

MOONRISE KINGDOM

DIRECTED BY: Wes Anderson

WRITTEN BY: Wes Anderson and Roman Coppola

RELEASE DATE: May 25, 2012

FILM RATING: ★ ★ ★

MURRAY RATING: ★ ★ ★

PLOT: A pair of lovesick teenage runaways confounds the scout troop sent out to retrieve them.

STARRING BILL MURRAY AS: Walt Bishop, flinty New England cuckold

In an odd bit of typecasting, Murray plays an outwardly successful, sexually frustrated older man for the fourth time in a film directed by **Wes Anderson**. It's also the fourth time he has played an attorney on-screen—edging out gangster and ghostbuster as his most-favored make-believe occupation. A return to form for Anderson after his previous live-action film, the irritating *Darjeeling Limited*, *Moonrise Kingdom* also pairs Murray auspiciously with his future *Olive Kitteridge* costar Frances McDormand. As Anderson explained to *Rolling Stone*: "I had this idea that I really wanted Bill and Frances McDormand to play a married couple. I just pictured it in my head, the two of them being these two lawyers. I always thought they would click and there would be a special chemistry. When I got them on set, that ended up happening for real. . . . There was some real emotion shared between them on that set. They

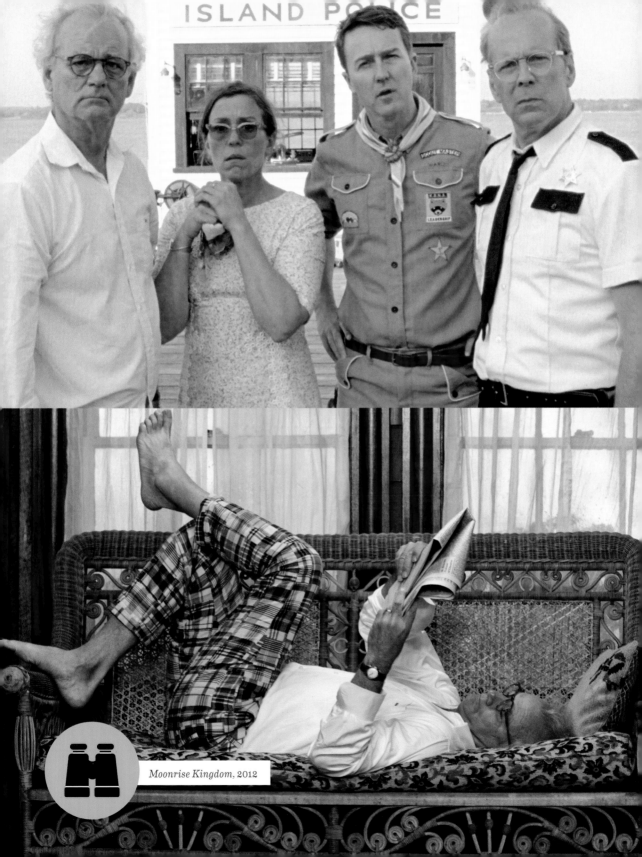

Moonrise Kingdom, 2012

were both brilliant, but also fun and charming friends." Adding to the good vibes on the Rhode Island shoot was the presence of **Cooper Murray,** Murray's fourteen-year-old son, who played one of the Khaki Scouts dispatched to capture the film's main characters.

NEXT MOVIE: *Hyde Park on Hudson* (2013)

MOUNTAINS

Murray has always been fascinated by mountains, although he never saw one firsthand until he moved to Denver to attend **Regis College** in 1968. He described the experience in a 1984 interview with *Rolling Stone* magazine: "It was just a matter of being high and seeing a different order—as opposed to whatever the hell I knew when I was eighteen years old. School and lunch. And beer. Aside from those three, I didn't have much experience. And girls. So there was just something different happening. I saw there was something else to see. I can't describe it. It's just a better feeling than usual. And yet it's perfectly ordinary because it's intended to be perfectly ordinary. It's not like lightning bolts hitting you on the head. It's just different." After seeing the Rockies for the first time, Murray could not get enough mountains. "Then I wanted to see them all," he said. Murray spent extensive time in the Himalayas while shooting *The Razor's Edge* in 1983.

MR. MAGOO

Murray is a huge fan of Quincy Magoo, the famously myopic 1960s cartoon character voiced by comic actor Jim Backus. "I thought there was a lot of truth in the exaggerated vulnerability of the near-sighted little cartoon guy," he once said. In another interview, he cited the squinting skinflint as a model for the types of roles he would like to play. "It sounds corny but I'd like all my stuff from here on out to be things you wouldn't be afraid to let your kids' kids discover decades from now. Like I discovered *A Tale of Two Cities* or even Mr. Magoo."

Murray considers the 1962 animated special *Mr. Magoo's Christmas Carol* the finest adaptation of Charles Dickens's holiday classic ever made. "My favorite Scrooge was Mr. Magoo," he told the *Boston Globe.* "It was funny, but it didn't lose any of the emotion, you know? And you're watching a cartoon, thinking, 'This isn't going to get me.' And then it gets you."

TALES FROM
MURRAYLAND

Nº 16 | The Time He Danced the Hammer Dance with MC Hammer

In the summer of 1990, Murray spent a month in southwest Virginia filming *What about Bob?* on scenic Smith Mountain Lake. When he found out that MC Hammer was playing a concert at the nearby Roanoke Civic Center, Murray called his agents requesting tickets for himself and the entire crew. When they arrived at the venue, Murray's entourage was seated on the side of the stage, where many jugs of moonshine were consumed. Murray later estimated that he had consumed "four or five ounces of 190 proof alcohol" by the time Hammer invited him on stage for his show-stopping number, "U Can't Touch This." "I did the dance," Murray told *Cigar Aficionado* magazine. "That's right, the Hammer dance. Surprisingly, I knew all the steps. But I learned why he wore those weird chef's pants, because I split my pants right up the back. And since it was the end of the month off on a remote location, all I had was my pants. I was going commando, if you know what I mean. I was working without a net."

Exposed and flailing, Murray staggered to the wings, where his costumer— later to become his second wife—managed to fasten up the breach in his britches with seven giant safety pins she happened to be carrying. "She fixed me up, and I went out and finished the number," Murray said. "Later [Hammer] told me that professional athletes would come up and not be able to finish the number. I wondered if it was because of the pants, and he said, no, they didn't have the stamina."

MR. MIKE'S MONDO VIDEO

DIRECTED BY: Michael O'Donoghue

WRITTEN BY: Michael O'Donoghue, Mitch Glazer, Dick Wittenborn, and Emily Prager

RELEASE DATE: September 19, 1979

FILM RATING: ★

MURRAY RATING: ★

PLOT: Sinister sleazebag "Mr. Mike" takes moviegoers on a globe-hopping cinematic *tour d'horizon.*

STARRING BILL MURRAY AS: The Honker, ever so briefly

Murray has a brief cameo in this wincingly unfunny video film from *Saturday Night Live* writer/provocateur Michael O'Donoghue. A self-indulgent, glacially paced parody of the 1962 documentary *Mondo Cane, Mr. Mike's Mondo Video* was bankrolled by *SNL* producer Lorne Michaels and scheduled to air in the *SNL* time slot during one of the show's off weeks in the 1978–79 season. But NBC executives balked when they saw the footage, refusing to broadcast it and forcing O'Donoghue to pad it out to feature length for a mercifully short-lived theatrical release. Several *SNL* regulars and guest hosts appear in the film. Murray plays his mush-mouthed drunk character, the Honker, in a man-on-the-street interview segment.

NEXT MOVIE: *Where the Buffalo Roam* (1980)

MTV EUROPE

During a visit to Rome in 2004 to promote *Lost in Translation*, Murray spent an evening in Sofia Coppola's hotel room watching MTV Europe with a group of friends from the movie. In an interview with the *New Yorker*, he described the channel's programming as "terrible, awful, like funeral music from another planet."

MURRAY, ANDREW THOMAS

Murray's younger brother, the seventh of the nine Murray siblings, was born in Evanston, Illinois, on April 5, 1956. An accomplished chef and restaurateur, Andy Murray developed the menu for the Murray Bros. Caddyshack, the family's golf-themed eatery in St. Augustine, Florida. An honors graduate of the New York Restaurant School, he previously worked in such fabled Manhattan hot spots as Mortimer's, the Tribeca Grill, and the Lone Star Roadhouse.

MURRAY, BRIAN

Murray's older brother, the second of the nine Murray siblings, was born on October 31, 1945, in Evanston, Illinois. An actor and writer, Brian Murray ad-

L M

opted the hyphenate Brian Doyle-Murray (after his maternal grandmother, Mary Agnes Doyle) to avoid confusion with a South African stage actor of the same name. Bill Murray has called Brian "my first great influence"

> ## "I LIKE TO SAY THAT THEY PEAKED WITH ME, AND IT WAS ALL DOWNHILL AFTER THAT."
>
> —MURRAY, on being the fifth of nine children

and said of him: "He made much of what I am possible."

After graduating from **Loyola Academy** in 1963, Brian Murray briefly attended Saint Mary's College of California before dropping out to become a railroad switchman. "He put a couple cars into San Francisco Bay once," Bill Murray once recalled. "But I guess all railroad men do something like that. He did a lot of weird things."

After family patriarch Ed Murray died in December 1967, Brian returned home to help support his widowed mother and eight siblings. He took a job as a peanut broker in downtown **Chicago** but lasted only six months. "If he'd stayed in it, he'd have ended up a very wealthy man," Bill Murray later claimed. When the legume game petered out, Brian devoted himself to acting full-time. He accepted a position at **Second City** and attended nighttime improv workshops with the legendary **Del Close**. In 1973, he left Chicago for New York to join the cast of *The National Lampoon Radio Hour*. That led to writing and performing stints on *Saturday Night Live*, recurring and guest roles on TV sitcoms throughout the 1990s and 2000s, and noteworthy supporting parts in films like *JFK*, *Wayne's World*, and *Cabin Boy*. Brian Murray also cowrote the screenplay for *Caddyshack* and appeared alongside his brother Bill in that film as well as *The Razor's Edge*, *Scrooged*, *Ghostbusters II*, and *Groundhog Day*.

MURRAY BROS. CADDYSHACK

Golf-themed restaurant in St. Augustine, Florida, co-owned by Murray and his brothers Brian, Joel, Andy, and Ed. The restaurant's official slogan is "Eat, Drink & Be Murray." The Murray Bros. Caddyshack, which opened for business on June 7, 2001, occupies an 8,000-square-foot space adjacent to the World Golf Hall of Fame. The dining area is decorated with *Caddyshack*-related memorabilia, including rakes, pails, lawnmowers, and assorted stuffed gophers. The menu was crafted by Murray's brother Andy, a professional chef, to reflect the food of the Midwest where the brothers grew up. Popular menu items throughout the years have included Sheboygan bratwurst, Chicago hot dogs, an Italian beef sandwich, the Double Bogey Cheeseburger, the BBQ Pulled Pork Sandwedge, the Caddyshake, and the Baby Ruth cheesecake.

MURRAY, CALEB JAMES

Murray's third son and first child by his second wife, **Jennifer Butler**, was born on January 11, 1993.

"MURRAY CHRISTMAS"

Since 2012, Murray has been sending friends a **Christmas** card bearing this greeting, featuring four photographs of himself wearing nothing but a red scarf. In 2013, he randomly mailed a "Murray Christmas" card to professional wrestling legend "Rowdy Roddy" Piper. "How and why I got this from Bill Murray, I have no idea," Piper tweeted.

MURRAY, COOPER JONES

Murray's fifth son and third child by his second wife, **Jennifer Butler**, was born on January 27, 1997. Cooper Murray appears as a Khaki Scout wearing a Native American headdress in his father's 2012 film *Moonrise Kingdom*.

MURRAY, EDWARD JOSEPH

Murray's paternal grandfather was born on February 3, 1886. He died on December 7, 1973, when Murray was twenty-three years old. "Grandpa Ed" Murray's family immigrated to the U.S. from County Cork, **Ireland**, shortly before his birth. The **Chicago** native drove a city bus, wore neatly tailored suits, and was known for his jocular disposition. "He always had licorice in his pocket, and he always had a Budweiser and a Camel," Murray said. "He had false teeth. There was always a baby in our family, and he'd always say, 'Come here, little baby.' And then he'd pop out his teeth exactly like the ghost in *Ghostbusters* and just scare the hell out of the baby. My mother'd get really pissed at him. 'Grandpa! How could you scare him like that?' He wouldn't say anything; he'd just drink his beer." An inveterate prankster, Murray's grandfather was known to set off firecrackers unexpectedly. His arsenal of novelties included a pair of chattering teeth, a bag of laughs, and a light-up bow tie, which, according to Murray, "he used very tastefully."

MURRAY, EDWARD JOSEPH II

Murray's father was born on January 4, 1921, and died on December 29, 1967, at age 46, of complications from diabetes. Ed Murray was a longtime employee of the J. J. Barney Lumber Company in **Wilmette**, **Illinois**, first as a salesman and later as vice president of sales. Bill Murray once described him as "an interesting combination of a thin, fragile man and a disciplinarian." Whenever one of his nine children misbehaved, he was known to whack

the offender with a yardstick brought home from the lumberyard. But Ed
Murray had a lighter side as well. Known for wearing pistol-shaped cufflinks
that fired blanks, he was likened by his oldest son and namesake to comedian Bob Newhart. "At the dinner table, he was very dry and quiet," Bill Murray told the *New York Times*, "but always triggered to laugh." A slow eater, Ed
Murray was notoriously difficult to impress. The children would compete to
see who could make their father spit out his food with laughter. Bill Murray
has likened the scene at the Murray family table to a Friar's Roast and the
feeling of making his father laugh to winning a National Merit Scholarship.
"If you weren't funny, you did the dishes," he said. One of Murray's most vivid
childhood memories is of the time he fell off his chair at the dinner table
while doing an impression of James Cagney. "I hit my head very hard on
the metal foot of the table leg, and it hurt terribly. But when I saw my father
laughing, I laughed while crying at the same time. I guess that was some
kind of beginning." Murray has called his father's death when he was just
seventeen "the worst pain I've ever known in my life."

MURRAY, EDWARD JOSEPH III

Murray's oldest brother, born on September 7, 1944, was the real-life model
for Danny Noonan in *Caddyshack*. Ed Murray attended Northwestern University on a Chick Evans Caddy Scholarship, awarded annually to outstanding caddies with financial need.
After a stint in the U.S. Air Force
and a brief foray into sports radio
(he once aspired to be the play-by-
play voice of baseball's Chicago
White Sox), Ed Murray enjoyed
a long and successful career as a
senior vice president and financial adviser with Morgan Stanley.
When he was working on the script
for *Caddyshack*, Doug Kenney

> ## "IT WAS HIS FORM OF REVOLT . . . AND IT WAS REVOLTING."
>
> —MURRAY, on his brother Ed's decision to root for the
> Chicago White Sox rather than the Cubs

interviewed Ed and incorporated many of his anecdotes into the screenplay.
For his contributions, Ed received a "special acknowledgment" in the credits
of the film.

MURRAY, HOMER BANKS

Murray's oldest son, by his first wife Mickey Kelly Murray, was born on
March 23, 1982. He is named after Homer's Homemade Gourmet Ice Cream,
an ice cream parlor in Murray's hometown of Wilmette, Illinois. His middle
name is a tribute to Murray's all-time favorite baseball player, Chicago Cubs
legend Ernie Banks. Homer Murray is a chef and restaurateur in Brooklyn,

> ## "I WANTED TO PICK A NAME I WOULD NEVER HEAR AGAIN IN CASE THE BABY WERE BORN LOOKING LIKE DAN [AYKROYD] AND I HAD TO PUT IT UP FOR ADOPTION."
>
> —MURRAY, on naming his firstborn son Homer

New York. He has a nonspeaking cameo in *Broken Flowers* as a young man who may—or may not—be his father's character's son.

MURRAY, JACKSON WILLIAM ("JACK")

Murray's fourth son and second child by second wife Jennifer Butler was born on October 6, 1995.

MURRAY, JOEL

Murray's younger brother, the ninth of the nine Murray siblings, was born on April 17, 1962, in Evanston, Illinois. Joel Murray, who "may be the funniest one of all," according to his brother John, attended Marquette University in Milwaukee. There he became a friend and frequent improv partner of future *Saturday Night Live* regular Chris Farley, who subsequently joined him at Second City in Chicago. Joel Murray is best known to television audiences for his recurring roles on *Dharma & Greg*, *Still Standing*, and *Mad Men*—in which he plays alcoholic, incontinent copywriter Freddy Rumsen.

MURRAY, JOHN COLLINS

Murray's younger brother, the eighth of the nine Murray siblings, was born on June 22, 1958, in Evanston, Illinois. As a young man, John Murray tended bar at the Hard Rock Café in New York City and wrote for *Inside Sports* magazine. ("The highlight of my career there was being assigned to find out how many hot dogs they served at Super Bowl II," he once said.) In the 1980s, he worked as an extra and production assistant on *Caddyshack* and joined the writing staff of former *Saturday Night Live* producer Lorne Michaels's prime-time sketch comedy series *The New Show*. In 1985, he starred in his own lowbrow comedy feature, *Moving Violations*. He also appeared opposite Bill as Frank Cross's brother in *Scrooged*. John Murray helped write and develop the Murray family travel documentary series *The Sweet Spot* and is currently a co-owner of the Murray Bros. Caddyshack restaurant. In 2013, he was charged with driving under the influence after he was caught driving his car through people's front yards at the World Golf Village near St. Augustine, Florida.

MURRAY, LAURA LUCILLE

Murray's younger sister, the sixth of the nine Murray siblings, was born on

May 21, 1952, in Evanston, Illinois. Laura Murray contracted polio when she was a toddler. (All the Murray children possess the polio gene, in fact, but only Laura was stricken with the disease.) Forced to wear excruciating leg braces, she compensated by developing formidable upper-body strength. "She could lift a table with one hand," Bill Murray once said. He drew inspiration for his portrayal of Franklin D. Roosevelt in the 2013 film *Hyde Park on Hudson* from Laura's struggle to overcome her disability. "That shaped the state I was in while I worked," he told an interviewer, "because I realized she didn't complain about anything."

Married in 1995 to Robert Dietrich, the former Laura Murray is retired from a job at an air freight import-export company. She lives in the Murray family home in Wilmette.

MURRAY, LINCOLN DARIUS

Murray's sixth son, the fourth and presumably final child borne him by second wife Jennifer Butler, was born on May 30, 2001.

MURRAY, LUCILLE COLLINS

Murray's mother was born on September 29, 1921, and died of cancer on November 2, 1988, at age 67. She was known for her strong singing voice. As a girl, she sang in the church choir and performed in school plays. She met Murray's father, Ed Murray, when they were in high school and married him on November 6, 1943. Lucille Murray bore nine children, losing another three—including a set of twins—to miscarriages. Her son Ed Murray III once likened her to Edith Bunker from the 1970s sitcom *All in the Family*. Like her husband, he said, "she had a wonderful sense of humor, too, just in a quieter way." Bill Murray once described her as "a real character, a talkative soul who can make friends with anyone" and who had "always been a massive influence on me."

After her husband died in 1967, Lucille Murray worked a series of jobs to provide for the family. She delivered phone books, worked at Marshall Field's department store, and operated a telephone switchboard. In 1969, she took a job as the mailroom clerk at the American Hospital Supply Corporation. She remained there for seventeen years before taking early retirement in 1986. She also served as president of her local chapter of NAIM, a Catholic widows' organization.

As a single mother raising nine kids, it fell to Lucille Murray to set expectations for her family—something Bill, the self-described black sheep of the family, initially chafed at. "We had no money, and my mother pressured us to pick up occupations," he once said. "She wanted a plumber, she wanted a dentist, a doctor, a priest, a nun, a carpenter. She wanted one of everything to do all those things we kept getting bills for." He later expressed regret that he did not listen to his mother's advice as a young man: "If I'd started paying attention to my mother when I was twelve instead of trying to sneak out of the house and avoid her, not only could I have handled her a little better, but I could have gotten a much better education about women and about people."

Over time, Murray's relationship with his mother improved. She was pleased by his early show business success because, he said, "I didn't turn out to be a complete wastrel." He came to appreciate her sense of humor. "I didn't used to think she was funny," he remarked to an interviewer in the early 1980s, "but now I realize she's like completely out of control, nuts. I just never noticed it. I sort of took it all seriously, you know, and acted like it was normal. Now I realize that she's funny to watch at least sixty percent of the time, like the way it's funny to watch a baby panda fall over stuff in the zoo." When he joined the cast of *Saturday Night Live*, Murray began surreptitiously taping his mother's telephone conversations and incorporating some of her "material" into his character work.

> ## "NINE WAS A LOT. MY MOTHER WAS A SPORT. SHE MUST HAVE ENJOYED A GOOD TIME AND WAS A SPORT ABOUT THE WHOLE THING. SOME PEOPLE LIKE THE PROCESS, BUT NOT THE PAPERWORK."
>
> —MURRAY, on his mother's decision to have nine children

As her son's fame grew in the wake of *Ghostbusters'* success, Lucille Murray began to revel in her new role as a celebrity mom. She retired from her job, moved to a condo in Fort Meyers, Florida, bought a mink coat, and dyed her hair blonde. In an interview published after her death, Murray describes her "sitting on the veranda . . . wearing her mink in 80-degree temperature, talking about 'my son the stockbroker' and 'my son the chef' and 'my son the actor' and 'my daughter the nun.'" Toward the end of her life, as she was battling cancer, Murray gave her an American Express card and encouraged her to spend as much as she liked on travel, clothing, and luxury items.

The loss of his mother in 1988 left Murray feeling "bereft," he said. "It seems strange to say now that I felt so lonely, yet I did. It was as if her passing put me into the same category of a kid who was an orphan. Crazy. And this is from a man in his forties."

MURRAY, LUKE FRANÇOIS

Murray's second son by first wife Mickey Kelly was born on April 1, 1985, in Paris, France, during Murray's mid-'80s sabbatical from filmmaking. His middle name is an homage to François Joubert, the protagonist of Murray's favorite novel, *A Story Like the Wind* by **Laurens van der Post**. Luke Murray currently works as a Division I men's college basketball coach.

MURRAY, MARGARET ANN ("PEGGY")

Murray's older sister and the fourth of the nine Murray siblings was born on May 6, 1949, in **Evanston, Illinois**. The closest to Bill in age, she is also the one with whom he has said he had the closest relationship. Peggy Murray worked for Marshall Field's in **Chicago** and had three children with circuit court judge Clayton "Jay" Crane, whom she married in 1971. She is the inspiration for the *Caddyshack* character Mrs. Crane, the older golfer whom Murray's **Carl Spackler** leers at while he pretends to masturbate.

MURRAY, NANCY MARY

Murray's oldest sister, the third of the nine Murray siblings, was born on November 1, 1947, in **Evanston, Illinois**. She is often described as the most serious of the Murray kids. A Dominican nun, she is referred to within the family as "our sister the sister" and "the white sheep of the family."

As a child, Nancy served as the director of the Murray family **nativity play** staged in the basement of their home. In 1966, shortly after graduating from high school, she entered the Dominican Sisters convent in Adrian, Michigan. She may have been driven to a life of celibacy by the antics of her brothers. On the occasion of Nancy's first date, the Murray boys greeted her beau at the door in stereotypical hillbilly costumes, complete with a banjo. "The poor guy must have been scared to death," John Murray later confessed. Nancy Murray, now Sister Nancy Murray, earned a theater degree from Florida's Barry University and a master's in pastoral studies from Loyola University in **Chicago**. She is the only Murray sibling with an acting degree.

Since 2000, Sister Nancy Murray has traveled around the world performing her one-woman show "St. Catherine of Siena: A Woman for Our Times." She plays fourteen characters in the ninety-minute show, which pays tribute to a fourteenth-century teenage nun known for her charitable work with the poor and sick.

MURRICANE, THE

Nickname given to Murray by his erstwhile *Saturday Night Live* colleague **Dan Aykroyd** because of his notorious mood swings. The Murricane is also the name of a cocktail inspired by Murray's 2009 visit to the Anchor, a nautical-themed dive bar in **New York City**. "He was commenting on the drinks," the bar's manager told the *New York Times*, "and we offered to name one after him. He was a good sport about it. He wanted something with **Chartreuse**, but we talked him into bourbon."

SISTER NANCY'S

TOP 3

In a 2009 interview with the *Chicago Tribune*, Sister Nancy Murray revealed her three favorite Bill Murray movies.

1. *Meatballs:* "I love that it was the first and I love that it reminded me so much of my father—Billy sounded so much like our dad. The way he talks to the young boy, Rudy—that kind of joshing thing, that was like an imitation of my dad."

2. *Scrooged:* "I love this one because it's Christmas, of course. But also because four of my brothers are in it. And the message was heartfelt, you know? At the time, I was doing work with the homeless and working on food pantries. I was working out of St. Sylvester Parish [in Humboldt Park] and that movie just kind of brought all that home."

3. *The Razor's Edge:* "It came out at the peak of the *Ghostbusters* thing and nobody wanted to see him in a serious role. But I loved that he wouldn't do *Ghostbusters* until they let him do this first. It showed a depth of character and another side, a serious side, that I knew he had. When I go on retreats for the seminary, sometimes we use it as a learning tool."

THE MURRICANE RECIPE*

INGREDIENTS

2 ounces fresh watermelon

4 or 5 basil leaves

1½ ounces bourbon

¾ ounce fresh lemon juice

¾ ounce St-Germain elderflower liqueur

Freshly ground black pepper, for garnish (optional)

Watermelon wedge, for garnish (optional)

PREPARATION

Combine watermelon and basil leaves in a mixing glass or shaker and muddle until watermelon is crushed and juicy. Add bourbon, lemon juice, St-Germain, and ice and shake vigorously. Strain into a cocktail glass and garnish, if desired, with a sprinkling of black pepper and a wedge of watermelon.

*Courtesy Lazy Point Bar (formerly the Anchor)

MUSIC MAN, THE

Murray has called his participation in the **Loyola Academy** production of this classic Broadway musical the high point of his high school experience, crediting it with inspiring him to pursue a career in show business. He originally auditioned for the lead role of Professor Harold Hill, the peripatetic con man who attempts to swindle the residents of an Iowa town by offering bogus music lessons. Considering himself a "dead ringer" for Robert Preston, who originated the role on Broadway, Murray was shocked when he lost the part to classmate Larry Basil. He did manage to win a slot in the show's roving barbershop quartet, the Buffalo Bills. But a teenaged Murray wasn't destined to warble high harmonies on "Goodnight Ladies" either. After noticing a number of scantily clad girls trying out for dancing roles, Murray switched gears and auditioned to become a chorus boy. "I just jumped up and said 'I'm a dancer," he recalled in a 1984 interview. "And people were like 'Huh? What? Come on.' So I went up onstage. I just wanted to sort of stand behind these girls, really, get as close as I could. I did my little audition, just clowning around, really. The woman said, 'Okay, you, you, you, and you,' and she pointed to me, and I was in. So I told my friends, 'Hey, I'm not going to be in the barbershop quartet—I'm a dancer now.' They said, 'What? *Why*?' I said, 'I don't know, man, I don't know. It's just an instinct.'"

Murray's instinct was right on the money. He wound up having a ball at nighttime dance rehearsals, hanging out with "slightly nuts" female dancers and sneaking liquor when no one was looking. "Sometimes the dance teacher would say, 'I have to leave early,' and we'd go 'Oh, that's too bad; that means we just have another hour to drink gin out of Coke bottles and jive around with these girls; that's just too damn bad.' And I'd come home half snookered on gin and Coke, and my mom would say, 'How was it?' and I'd say, 'Uh, I hurt my foot.'"

Apparently, Murray's fascination with *The Music Man* endured long after he left high school. Some years later, while visiting the University of Notre Dame with the **Second City** touring company, Murray disappeared from the troupe for several days to go skylarking at a nearby all-girls college. During his walkabout, he was thrown out of a restaurant for singing "(Ya Got) Trouble," the showstopping number from *The Music Man*, on top of a table.

L
M

TALES FROM
MURRAYLAND

Nº 17	The Summer He Played Minor League Baseball

In July 1978, *Saturday Night Live* sent Murray to Aberdeen, Washington, to film a segment for a special titled "Things We Did Last Summer." The premise was that Murray was quitting comedy to pursue his lifelong passion of playing professional baseball. On July 28, Murray strapped on the flannels of the Grays Harbor Loggers, a minor league team in the Pacific Northwest League. In his first game, against the Victoria Mussels, he went one for one during a 7–4 Loggers victory. He returned to the lineup a few days later in a game against the Walla Walla Padres and struck out on three pitches. "I don't know a TV actor who can hit a decent sinker," Murray said. "He was not like us, but he was a good athlete," said one of Murray's teammates, pitcher Tracy Harris. "He got in some cuts, he threw the ball, and he could catch flies." The brief bush league stint endeared Murray to fans and fellow ballplayers. He won a dance contest in Aberdeen, sang "The Star-Spangled Banner" before a game, and recited Lou Gehrig's farewell speech to the crowd before he "retired." Murray also developed a reputation for always picking up the check in restaurants. Once, in an airport bar, when a woman recognized Murray and sat down next to him, he pointed to Harris. "Do you know who this is?" he asked her. "This is Don Drysdale."

Murray's stint in the bushes was a brief one, but it was not soon forgotten. Nearly thirty years later, on July 8, 2006, the Class A Fort Myers Miracle honored him with a Bill Murray bobblehead doll giveaway. The doddering figurine depicted Murray in his Grays Harbor Loggers jersey.

NADER, RALPH

Murray has called this crusading consumer advocate and two-time U.S. presidential candidate "the greatest living American." He has credited Nader with saving the lives of several million people through his promotion of seat belt use and compared him favorably to Oskar Schindler, the German industrialist whose efforts to rescue Jews during the Holocaust were chronicled in the 1993 film *Schindler's List*. "[Schindler] saved hundreds," Murray told the *Guardian*. "Great man. Deserved a movie. Spectacular. Great film and a great human being. But this guy, Ralph—there's no movies about Ralph."

Murray campaigned for Nader during his first unsuccessful run for the presidency in 2000. But their association goes back much further than that. Nader was the guest host for Murray's first *Saturday Night Live* episode on January 15, 1977. Backstage, Nader jawboned Murray about the importance of safety features in automobiles. Murray promised Nader that he would buy the first-ever mass-produced car with dual airbags. Eighteen years later, he made good on his pledge. In 1995, Murray purchased a Chrysler LHS, fully equipped. He did make some major aesthetic alterations. "I had to pay a lot to make it look acceptable to me," he said. "I painted it black, took the chrome off. It has some very styling hubcaps."

NATIONAL LAMPOON RADIO HOUR, THE

Upon moving to New York in 1974, Murray joined the cast of this weekly radio comedy series from the creative brain trust behind *National Lampoon* magazine. He remained with the program through the end of its run. Murray's brother Brian, **Harold Ramis**, and future *Saturday Night Live* cast members **Chevy Chase**, **John Belushi**, Christopher Guest, **Gilda Radner**, and Harry Shearer all appeared on the *Radio Hour* its 59-episode lifespan, from November 1973 to December 1974.

NATIONAL LAMPOON'S ANIMAL HOUSE

Murray was briefly considered for the role of Donald "Boone" Schoenstein in this classic 1978 comedy about bawdy hijinks at a fictional 1960s fraternity. Peter Riegert ended up playing Boone, although screenwriter **Harold Ramis** claimed to have written the part with himself in mind. In early stages of production, Murray's brother **Brian Doyle-Murray** was envisioned for the part of Hoover, with **Chevy Chase** as Otter and **Dan Aykroyd** as D-Day—roles that eventually went to James Widdoes, Tim Matheson, and Bruce McGill, respectively. Murray and Aykroyd reportedly backed out because of their *Saturday Night Live* commitments; Chase elected to make the lightweight thriller *Foul Play* instead.

NATIONAL LAMPOON SHOW, THE

In late 1974, at the invitation of his brother Brian, Murray traveled to **New York City** by overnight bus from **Chicago** to join the cast of this theatrical comedy revue. When he arrived, Murray was so disheveled that one of the show's writers, Sean Kelly, mistook him for a homeless person. But he soon earned a place in a company of up-and-comers that included, at one time or another, **John Belushi**, **Gilda Radner**, **Harold Ramis**, Joe Flaherty, and Richard Belzer.

After a brief, chaotic tour of American colleges and Canadian bars, *The National Lampoon Show* opened off-Broadway at the New Palladium Theatre on March 2, 1975. It ran for 180 performances over four months. Audiences were sparse but spirited. "The show was hostile and abusive to the audience, and it was a very rowdy crowd," said Harold Ramis. Theatergoers often smuggled in bottles of whiskey, precipitating regular altercations with the cast. "It was like crowd-control theater," Murray later recalled. "It was a brawl every single night, and they were going to take the stage, if you didn't. It was really an ugly audience. It's what biker bars are all about."

Critics were revolted by the show's irreverent, slash-and-burn style of comedy. "*Lampoon* sets new boundaries for impropriety," wrote Mel Gussow in the *New York Times*. "But unlike its cousin-in-vulgarity, the Madhouse Company of London, it does not match its bad taste with good humor." The reviewer for *Cue* magazine opined: "There's obviously a large market for this sort of disrespectful slop-jar humor. If you can laugh at the physically handicapped, the mentally retarded, or—perhaps the single most odious moment in the show—[First Lady Betty] Ford's mastectomy, you'll enjoy it."

Although Murray would later grouse that "nobody saw it," *The National*

> # "THERE WAS ONLY ONE AUDIENCE'S WORTH OF PEOPLE IN THE WHOLE TOWN. AND THEY HATED US."
>
> —MURRAY, after a raucous *National Lampoon Show* in London, Ontario

Lampoon Show did attract the attention of two men who would play important roles in the next stage of Murray's career: **Lorne Michaels** and **Howard Cosell**.

NATIVITY PLAY

As a child, Murray took part in numerous nativity plays reenacting the events surrounding the birth of Jesus Christ. His brothers and sisters staged one such pageant in the family basement, with two blankets stretched across a clothesline serving as stage curtains. Murray played Joseph in that production, with his sister directing and starring as the Virgin Mary. A towel festooned with one of his father's neckties made up his shepherd's costume.

When it came time to stage the Nativity for his grade school **Christmas** pageant, Murray had not nearly so happy an experience. He hoped to reprise his triumph as Joseph but was rejected for reasons that were not made clear to him. "I suppose I wasn't holy at the time," he later complained. Next, he was edged out by another student for the part of the innkeeper who turns the baby Jesus away at the door. Finally, Murray was placed in the choir and outfitted with a yellow cardboard halo. "I ended up on a riser, with all the other no-talents, singing carols between acts," he carped. Murray gabbed with his fellow extras throughout the show. Decades later, he admitted that he was still bitter over the slight.

NBC'S SATURDAY NIGHT

See Saturday Night Live.

NERDS, THE

See **DiLaMuca, Todd**.

NEW {FAKE} TRAILER

This 2011 web video inspired by the work of **Wes Anderson** features Murray taking a slow-motion walk through the halls of a **South Carolina** elementary school. Murray was visiting Trident Academy, his son's school, to film a promotional video when director of photography David Walton Smith came up with the idea to shoot an impromptu homage to Murray's perambulation at the end of *The Life Aquatic with Steve Zissou*. Set to the tune of "Powerman" by the Kinks, *New {fake} Trailer* depicts a glowering Murray strolling through the school corridors, accompanied by Smith and three of his friends (one of whom, camera assistant Crynma Jang, had no idea who Murray was). When the camera stopped rolling, the star kept on walking, right out to his car and into viral video history. The one-minute short has garnered more than two million views during its lifespan on Vimeo and YouTube.

"NEW GUY" SPEECH

Direct-to-camera oration delivered by Murray on the March 19, 1977, episode of *Saturday Night Live*, often credited with turning around his sagging fortunes on the show. Murray had been on *SNL* for two months at that point, but after a first episode in which he'd been prominently featured in multiple sketches he languished in nondescript supporting parts. Writers were reluctant to write for him after he flubbed his lines on several early shows. After weeks of being relegated to playing "the second cop, the second FBI guy," as he put it, Murray approached *SNL* producer **Lorne Michaels** with the idea of addressing his struggles on the air. The result was a heartfelt, self-penned plea for support that incorporated elements of Murray's personal biography. It played well in the studio and earned him a second chance with viewers who still looked at him as **Chevy Chase**'s ungainly replacement. Murray continued to fight for air time for the rest of his first season, but after the "New Guy" speech, he was no longer in danger of being dropped from the show.

NEWLEY, ANTHONY

British singer and songwriter, best known for cowriting the lyrics to the classic James Bond theme "Goldfinger" and his Oscar-nominated score for *Willy Wonka & the Chocolate Factory*. In a 1999 *New York Times* profile, Murray confessed his admiration for Newley, whom he considers underrated.

"NEW MURRAY"

Nickname bestowed on Murray by legendary **Indian Hill Club** caddy master Lou Janis, to distinguish Bill from his older brothers Ed and Brian.

NEW YORK CITY

Murray first moved to Manhattan in 1974, when he joined the cast of *The National Lampoon Show* and *The National Lampoon Radio Hour*. He arrived in the Big Apple, he later told *GQ*, "just as everything went to shit.... Subways were insanely cold in the winter and insanely hot in the summer. The windows were all open, so you'd get metal filings and dust in your face. It was like being on a prison train, or working in a mine. I used to run all the time. I would get off that train and just start running." He rented an apartment formerly occupied by actor **Gene**

> ## "NEW YORK CITY AT ITS MOST HEARTWARMING IS A DEATH DANCE TWIXT VEHICLES AND PEDESTRIANS."
>
> —MURRAY, on New York traffic

Hackman and has maintained an almost continual presence in the city and its environs ever since.

"My favorite thing about New York is the people," Murray once said, "because I think they're misunderstood. I don't think people realize how kind New York people are. The drivers are far more considerate, they're just very aggressive." He has also spoken admiringly of New York as a "crucible" where talented newcomers go to test their mettle. "Every year you see a new crop of people thinking they got it coming into town. You see them. They come in in the fall and you can see it and it's amazing to walk down the street, you go, 'New, new, new, new.' You can spot 'em. . . . It's exciting. It's a cycle of life and this is the place where it happens."

On one of his first car rides into the city, Murray passed by one of the enormous cemeteries that line the route from John F. Kennedy International Airport to Manhattan. "I always say to people, those are the people that *didn't* make it. They just threw them over here and then buried them."

NEXT STOP, GREENWICH VILLAGE

DIRECTED BY: Paul Mazursky
WRITTEN BY: Paul Mazursky
RELEASE DATE: February 4, 1976
FILM RATING: ★ ★ ★
MURRAY RATING: ★ ★

PLOT: A Brooklyn nebbish pursues a show business career in 1950s Greenwich Village.

STARRING BILL MURRAY AS: Nick Kessler, mustachioed bohemian

Murray made his feature film debut with a blink-and-you'll-miss-it cameo in this semi-autobiographical drama from director Paul Mazursky. Sporting an anachronistic 1970s porn 'stache, he appears in the background as a reveler in the film's rent party sequence. Stuart Pankin, Vincent Schiavelli, and Jeff Goldblum also have small roles in the film.

NEXT MOVIE: *Meatballs* (1979)

NICK THE LOUNGE SINGER

Nightclub performer known for his bombastic renditions of movie themes and popular songs whom Murray played onstage at **Second City** and in twelve *Saturday Night Live* sketches spanning three decades. Nick, whose last name changes with each appearance, made his *SNL* debut on April 16, 1977. Murray brought him back eight times over the course of his four seasons in the show's main cast. Nick's most notable appearance may have been his second, on the January 28, 1978, show hosted by Robert Klein, during which he sang his version of John Williams's *Star Wars* theme:

Star Wars
Nothing but *Star Wars*
Gimme those *Star Wars*
Don't let them end
Star Wars
If they should bar wars
Please let these *Star Wars* stay

Murray based the character of Nick on **Chicago** nightclub fixture Jimmy Damon, whose act he had caught during his early days at **Second City**. Like Nick, Damon was famous for wearing tight leather pants and an unbuttoned shirt on stage—the better to show off his copious chest hair. "I wasn't upset," Damon told an interviewer regarding Murray's homage. "I just wish he'd sent me a check. He owes me a lot of money."

Although he has generally avoided commenting on the Damon connection—possibly out of fear of being sued—Murray has opined about his overall approach to parodying lounge singers: "You have to see what the original center of the song was and how they destroyed it. It's the ruining of a good song that you want to recreate. You have to like the stuff and you have to, I guess, know that when you have the microphone you have the opportunity to

SNL
Saturday Night Live, 1977

touch somebody. And when you don't do it with the lyric of it, and your own excuse for technique comes in and steps on top of it, that's, I guess, what I object to when I'm mimicking something."

Murray has brought Nick out of the mothballs each of the four times he's hosted *Saturday Night Live*. He performed a Nickified rendition of the "Love Theme from *Jaws*" on the *SNL* fortieth-anniversary special in February 2015. He's also been known to break into the character on movie sets. In a 2014 interview with the Onion's A.V. Club, actor Kurtwood Smith recalled the time Murray "did" Nick during the filming of the climactic scene in 1990's *Quick Change*:

"We had a scene in the first-class section of this airliner.... The plane was full. Jason [Robards] was in the scene. I think Randy [Quaid] and Geena [Davis] were, too. So there were just tons of people. And we got ready for Bill to call, 'Action!' So he said, 'Okay, everybody ready? Sound? Everybody ... ?' And then he starts singing. You know the song 'Brandy (You're a Fine Girl)'? He starts singing it kind of like the lounge guy he used to do on *Saturday Night Live* ... and he sings the entire song. All the verses. The entire song. *Then* he says, 'Action!' It had nothing to do with anything. But we were all quite entertained. It was great!"

NIKO

Dim-witted fry cook played by Murray in six Olympia Café sketches on *Saturday Night Live*.

NINETEEN EIGHTY-FIVE

Stillborn sci-fi comedy that would have paired Murray and **Dan Aykroyd** several years before *Ghostbusters*. A parody of George Orwell's *1984*, *Nineteen Eighty-Five* is set in a dystopian future society ruled by a pair of scientists known as the Big Brothers. Murray and Aykroyd were tapped to play "thoughtcops" who enforce the edicts of the state—including strict regulations on when and where citizens can masturbate. *Saturday Night Live* writers Al Franken, Tom Davis, and Jim Downey collaborated on the script for *Nineteen Eighty-Five*, which MGM hoped would be the first big "*SNL* movie" following the success of *National Lampoon's Animal House*. However, budget problems and financial dysfunction at the ailing studio ultimately torpedoed the project.

NORTH BY NORTHWEST

This 1959 spy thriller is one of Murray's favorite movies. He was particularly enamored of the film's two romantic leads. "I always just thought **Cary Grant** was the coolest," he told *Empire* magazine. "His chops were so crisp and so clean. And then you throw in Hitchcock and you've pretty much got his ticket." In another interview, Murray noted, "I'm crazy about that Eva Marie Saint."

NOTHING LASTS FOREVER

DIRECTED BY: Tom Schiller

WRITTEN BY: Tom Schiller

RELEASE DATE: September 1984

FILM RATING: ★★

MURRAY RATING: ★★

PLOT: An aspiring artist seeks his métier in a dystopian future New York City run by the Port Authority.

STARRING BILL MURRAY AS: Ted Breughel, moon bus flight steward

While filming *Tootsie* in the spring of 1982, Murray took time out from his schedule to appear in this black-and-white art house curiosity from writer/director Tom Schiller. Murray took on the extra project as a personal favor to Schiller, the impish auteur behind numerous classic *Saturday Night Live* short films—including the Honker showcase *Perchance to Dream*. Murray has called Schiller "one of the few people I think of as being truly brilliant." The director's feature debut, alas, is more baffling than brilliant, though it has attained a modest cult following.

A plaintive cinematic reverie that combines elements of classic science fiction and old MGM musicals, *Nothing Lasts Forever* plays like one of Schiller's dreamlike *SNL* shorts stretched out to eighty-two minutes. Twenty-year-old Zach Galligan, soon to hit it big in the Steven Spielberg–produced blockbuster *Gremlins*, stars as Adam Beckett, a naive young classical pianist struggling to find his place in a *Brazil*-like future Manhattan. The decidedly nonlinear plot has Adam falling in with a group of pretentious downtown scenesters—the film's most effective scenes parody the SoHo art milieu of the 1980s—and taking a trip to the moon at the urging of a magical homeless man played by geriatric Oscar nominee Sam Jaffe. The supporting cast is a curious mix of Schiller's *SNL* pals (Murray, Dan Aykroyd), Old Hollywood fossils (Imogene Coca, Eddie Fisher), and Mort Sahl. Murray plays Ted Breughel, a belligerent flight attendant on a lunar-bound space bus. "At that time Bill hadn't played many mean characters and I always thought it would be fun to portray those airline stewards as sort of secretly hostile," says Schiller. The part started out as a cameo but expanded during filming as Murray improvised new scenes.

Murray spent about a week on the set, cramming in his scenes whenever he wasn't needed on *Tootsie*. According to author Michael Streeter's biography of Tom Schiller, *Nothing Lost Forever*, Murray was tired and cranky during much of the shoot, which led to some conflicts with his costars. "There were times when he was very nice to me—very generous and funny," Zach Galligan told Streeter. "And then there were times that he was sullen and unhappy and kind of moody. You didn't really know which Bill Murray was going to show up on the set that day. My whole relationship with him left me very confused." Actress Lauren Tom, who played Galligan's love interest, Eloy, was less diplomatic. "Bill Murray liked to tease me about being the 'young starlet' or something like that," she said. "It bothered me a bit. Actually, I thought he was sort of an ass." But Tom Schiller dismisses the complaints: "Bill was a perfect gentleman. He was always so focused that any 'tension' around him was due to his pinpoint attentiveness and enlightened consciousness."

Murray worked for scale on the condition that his name and likeness not be used in the marketing of the film. As a result, though Murray has one of the meatier supporting roles in *Nothing Lasts Forever*, he doesn't appear in the film's trailer, and his name is completely absent from the official poster. Perhaps he didn't want to mislead audiences into expecting another *Caddy-shack*-style comedy. Or perhaps he sensed the movie's uncertain commercial prospects. Murray admitted that the script for Schiller's black-and-white fantasia left him somewhat perplexed. "I didn't quite understand what it was," he said.

He wasn't alone. Executives at MGM had high hopes for *Nothing Lasts Forever*, which they thought would be a crowd-pleasing "*Saturday Night Live* movie" in the mold of *The Blues Brothers*. But they were mortified by the film that Schiller delivered. Producer **Lorne Michaels**, who had convinced the studio to bankroll the project, was quietly relieved of his authority. All plans to promote and distribute the film were shelved. Ultimately it was dumped into one theater in Seattle in the summer of 1984, in a halfhearted attempt to cash in on the success of *Ghostbusters*. Since then, it has been screened only rarely in the United States, though dubbed versions do occasionally air on European television.

"It just needs to be seen," Murray told author Michael Streeter twenty years after *Nothing Lasts Forever*'s abortive release. "It should be on a midnight movie list on television so people can see it. . . . It's the kind of movie where people would be taken by it if they saw it." Anyone interested in testing the validity of Murray's proposition can watch the film online, where it currently resides in perpetuity.

NEXT MOVIE: *The Razor's Edge* (1984)

NUDITY

Murray has never done a nude scene in a film. In fact, it is one of his few inhibitions. *Groundhog Day* screenwriter Danny Rubin wrote a scene wherein Phil Connors sheds all of his clothes and walks into the teeth of an approaching snowstorm, but Murray nixed it. "I don't do naked," he told Rubin. And that was that.

TALES FROM
MURRAYLAND

Nº 18 | The *Road House* Prank

Murray is a huge fan of the 1989 action film starring Patrick Swayze as a bouncer at a small-town Missouri bar. He is especially fond of the film's celebrated love scene, in which Swayze and costar Kelly Lynch have sex against a rock wall. According to Lynch, Murray watches the film whenever it comes on TV and makes a point of calling her husband, screenwriter Mitch Glazer, during her sex scene with Swayze. "Kelly's having sex with Patrick Swayze right now," Murray reportedly exults in his Carl Spackler voice. "They're doing it. He's throwing her against the rocks." If Murray is unavailable, one of his brothers will call instead. Glazer admitted to an interviewer that he is dismayed by the calls, which come in at all hours of the day or night from wherever Murray happens to be at the time—including at least one call from Russia. "It was funny the first dozen or so times," Glazer said.

OKLAHOMA!

Murray is a big fan of this 1943 Broadway musical from the creative team of Richard Rodgers and Oscar Hammerstein. He once told an interviewer that he rated *Oklahoma!* as "the best musical ever."

See also **Mame**.

OLIVE KITTERIDGE

Continuing the transition into "sad old man" roles that began with *St. Vincent*, Murray plays a forlorn widower learning to love again in this 2014 HBO miniseries based on the Pulitzer Prize–winning novel by Elizabeth Strout. Frances McDormand stars as Olive Kitteridge, a crabby New England schoolteacher who enjoys an unlikely late-life romance with Murray's character.

OSMOSIS JONES

DIRECTED BY: Tom Sito, Piet Kroon, and Peter and Robert Farrelly

WRITTEN BY: Marc Hyman

RELEASE DATE: August 10, 2001

FILM RATING: ★★⯨

MURRAY RATING: ★★

PLOT: A dyspeptic slob successfully fights off a bout of food poisoning.

STARRING BILL MURRAY AS: Frank Detorri, gluttonous zookeeper

Murray reunited with the Farrelly brothers for this curious comedy mixing live-action with hand-drawn animation in the glorious tradition of *Space Jam*. Playing a slovenly widower who contracts a life-threatening virus after eating a tainted egg, Murray delivers the sweatiest, seediest, least appealing character turn of his career. Most of the action takes place inside his disease-ravaged body, where a cartoon buddy-cop duo voiced by Chris Rock and David Hyde-Pierce join forces to vanquish the killer germs trying to do him in. Bobby Farrelly called *Osmosis Jones* "the best script I've seen my whole time in the business," and though that is more than a little hyperbolic, there are many clever moments here that evoke the golden age of Warner Bros. animation. As a twenty-minute educational short about the human digestive system, this film might have been a minor classic. At ninety-five minutes, the joke goes on far too long. The cartoon sequences are intermittently amusing, but the Farrelly-directed live-action inserts push the envelope of gross-out humor to its stomach-turning extreme. In two separate scenes, Murray disgorges himself all over the kindly schoolteacher played by Molly Shannon. Equally revolting is Chris Elliott, outfitted in an Edgar Winter fright wig, as Murray's lackwit younger brother. This is not the *Groundhog Day* reunion moviegoers were expecting.

NEXT MOVIE: *Speaking of Sex* (2001)

OVITZ, MIKE

This legendary Hollywood talent agent represented Murray from the early 1980s until the mid-'90s. "He was my monster," Murray once remarked of the Creative Artists Agency founder. "He was great. He's a famous character, but he was my character. And when he's on your side, he's a weapon. He's really something." Murray has Ovitz to thank for the big-money studio deals that defined his career in the 1980s. "He did things that no one did before and made things happen," Murray has said. In 1995, Ovitz left CAA to become president of the Walt Disney Company. Murray remained with the agency for another five years before firing his **agents** in 2000.

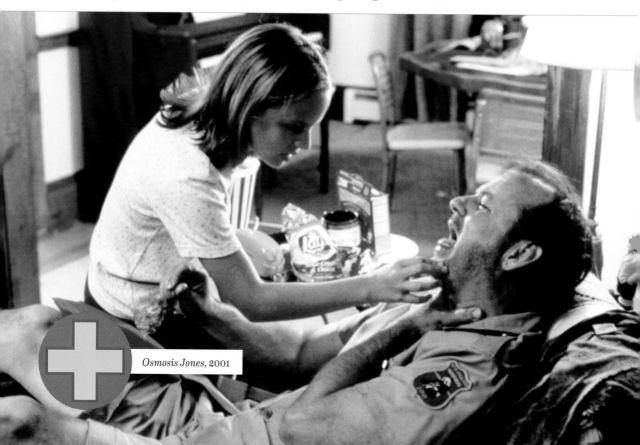

Osmosis Jones, 2001

PALIN, SARAH

In an interview conducted during the 2008 presidential campaign, Murray expressed reservations about several candidates, including this Alaska governor turned Republican vice presidential nominee. "I don't know where that voice comes from," he said of Palin. "It sounds like northern Wisconsin or Minnesota or something; not what I imagine Alaskans sound like. It's a disturbing pitch."

PARKS AND RECREATION

In November 2014, Murray filmed a surprise cameo for the penultimate episode of this popular TV sitcom about a midlevel parks department bureaucrat and her friends and coworkers in Pawnee, Indiana. In the episode "Two Funerals," which aired on February 17, 2015, Murray plays Walter Gunderson, the oft-mentioned, never-before-seen, and recently deceased mayor of Pawnee. He appears briefly as a corpse lying in an open casket and in a prerecorded video message played at his funeral service. According to published reports, Murray improvised much of his monologue.

PASSION PLAY

DIRECTED BY: Mitch Glazer

WRITTEN BY: Mitch Glazer

RELEASE DATE: September 10, 2010

FILM RATING: ★⸍

MURRAY RATING: ★

PLOT: A burned-out jazzman falls in love with a winged sideshow oddity.

STARRING BILL MURRAY AS: Michael "Happy" Shannon, bewigged, bespectacled gangster

Twenty years in the making, this directorial debut of Murray pal **Mitch Glazer** is an over-the-top gonzo fable about a smack-addicted jazz musician (Mickey Rourke) who becomes emotionally and erotically transfixed by a woman with angel wings (Megan Fox). Watching it, one gets the sense Glazer started his script with a sex scene between a man and a bird woman, then worked backward from there. The whole thing plays like someone's twisted bestiality fantasy captured on film.

Passion Play, 2010

If Murray's performance seems phoned in, as if he was doing the movie as a favor to a friend, it's because he was. Glazer's first choice for the role of mobster Happy Shannon, Toby Kebbell, quit after three days of filming. (According to reports, he was terrified at having to share the screen with Rourke.) Murray volunteered to take the part, the latest in a long line of doomed passion projects to which he has lent his imprimatur. "The movie is such a long shot. So impossible," he said shortly after *Passion Play*'s release. "But I live to go down with those guys that have no fuckin' chance."

Glazer later admitted he "fell to his knees" when Murray agreed to come on board—oddly enough, on **Christmas** Day. But if he was expecting another gift in the form of a fully committed performance, he was sorely mistaken. Outfitted with Glazer's eyeglasses and one of the worst toupees of his career, Murray brings little or nothing to the hazily written role of the underworld boss who competes with Rourke for Fox's affection. Tellingly, the actor originally tapped to play Happy was more than thirty years younger than Murray, suggesting that even Glazer had no fixed idea of who the character was supposed to be.

Passion Play opened to widespread derision at the 2010 Toronto International Film Festival and then was shelved for several months as Glazer performed meatball surgery on his original cut. He needn't have bothered.

TALES FROM
MURRAYLAND

N° 19   The Day He Dunked
an Autograph Hound

Murray took a break from filming *Scrooged* to enjoy a little R & R at Rancho La Puerta, a vegetarian health spa in Baja California. Joining him at the tony desert resort were *Scrooged* screenwriters Mitch Glazer and Michael O'Donoghue. They were the only three men in a spa full of wealthy Beverly Hills housewives. Murray spent the weekend hiking, swimming, and signing autographs for guests. By his final day, he was weary from all the unwanted attention. When a middle-aged woman in a fur coat approached him and requested yet another autograph, Murray complied on one condition. "I'll have to have something in return," he told her. "I get to throw you in the pool." "Sure, you do that," the woman replied with a laugh, sticking a pen in his hand. With that, Murray scooped her up, carried her over to the deep end of the pool, and dropped her—fur coat and all—into the water. As Glazer summed up: "He'd made the deal and that was it."

By the time it hit theaters in the fall, the film had been disowned by its star, Mickey Rourke, who branded it the latest "terrible movie" in his less-than-stellar canon. After a brief theatrical run, *Passion Play* was consigned to the direct-to-DVD birdcage, never to fly in public again.

NEXT MOVIE: *Moonrise Kingdom* (2012)

PEANUT BUTTER, LETTUCE, AND MAYONNAISE ON PUMPERNICKEL

Ingredients of Murray's favorite sandwich.

PEOPLE VS. LARRY FLYNT, THE

Murray was up for the role of pornographer Larry Flynt in this 2006 biopic from *Ed Wood* screenwriters Scott Alexander and Larry Karaszewski. But director Milos Forman claims Murray never returned his phone calls. Tom Hanks was also considered for the part, which earned Woody Harrelson an Oscar nomination for best actor.

PERCHANCE TO DREAM

Black-and-white short film from director Tom Schiller that aired during the March 10, 1979, telecast of *Saturday Night Live*. Murray plays **the Honker**, a homeless drunk who takes a swig from an enchanted liquor bottle and dreams he is an actor performing Shakespeare on stage.

PETTY CASH

Murray prefers to carry cash in denominations of fifty and ten, reasoning that "people like fifties, twenties are too big for most things, and hundreds are hard to break."

PHILADELPHIA

Director Jonathan Demme considered Murray for the role of Joe Miller, the homophobic lawyer who helps an AIDS-afflicted colleague wage a wrongful termination lawsuit, in this Oscar-winning 1993 drama. At the time, Daniel Day-Lewis was slated to headline the film. When Tom Hanks replaced Day-Lewis as the lead, Demme opted to go with a dramatic actor for the second banana. Murray gave way to Denzel Washington.

PICKLES

During his 2014 Reddit "Ask Me Anything" session, Murray confessed his fondness for pickles. "I like pickles. I put pickles in lots of sandwiches. I'm big on pickles, but I've never had them with peanut butter. I really like peanut butter though. I'm kind of surprised because I like them both so much that I haven't combined them."

PLAYER PIANOS

Murray became fascinated by player pianos after buying one from *Saturday Night Live* short filmmaker Tom Schiller in the 1990s. "There was a period after leaving the show when I was kind of down on my heels," Schiller says. "I had this magnificent player piano and I told Bill I was strapped for money. He generously offered to buy it and said I could buy it back later on. He kept it for a few years and when I had the cash, he made good on his promise and I was able to buy it back." "I was really torn," Murray told author Michael Streeter. "I was happy that he bought it back, but I really loved that piano."

POLITICS

Murray has rarely spoken publicly about his political affiliation. In an interview with the *Chicago Tribune* conducted shortly before the 2008 presidential election, he declared then-candidate Barack Obama "interesting to watch" but expressed disinterest in vice presidential nominees Joe Biden and **Sarah Palin**. In a 2012 appearance on CNBC's *Squawk Box*, Murray espoused a personal weltanschauung that emphasized the virtues of self-reliance:

"I think we ought to be personally responsible," he said. "I think if you can take care of yourself and then maybe try to take care of someone else, that's sort of how you're supposed to live. . . . I think we've sort of gotten used to someone looking out for us and I don't think any other person is necessarily going to be counted on to look out for us. I think there's only so many people that can take care of themselves and can take care of other people. The rest of the people—they're useful in terms of compost for the whole planet." Speaking about the taming of the frontier, he lauded the heroism of the early settlers: "This country is really a pioneer country, the people that came here. We forget the kind of discipline they had to have. . . . They came in wagons and the wheels broke. . . . There was no option but to do it yourself, to have your own responsibility. There is no turning back."

Later in that same *Squawk Box* appearance, Murray decried the sad state of partisan politics in America. Politicians, he said, "spend all their time just trying to destroy the other guy, not to work together but to humble and humiliate the other so that they can't have success. It's not working to serve anyone anymore. If you're not serving some sort of common good, and you're only serving your sort of partisan alliance, you're part of what's destructive. You're destroying something."

In a 2014 profile for the *Guardian*, Murray doubled down on his criticism of political partisanship: "Political parties work to cripple their opponents," he railed. "They spend all their time in office trying to paralyze the work of the others. They try to stifle. It's cruel, cruel. . . . I wish you could hold all of Congress prisoner and they'd get Stockholm syndrome and have to go along

P
Q
R

with their captors. And their captors would be people who were real true American citizens." He also issued a vague premonition about an upcoming national apocalypse: "Eventually something horrible will happen, something dynamic and powerful. It's going to have to be cataclysmic for people to wake up and say: 'Okay, is anyone gonna do this?' There's going to have to be a shock of another kind. I think something's gonna have to change. Usually it's something like war or 9/11 that makes people come together."

POLYESTER

Murray sang the "love theme" for this 1981 film from cult auteur John Waters. For more details, see **Waters, John**.

POPE JOHN XXIII

This Roman Catholic pontiff, who reigned from 1958 to 1963 and presided over the historic Second Vatican Council, is one of Murray's all-time favorite popes. "He's my guy," the actor told the *Guardian* newspaper. "An extraordinary joyous Florentine who changed the order." Not all of John XXIII's reforms met with Murray's approval, however. The elimination of the traditional Latin mass in particular sticks in Murray's craw. "I tend to disagree with what they call the new mass," he has said. "I think we lost something by losing the Latin. Now if you go to a Catholic mass even just in Harlem it can be in Spanish, it can be in Ethiopian, it can be in any number of languages. The shape of it, the pictures, are the same but the words aren't the same. There's a vibration to those words. If you've been in the business long enough you know what they mean anyway. And I really miss the music—the power of it, y'know? Yikes! Sacred music has an effect on your brain."

PRESLEY, ELVIS

Murray is fascinated by the life of this rock 'n' roll legend. He famously crashed Presley's funeral in 1977. "He was an extraordinary guy," Murray once observed of the King. "He could have really been good. I mean his movies, some of them were absolutely terrible, but I don't think people know how hard it is to be as natural as he came off in his movies." He went on to rhapsodize about the hip-swiveler's romantic mystique. "The amazing thing about Elvis, or another amazing thing, was the guy did some dating in his life, and not one woman that he

> **"WHEN ELVIS DIED, I THOUGHT, 'IF ELVIS CAN DIE, WHAT IS GOING TO BECOME OF ME?'"**
>
> —MURRAY, on the 1977 demise of the King of Rock 'n' Roll

dated will say a bad thing about Elvis—they were all nuts about him. I mean none of them really ended up with him, but we knew a girl in Illinois who met Elvis once and he bought her a car! And we'd ask her, 'So what's the deal with the King?' He was still alive at that point. And she wouldn't tell us a thing. She was crazy about him. She thought he was just, you know, the cat's meow."

PRESS YOUR LUCK

In 2000, Murray signed on to star in this film based on the true story of Michael Larsen, an unemployed ice cream truck driver who won more than $100,000 on the TV game show *Press Your Luck* by memorizing the patterns on its vaunted "big board." Frequent Murray collaborator Howard Franklin would have directed the comedy, which never made it past the development stage.

PRIMARY COLORS

Murray walked out on this 1998 big-screen adaptation of political journalist Joe Klein's novel. In an interview, he disparaged the film for its unflattering portrayal of a thinly veiled President Bill Clinton. "I despised it," he said.

PUBLIC TRANSPORTATION

When visiting big cities, Murray enjoys taking public transportation—especially buses. "It's not crowded and you're above everything so you can see the sights. You even get your own bus lane." He likes taking subways as well. "People are always like, 'What are *you* doing here?' I go, 'It's the fastest way to get to Yankee Stadium.' To get from the airport to his hotel, he often eschews taxis in favor of trains, which he calls "self-normalizing."

Despite his enthusiasm for public transport, Murray is invariably disappointed with the service he receives from bus and train operators. "I've been treated badly on various types of transportation in my life," he says, "and I've always felt that inherent schoolteacher mentality where there are teachers that resent you because you're going to graduate this class, and they're going to be here next year. There are some that don't belong in the transportation business and that's why they stick out. They have the job and they have the position but they don't have the grace." Murray channeled his disappointment into his portrayal of a surly bus attendant in the 1984 film *Nothing Lasts Forever*.

P
Q
R

QUICK CHANGE

DIRECTED BY: Howard Franklin and Bill Murray

WRITTEN BY: Howard Franklin

RELEASE DATE: July 13, 1990

FILM RATING: ★★

MURRAY RATING: ★★

PLOT: Three bank robbers try to make their getaway through the nightmarish streets of "No Radio"-era New York City.

STARRING BILL MURRAY AS: Grimm, a bank robber who dresses up as a clown

Following the success of *Scrooged* and *Ghostbusters II*, Murray once again had the juice to call his own shots in Hollywood. But rather than roll the dice on another ambitious passion project like *The Razor's Edge*, he opted to play it safe with this unconventional caper comedy based on a 1981 novel by newspaper columnist Jay Cronley. *Quick Change* had already been adapted once for the screen, as the 1985 French-Canadian feature *Hold-Up* starring Jean-Paul Belmondo, but Murray was excited enough about the prospects for a remake to hop on board as a producer. Howard Franklin wrote the script, the first of three collaborations with Murray during the 1990s. When both Jonathan Demme and **Ron Howard** turned down offers to direct, Franklin and Murray took the reins. To date, *Quick Change* remains Murray's lone directorial effort.

The film follows a trio of bank robbers as they make their escape from Manhattan through Brooklyn and Queens to John F. Kennedy International Airport. Murray plays Grimm, a dour city planner driven to a life of crime by **New York City**'s slide into decrepitude in the 1980s. Geena Davis plays Murray's girlfriend. Randy Quaid plays the same hulking, dim-witted man-child he plays in every movie. The superb supporting cast includes Jason Robards, Phil Hartman, Stanley Tucci, and Tony Shalhoub. Murray spends the opening half hour of *Quick Change* in clown **makeup**, a plot element that was unwisely emphasized in posters and marketing materials for the film, making it look like a circus comedy. Murray voiced reservations about the get-up in an interview he did with Roger Ebert shortly before the movie opened: "You do kind of worry because you wonder if they're going to know who you are. You could be so disguised they can't recognize you. We tried to let the face come through, so I could use my facial expressions. We didn't want to make it such a mask that I couldn't react."

Once Murray's character ditches the clown white, *Quick Change* does have a certain ramshackle charm. But it lacks the comic velocity of similar films like Martin Scorsese's *After Hours*, and its central conceit—that New York is an open sewer overflowing with criminals and eccentrics—seems more quaint and dated with each passing year. Murray and Franklin shot on location in some of the city's worst neighborhoods, a choice that may have sapped the spirit of some of the performers. "It's very hard to be funny when you see how people are living," Murray said later. One night while filming, the set was targeted in a drive-by shooting. A member of the crew narrowly escaped having his head blown off. "That's good for morale; keeps the crew tight," Murray quipped.

Despite all the on-set tsouris, Murray called *Quick Change* "the most fun movie experience I've ever had—until the release." Though he did everything he could to promote the film, he was disappointed by the efforts of the Warner Bros. marketing department. "They were doing everything but selling that movie," Murray carped. Shortly before *Quick Change* was scheduled to hit theaters, Murray begged the studio to pull the plug. "The week before it came out I said, 'Don't even open the movie now. Let's start over and I'll do another round of press junkets. Don't spend this money, it's a waste of time.' But they spent it anyway." The proof was in the pudding. *Quick Change* tanked, grossing a paltry $15.2 million. Its codirector and star remains one the film's staunchest supporters. "I think in ten years people are going to say, 'That was a really good movie,'" Murray declared of *Quick Change* in 1993.

NEXT MOVIE: *What about Bob?*

¿QUIÉN ES MÁS MACHO?

With **Dan Aykroyd** and **John Belushi** increasingly absorbed by their movie careers, Murray did some of his finest character work during his final two seasons on *Saturday Night Live*. In this classic February 17, 1979, sketch, he plays Paco Valenzuela, the debonair host of a Spanish-language game show on which contestants must decide which of two male celebrities is more macho. **Gilda Radner** and guest host Ricky Nelson compete to assess the manliness of such '70s-era stars as Fernando Lamas and Ricardo Montalbán. Oddly enough, Murray had previously performed an impression of Lamas (opposite Aykroyd as Montalbán) in a sketch on the May 14, 1977, *SNL* episode, which was hosted by Shelley Duvall.

Quick Change, 1990

TALES FROM
MURRAYLAND

Nº 20	The Party on Strother Martin's Grave

During production on *Stripes* in 1980, Murray and Warren "Sergeant Hulka" Oates took a break from filming to visit the grave of recently deceased character actor Strother Martin at Forest Lawn Cemetery in Los Angeles. Murray had bonded with Martin when the latter hosted *Saturday Night Live* a few months before his death. Oates had worked with him on *Gunsmoke* and *The Wild Bunch*. Determined to show their friend out in style, Murray and Oates got drunk on Armagnac, poured some for Strother, passed out on his grave, and woke up several hours later covered in cuts and bruises. "We figured Strother took us somewhere and beat us up," Murray said.

RADNER, GILDA

Murray had a tumultuous on-again, off-again romantic relationship with his *National Lampoon Radio Hour* and *Saturday Night Live* castmate, with whom he collaborated on the popular Nerds sketches. "I've always had a thing for funny girls," he once declared. "Gilda was the greatest laugher and she was funny herself. To me that was incredibly attractive." By all accounts, their liaison had ended by the early 1980s, when Radner married guitarist G. E. Smith and Murray wedded Mickey Kelly. The creator of such breakout characters as Baba Wawa, Emily Litella, and Roseanne Roseannadanna, Radner was known as the heartbreaker among the early *SNL* cast. "Anyone that knew Gilda fell in love with her," Murray once said. "She was really something." In interviews, he has credited Radner—the daughter of a prominent Detroit hotelier—with teaching him the importance of saying no to people. "Gilda had money from her family, and when she went in to talk about a job, she didn't need it. And there's something about work, just like there's something about romance, that if you don't have to have someone, you're more desirable."

RAIDERS OF THE LOST ARK

Murray was one of several actors considered for the role of Indiana Jones in this 1981 blockbuster. Tom Selleck, Nick Nolte, Steve Martin, Chevy Chase, Tim Matheson, Jack Nicholson, and Jeff Bridges were also up for the part, which eventually went to Harrison Ford.

RAIN MAN

Dustin Hoffman won an Oscar for his portrayal of autistic savant Raymond Babbitt in this 1988 film. But according to screenwriter Barry Morrow, Murray was offered the role first. In the original casting configuration, Hoffman would have played Raymond's brother Charlie, the role played by Tom Cruise in the finished film.

RAMIS, HAROLD

Curly-haired comic writer, actor, and director who collaborated with Murray on numerous projects over a twenty-year period beginning in the mid-1970s. A native of **Chicago**, Ramis attended college at Washington University in St. Louis. After graduation, he worked for seven months as an orderly in a mental institution. There he learned "how to speak to schizophrenics, catatonics, paranoids, and suicidal people," an experience, he often said, that was perfect training for working with actors.

> ## "HE JUST PUNISHES PEOPLE, FOR REASONS THEY CAN'T FIGURE OUT."
>
> —HAROLD RAMIS, on why Murray chose to cut off all contact with him in the 1990s

Ramis first met Murray in 1968 at the introduction of Murray's brother Brian. "Brian and I were in **Second City** together and he said, 'Why don't you come up and have dinner at my mother's house?'" Ramis recalled in a 2010 interview. Along the way, they stopped off at the **golf** course where Murray operated a ninth-hole hot dog stand. Their paths would cross again a few years later in New York, when Murray joined the casts of *The National Lampoon Radio Hour* and the Off-Broadway revue *The National Lampoon Show*. Ramis was immediately struck by Murray's electrifying stage presence. He repeatedly called Murray the best verbal improviser he had ever seen. The two eventually struck up a creative partnership that lasted through six feature films. "I always tell students to identify the most talented person in the room and, if it isn't you, go stand next to him," Ramis once said. "That's what I did with Bill."

Ramis has often been credited with helping to cultivate Murray's 1980s big-screen persona—the sardonic slacker-trickster who charms his way out of precarious situations. "I had Bill's voice down," he told *GQ*. "When people would read something I'd written for him, they'd say, 'That is so perfectly Bill Murray.' Of course, the irony is that he'd read it and say, 'Bullshit, I can't say this.'" In a 2009 interview with the Onion's A.V. Club, Ramis likened his creative bond with Murray to an alliance between great powers: "I could help him be the best funny Bill Murray he could be, and I think he appreciated that then."

In time, however, Murray may have come to resent Ramis's outsize role in his career. "Bill owes everything to Harold," a mutual friend, producer Michael Shamberg, told the *New Yorker*, "and he probably has a thimbleful of gratitude." The rift between the two men came to a head on the set of *Groundhog Day* in 1992. Creative differences centered on Ramis's rewrites to Danny

"SHE WAS ABLE TO WALK THROUGH LIFE WALKING DOWN THE STREET PAST ELEVEN GUYS THAT EITHER WERE IN LOVE WITH HER, HAD BEEN IN LOVE WITH HER, OR WERE GOING TO BE IN LOVE WITH HER."

—MURRAY, on the unbearable cuteness of Gilda Radner

Rubin's screenplay, as well as Murray's belief that Ramis was becoming too much of a "mogul," led to a more or less permanent cold war between the two men that lasted until Ramis fell mortally ill with autoimmune inflammatory vasculitis in late 2013.

Over the last two decades of his life, Ramis made repeated efforts to patch things up with Murray. But except for brief exchanges at a wake and a bar mitzvah, the two men never spoke to each other. Ramis remained puzzled by his former friend's refusal to engage. "I have no clue" why Murray cut him off, he once said. "And because it's unstated, it sends me to my worst fears. Did he think I was weak? Or untrue? Did I betray him in some way? With no clue or feedback from him, it's this kind of tantalizing mystery. And that may be the point."

Only in Ramis's final hours did Murray make the decision to reconcile with him. "He became ill and I thought, 'Well, this is stupid,'" Murray told an interviewer for *Grantland*. Shortly before Ramis passed away, Murray visited him unexpectedly at his home in the Chicago suburbs to say goodbye. After his death, Murray issued a statement to the press through his lawyer, David Nochimson. It read in full: "Harold Ramis and I together did *The National Lampoon Show* off-Broadway, *Meatballs*, *Stripes*, *Caddyshack*, *Ghostbusters*, and *Groundhog Day*. He earned his keep on this planet. God bless him."

RASCALS, THE

Blue-eyed soul quartet of the 1960s, best known for their hits "Good Lovin'" and "Groovin'." In 2010, Murray attended a reunion concert by the band, which he called "maybe the best thing I've ever seen."

RAZOR'S EDGE, THE

DIRECTED BY: John Byrum

WRITTEN BY: John Byrum and Bill Murray

RELEASE DATE: October 19, 1984

FILM RATING: ★ ★

MURRAY RATING: ★ ★

PLOT: A battle-scarred World War I veteran abandons his comfortable life in America to go on a vision quest through Paris and India.

STARRING BILL MURRAY AS: Larry Darrell, burned-out World War I ambulance driver

According to Hollywood legend, actor Tyrone Power was so transfixed by W. Somerset Maugham's 1944 novel *The Razor's Edge* that he pulled an audacious power play in order to get a movie version made. Burned out after years of cranking out Zorro movies, Power agreed to play the masked swordsman one last time if Twentieth Century Fox would let him star as Larry Darrell, Maugham's idealistic hero, in a big-screen adaptation of the novel. The story is apocryphal—Power played Zorro only once, and that was in 1940—but it illustrates the powerful hold a prestige project like *The Razor's Edge* can exert over a young star wary of being typecast. Nearly forty years after Larry Darrell breathed new life into Tyrone Power's career, Bill Murray successfully maneuvered Columbia Pictures into giving him a crack at the role, one he hoped would establish him once and for all as a bankable dramatic actor.

In the early 1980s, Murray became friends with John Byrum, a young director who had grown up about a mile from Murray's hometown. In March 1982, shortly after Murray's wife gave birth to their first child, Byrum sent Murray a copy of *The Razor's Edge* to keep him occupied during her recovery. After reading the first fifty pages, Murray had an epiphany: he *was* Maugham's disillusioned seeker and he wanted to make the character his first great dramatic role. The next night, he called Byrum at four in the morning. "This is Larry, Larry Darrell," Murray said when the director picked up the phone. The two friends began spitballing plans to bring *The Razor's Edge* back to the screen.

Murray and Byrum spent the next year working on the script. At Murray's suggestion, they set off on a Darrell-like road trip across America, writing up scenes in bars, bus stations, and restaurants they stopped in along the

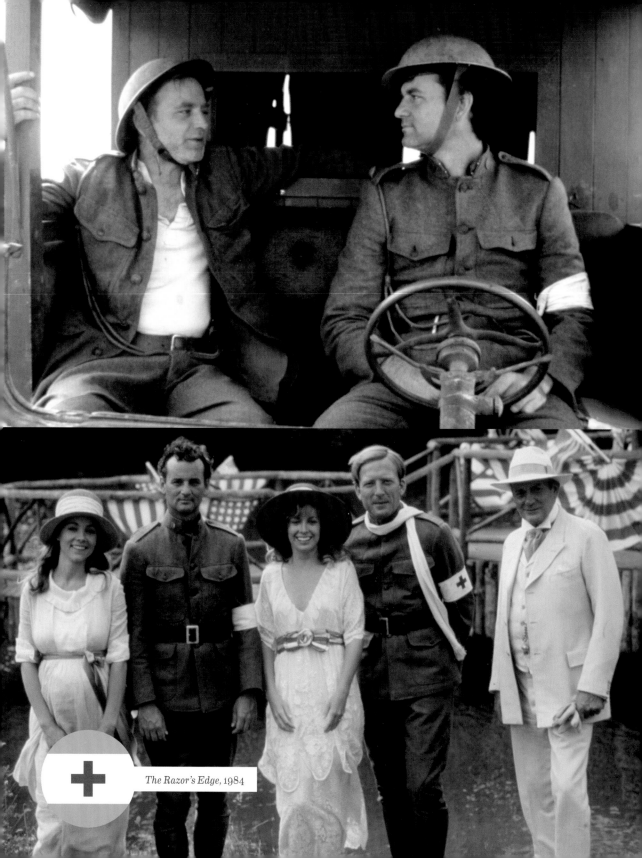

The Razor's Edge, 1984

way. "We went to northern California ashrams and nudist colonies, visited strange religious cults with aerobic classes," Byrum later told *Film Journal*. "We did a lot of our best writing in a car driving across Nebraska."

Securing studio backing for the unusual venture proved surprisingly easy, once Murray realized he could leverage his participation in the new paranormal comedy that **Dan Aykroyd** was writing for him. "As soon as people heard about *Ghostbusters*, every studio wanted it," Murray said. "But I still wanted to do *The Razor's Edge*. Finally Dan said, 'Tell whoever wants *Ghostbusters* that they have to take *The Razor's Edge*, too.' We didn't have to tell them. They figured it out real quick. You didn't have to be a rocket scientist to see what the deal was going to be. Finally the people at Columbia said, 'We're really nuts about that *Razor's Edge*. Now about this other movie . . .'"

> ## "PEOPLE SAID I WAS VERY COURAGEOUS MAKING THAT MOVIE. SURE. SO'S SETTING YOURSELF ON FIRE. AFTER THAT MOVIE, I FELT RADIOACTIVE."
>
> —MURRAY, on the negative public response to his labor of love, *The Razor's Edge*

Filming took place on location in France and India in the summer of 1983. Murray's wife Mickey and infant son Homer joined him for the first leg of the shoot. "Nobody wanted to come to India," he said. "They all thought it was pretty good to be in Paris spending money, but when we said, 'Well, now we're going to go eat dried dog and yogurt,' they said 'No, we think we'll go home.'" Consistent with his view that *Razor's Edge* was a film he had been called to make, Murray took no salary for acting in it (though he did get $12,000 for cowriting the script). Principal photography wrapped up in early October, just in time for Murray to report to the *Ghostbusters* set in **New York City**.

After viewing a rough cut of *The Razor's Edge* that fall, Murray waited nervously for the audience's verdict. Originally scheduled to come out before *Ghostbusters*, the film was held back until the following autumn, allowing the negative buzz to build. "I don't know what my **fans** are going to think," Murray told an interviewer in anticipation of the release. "It's definitely not what they're used to from me."

He was right to be worried. *The Razor's Edge* opened in October 1984 to harshly negative reviews. The *New York Times* called it "slow, overlong, and ridiculously overproduced." "Huge chunks of hackneyed drama are inter-

P
Q
R

spersed with Murray doing Murray," carped the reviewer for the New York *Daily News.* J. Hoberman of the *Village Voice* called Murray's Larry Darrell "a leering goofball, even in deepest Tibet." Murray's earnest attempt to portray a spiritual seeker was fatally burdened by his past life as a clown, Hoberman wrote. "When he finally dons the saffron robes, he's like a conehead who's lost his cone." The public wasn't convinced either. "I remember arriving a few minutes late on the opening day," John Byrum recalled. "They were streaming out of the theater and shouting to people waiting in line for the next show: 'Don't waste your money, it isn't funny!'"

Watching *The Razor's Edge* today, it is hard to justify such an angry response. True, the movie is excruciatingly slow and ponderous—but no more so than such "masterpieces" of the era as *Chariots of Fire* or *Gandhi.* It deserves props for its ambition, though it is weighed down by a number of terrible performances (the two female leads, Catherine Hicks and Theresa Russell, are especially dreadful) and by Murray, who thrives in the early comedic scenes but seems totally out of his element moping around World War I–era Paris. His attempts to convey Larry Darrell's spiritual detachment come off as mere blankness—an affect he would perfect later in his career but had not mastered at this point in his development as an actor.

What makes *The Razor's Edge* so fascinating is the window it opens onto Murray's mind-set at this stage of his life. Having turned thirty, and newly minted as one of the rising stars in Hollywood, he was struggling with the demands of fame and family. Shortly before he started work on the project, his friend **John Belushi** died of a drug overdose; *Caddyshack* screenwriter Doug Kenney had lost his life just two years earlier. *Razor's Edge* executive producer Rob Cohen attributed Murray's obsession with making the film to the changes going on in his personal life: "He got married. He had a child. There were the deaths of some friends. All these things came up on him, and I believe he began to think a little more deeply about life."

Murray explained the project's appeal in similar terms: "The story I got was of a guy who sees that there's more to life than just making a buck and having a romantic fling. I'd experienced that, and I knew what that was, so I had my own ideas about how it played. . . . There are things in it that came from our own lives or that were happening to us while we were doing the movie." Indeed, some of the lines Murray wrote for Larry Darrell seem like they could have come out of his own mouth circa 1984. "This isn't the old Mr. Sunshine," Larry declares at one point, in what could have been a warning to moviegoers expecting another *Stripes* or *Caddyshack*. Speaking about the hollowness of material success, Larry says: "I've got a second chance, and I'm not gonna waste it on a big house, and a new car every year, and a bunch of friends who want a big house and a new car every year!"

When *The Razor's Edge* tanked, Murray was left to pick up the pieces. In interviews conducted after the film's release, he conceded that it had been a mistake to do it as a period piece, suggesting that a Larry Darrell story set in the aftermath of Vietnam might have had more appeal for modern audiences. "I kind of deluded myself that there would be a lot of interest" in the film, he said. "I made a big mistake." With the passage of time, he came to see it as a noble error: "People say that was a flop of a movie. They don't know what a flop is. A flop is where nothing is good. I loved the process of making it. The fact that it wasn't a commercial hit . . . I'm a half-smart guy. I can see where a movie about a man's spiritual search might not do as well as *Home Alone*." But he also bristled at the pasting he had taken from critics, accusing them of bias against comedians taking on dramatic roles: "It angers people, like you're taking something away from them. That's the response I got. I thought, 'Well, aren't we all bigger than that?' I wasn't shocked by it, but I thought that the professional critics would be able to say, 'Okay, we shouldn't rule this out, because the guy normally does other stuff.'"

Murray was able to recover from the disappointment of *The Razor's Edge*, though friends report that he did not react well at the time. "I think Bill was completely trashed by the film's failure," said John Byrum. "It was his first serious film and he wanted to extend himself as an actor. The critics and audiences wanted him to be the guy in *Meatballs* for the rest of his life." In fact, Murray was so mortified by the burden of public expectations that he closed up shop, moved to Paris, and did not star in a Hollywood film for the next four years.

NEXT MOVIE: *Little Shop of Horrors* (1986)

P
Q
R

REGIS COLLEGE

Jesuit college in Denver, Colorado, that Murray attended from 1968 to 1970. He later admitted that he chose the school because a couple friends were going there. Murray took only one acting class at Regis (now known as Regis University). "I thought it'd be a piece of cake and there were a lot of girls in it," he said. "I knew I could act as good as these girls could, just by seeing them around the coffee shop." His acting teacher was even more of a horndog than he was. "So long as you never looked funny at him while he was staring at a girl, you got a good grade. But I only hung in there for one semester. That was that." Murray then enrolled in the premed program but was forced to drop out of school after he was arrested for **marijuana** possession while flying back to Denver from **Chicago** in September 1970. "I was not really college material," he once confessed to an interviewer. "I didn't know how to study, but I liked the lifestyle. You could dress any way you wanted. I was wearing pajamas and a sports coat to school and pajamas and loafers to formal events. College was terrible. I didn't get it at all, but it got me out of the house." Despite his misgivings, Murray returned to Regis for what would have been his twentieth class reunion, in 1992. He was spotted at the reception wearing a badge bearing the legend "Hi! I'm Bill Murray." In July 2007, Regis awarded Murray an honorary doctorate in humanities. He accepted the degree wearing a suit jacket over a pair of pajama shorts.

> ## "WHY SHOULD I SPEND MORE TIME ON YOUR COLLEGE GRADUATION THAN I SPENT ON MY OWN? I HAVE A DEGREE, FROM HIGH SCHOOL, BUT I'M A FUCKING MILLIONAIRE."
>
> —MURRAY, in a commencement address to graduating seniors at Columbia University in 2000

REITMAN, IVAN

Slovak Canadian filmmaker who directed Murray in *Meatballs*, *Stripes*, and both *Ghostbusters* movies. In the early 1970s, Reitman worked as a theatrical producer in Toronto. In that capacity, he was instrumental in bringing *The National Lampoon Show* off-Broadway in 1975. He later likened the experience of working with Murray, **John Belushi**, **Harold Ramis**, and other *Lampoon Show* cast members to taking "an inspirational shower." "I immediately knew I would have to make movies with them, that they would all be famous, that this was where comedy was going." Of his subsequent collaborations with Murray, Reitman has said: "One thing I've tried to do as a director is show Bill as a human being. On *Saturday Night Live*, all you saw was this wacky sort of side, but he has a very warm, genuine quality. I think I brought out some glimpses of that."

RELIGION

Murray was raised Roman Catholic and educated by nuns at **St. Joseph School** in **Wilmette, Illinois.** In early childhood, he developed his own personal form of spirituality. "When I was little, and alone, I used to sing songs to God," he once said.

Although he maintains a nominal affiliation with the church, he no longer identifies as Catholic. In a 1984 interview, Murray talked about his faith: "I'm definitely a religious person, but it doesn't have much to do with Catholicism anymore. I don't think about Catholicism much." He attributes his drift away from organized religion to the harsh discipline imposed by the nuns in his grade school: "You really get, you know, the fear of hell and confession and Mass and the sacraments. You get it real hard, but because it's sort of by rote, sometimes the feeling of it is sort of lost to you."

ROMANCE OF HAPPY VALLEY, A

Murray credits this 1919 silent film from director D. W. Griffith with convincing him to make better career choices. The story follows a young man who leaves his Kentucky farm to make his fortune in **New York City.** After several years, he returns home a wealthy man. But his father no longer recognizes him and hatches a plan to murder him and steal his money. The film ends on a happy note, with the family members reconciled and their imperiled farm saved from bankruptcy.

Murray first saw *A Romance of Happy Valley* at the Cinémathèque Française in Paris during his **sabbatical** from Hollywood in the mid-1980s. The film was presented with Russian subtitles, which Murray couldn't understand, but it still managed to move him to tears. "This movie just destroyed me," he told an interviewer. "And I thought 'How the hell can you go make *The Love Bug* if you've seen *this*.'" In addition to inspiring him to seek out more meaningful projects, *Happy Valley* also prompted Murray to muse on what his life would have been like had he been born in the silent film era. "What would a guy like me do at that time? I wouldn't be working in the movies. Without a tongue, who am I?"

ROMANTIC COMEDIES

Although he has been offered numerous plum parts, Murray has avoided making romantic comedies since *Groundhog Day.* "The romantic figure has

P
Q
R

to behave romantically even after acting like a total swine," he has said. "It's, 'I'm so gorgeous, you're going to have to go through all kinds of hell for me,' and that isn't interesting to me. Romance, like comedy, is very particular. There's something about romance that if you don't have to have someone, you're more desirable."

ROYAL TENENBAUMS, THE

DIRECTED BY: Wes Anderson

WRITTEN BY: Wes Anderson and Owen Wilson

RELEASE DATE: December 14, 2001

FILM RATING: ★ ★ ★

MURRAY RATING: ★ ★

PLOT: A family of eccentrics reconciles with its vagabond patriarch.

STARRING BILL MURRAY AS: Raleigh St. Clair, cuckolded neurologist

Wes Anderson to the rescue once again. After a year in which his talents were largely wasted in the sick-making *Osmosis Jones* and the slapdash *Speaking of Sex*, Murray filled his tank with hipster cred by appearing in Anderson's twee family fable. *The Royal Tenenbaums* is not quite as good as *Rushmore*, and Murray's role is not nearly as meaty. But he took the part sight unseen, without even reading the script, on the strength of his affinity for the young director. Proximity also had something to do with it. "We filmed in New York," Anderson told *Rolling Stone*, "and as he didn't live that far away, Bill thought that it would be fun to do it." Another important consideration: Murray's uncanny ability to grow a beard quickly, which allowed him to disappear into his role as the lugubrious neurologist Raleigh St. Clair. On

the set, Murray became fast friends with Royal Tenenbaum himself, the seventy-year-old acting legend whose old **New York City** apartment he had once sublet. "**Gene Hackman** took a real liking to him during that shoot," Anderson said. "They got along *very* well."

NEXT MOVIE: *Lost in Translation* (2003)

RUSHMORE

DIRECTED BY: Wes Anderson

WRITTEN BY: Wes Anderson and Owen Wilson

RELEASE DATE: October 9, 1998

FILM RATING: ★ ★ ★ ★

MURRAY RATING: ★ ★ ★ ★

PLOT: A twee übermensch competes with a depressed millionaire for the affections of a morose widow.

STARRING BILL MURRAY AS: Herman Blume, sad-sack steel magnate

After failing to cast Murray in his debut feature, *Bottle Rocket*, director **Wes Anderson** finally snagged the White Whale for his sophomore effort. The delightfully idiosyncratic *Rushmore* marked a critical turning point in Murray's career, as the dark, forlorn, yearning quality that had existed as an undertone in his characters finally came roaring to the surface. The era of "Sad Bill Murray" had officially begun.

To his credit, Anderson was among the first filmmakers to spot the potential for pathos in Murray. He and coscreenwriter Owen Wilson wrote the part of Herman Blume specifically for him. "I thought he'd be funny, and real," Anderson explained. "And also there was a sort of a sadness about him." As he had with *Bottle Rocket*, he sent the script for *Rushmore* to Murray with little expectation that he would even read it. But Murray was impressed by the precision of the writing and called Anderson to talk about the role. "Anybody that writes it that way knows exactly what they want to show," he told the *New York Times*.

At the time, Murray was still reeling from a series of personal and professional setbacks—including his first divorce and the critical and commercial failure of *The Man Who Knew Too Little*—and was eager to tap that vein of disappointment in his work. "A lot of *Rushmore* is about the struggle to retain civility and kindness in the face of extraordinary pain," he explained. "And I've felt a lot of that in my life. Movies don't usually show the failure of relationships; they want to give the audience a final, happy resolution. In *Rushmore*, I play a guy who's aware that his life is not working, but he's still holding on, hoping something will happen, and that's what's most interesting." Elsewhere, Murray admitted that he drew inspiration for his performance from the breakup of his **marriage**: "You've had to have really suffered to realize how badly someone can feel, not just for an act or an incident, but a wave, a time period of bad feeling, of low self-esteem."

Murray agreed to work on the film for scale, or $9,000, plus a percentage of the profits. His standard salary at the time was a thousand times that amount, or $9 million a picture.

Rushmore, 1998

In his book *The Wes Anderson Collection*, Matt Zoller Seitz reveals that Murray might have taken a loss on *Rushmore* if Anderson had cashed the blank check Murray gave him to cover the cost of a $25,000 helicopter scene that the studio refused to pay for. Anderson ended up cutting the sequence from the film, but he was so touched by Murray's gesture that he saved the uncashed check as a memento.

Anderson's other memories of working with Murray all involve eating, drinking, and general merriment: an evening in a hotel bar in **Los Angeles** when "Bill took the place over and started dancing," and the happy aftermath of a disastrous table read with the film's inexperienced star Jason Schwartzman. "It didn't go well at all," Anderson told *Rolling Stone*. "We beat ourselves up over whether we should change the dialogue, but Bill said that the dialogue is why he signed on. A day later, Bill took us out to a restaurant where we ate chicken-fried steak. After that, everything was fine. I like to think that he was great in the role— but beyond that, he was the godfather of that film."

NEXT MOVIE: *Cradle Will Rock* (1999)

RUTLES, THE

See All You Need Is Cash.

PQR

TALES FROM
MURRAYLAND

Nº 21	Operation Murray Drop

In August 2008, Murray helped kick off the annual Chicago Air and Water Show by jumping out of a plane two and a half miles above the city with skydivers from the U.S. Army Golden Knights parachute team. Murray managed to play air guitar and perform a brief hand jive before his chute deployed.

At the time, the fifty-seven-year-old actor was in the depths of a depressive spiral precipitated by his recent bitter divorce from his second wife, Jennifer Butler. "I was just dead, just broken," he said of his mind-set that summer. Friends thought a bracing skydive might be good therapy for him. "They asked me on a day I didn't care," said Murray. "I didn't even care if there was a parachute. Of course, by the time I got there I had had a few good days and I thought, 'What am I doing?'" In a postdive interview with the *Chicago Tribune*, Murray described the experience as a mix of terror and exhilaration:

"Once you go, and you hit the air, all that's gone. The physical sensation overwhelms your body. Overwhelms your mind. You can't think anymore. You're just in a washing machine of air. You're trying to move your arms and move your hands. Meanwhile, you've got this guy on your back. And then he starts steering you. And they're filming you, so you feel like, 'Oh, I'm supposed to be funny now.' When the chute opens, it's not that ka-kunk thing you see in the movies. It's just that the people you're talking to or looking at just sort of drop through the bottom of the floor. Then it became extremely peaceful and really dreamy. I was like, 'Hey, there's Wrigley Field, can we go over there?'"

SABBATICAL

In late 1984, following the success of *Ghostbusters* and the critical and commercial implosion of *The Razor's Edge*, Murray fled Hollywood for Paris, France. He remained there for six months, studying philosophy and history at the celebrated French university La Sorbonne. Murray has called his hiatus from moviemaking "the best thing I ever did."

"I thought that *Ghostbusters* was the biggest thing that would ever happen to me," he told film critic Roger Ebert. "It was such a big phenomenon that I felt slightly radioactive. So I just moved away for a while." While at the Sorbonne, Murray immersed himself in the writings of the Greco-Armenian mystic **George Ivanovich Gurdjieff**. His second son, **Luke François Murray**, was born in Paris during his time away from home.

Years later, Murray described his Parisian daily routine to the *Times* of London: "I spent the morning in a class of other idiots learning French, and then in the afternoon I went to the Cinémathèque, and that was a fantastic life. At lunchtime I stopped by at a chocolatier, and I was always walking around with 150 grams of chocolate in my pocket, and offering a piece was a great way to start a conversation."

At the famed Cinémathèque Française, Murray took a self-taught course in film studies with an emphasis on the silent era. He devoured the works of Buster Keaton, watched a print of D. W. Griffith's *The Birth of a Nation* with Russian subtitles, and discovered the 1919 melodrama *A Romance of Happy Valley*. Murray later credited that film with changing the way he thought about picking his own projects.

According to Murray, the half year he spent in France had little effect on his viability in Hollywood. "It took everyone a long time to stop counting the *Ghostbusters* money," he once said. "They were distracted, and they left me alone for a while. There were times when they wanted me to make movies that were part of packages, and I would never bite. I knew certain movies—like *Airplane!*—were going to be successful, but I didn't want to do it. It's just not my thing. I don't lie awake and think, 'If only I'd done *Revenge of the Nerds.*'"

Although Murray returned to the United States in the spring of 1985, he remained disinclined to get back on the superstar treadmill. He canceled the

S
T

one project he had agreed to do and declined another lead in a film for three years. He spent most of his time with his wife and sons at their renovated farmhouse in New York's Hudson River valley, reading historical novels about **Ireland**.

"I would get twenty phone calls a day from people wanting to do a movie," he told Roger Ebert, "and there would be this incredible amount of pressure. On Friday I'd get like thirty phone calls, and then on Monday no one would call, and I'd look in the paper, and someone else was doing the movie because I didn't say yes."

SANDLER, ADAM

Murray is not a fan of the comic actor whose imbecilic brand of humor defined *Saturday Night Live* in the 1990s. "Adam Sandler doesn't make me laugh," he once admitted. "I would enjoy driving in L.A. with the windows open more than I would enjoy watching *The Waterboy*."

SANTA CLAUSE, THE

Family-friendly 1994 comedy about a shlubby **Chicago** dad who is contractually obligated to assume the role of Santa Claus on **Christmas** Eve. The lead role of Scott Calvin was originally written for Murray, but after his unpleasant experience on *Scrooged* he had no interest in pursuing another holiday-themed project. The part went to Tim Allen, who milked it for two sequels.

SATURDAY NIGHT LIVE

Murray first achieved nationwide fame as a cast member on this late-night TV sketch comedy series from 1977 to 1980. He replaced the departing **Chevy Chase**, who quit the show midway through its second season to pursue a movie career in Hollywood. Murray remained with the program through its brilliant, erratic fifth season, when the departures of original cast members **John Belushi** and **Dan Aykroyd** left him with a virtual monopoly on "first white guy" parts in nearly every sketch. He has since returned to host the show four times. While many *SNL* alums have left feeling embittered by the experience, Murray has had nothing but nice things to say about the series that gave him his big break. "I'm not gonna bitch about *Saturday Night Live*," he once declared. "Before *Saturday Night Live*, I was eating brown rice and cereal. It was so goofy, that show. You could say or do anything you like in the name of entertainment. I was water-skiing behind some very powerful animals."

See also **Aykroyd, Dan**; **Belushi, John**; **Chase, Chevy**; **DiLaMuca, Todd**; **Eldini, Jerry**; **Honker, The**; **Michaels, Lorne**; **New Guy Speech**; **Nick the Lounge Singer**; **Niko**; **Radner, Gilda**; "**Shower Mike**."

SNL

Saturday Night Live, 1977

SATURDAY NIGHT LIVE WITH HOWARD COSELL

After he was passed over for a spot in the original *Saturday Night Live* cast, Murray was personally selected by bewigged sportscaster **Howard Cosell** to join the repertory company for this freewheeling prime-time variety hour on ABC. Cosell had "discovered" Murray after seeing him perform off-Broadway in *The National Lampoon Show*. Murray's brother Brian and fellow *Lampoon* alum Christopher Guest were also hired to impart some youth and hipness to the *Saturday Night Live with Howard Cosell* cast, officially dubbed the Prime Time Players.

The series, which a *People* magazine preview noted was "conceived by Cosell and his high-rolling boss at ABC Sports, Roone Arledge," was intended to evoke the eclectic spirit of the old *Ed Sullivan Show*. But Cosell was incredibly uncomfortable on camera, the comedy players were seldom used, and the show quickly devolved into an ungainly mishmash of vaudeville schtick, video trickery, and circus acts. Guests included John Wayne, Ted Kennedy, Barbara Walters, Muhammad Ali, Evel Knievel, Frank Sinatra, John Denver, Paul Anka, Shirley Bassey, Jimmy Connors, Siegfried and Roy, and the cast of the Broadway musical *The Wiz*. Although the Cosell show aired at eight o'clock, **critics** couldn't resist measuring it against the NBC *Saturday Night* program. As Murray also noted, it was not a flattering comparison: "Everybody else was on the other show. So we were on TV, and they were on TV. But they were *the show*, and we were on with the Chinese acrobats and elephants and all sorts of crazy acts, and we would get cut almost every other week."

Two months into its run, ABC abruptly canceled *Saturday Night Live with Howard Cosell*. Only fifteen live episodes ever aired, all of which remain buried deep within the network archives.

SCROOGED

DIRECTED BY: Richard Donner

WRITTEN BY: Mitch Glazer and Michael O'Donoghue

RELEASE DATE: November 23, 1988

FILM RATING: ☆

MURRAY RATING: ☆

PLOT: A loathsome network television executive learns the true meaning of Christmas at the hands of three increasingly abusive ghosts.

STARRING BILL MURRAY AS: Frank Cross, president of the IBC network

---

After a four-year **sabbatical** from Hollywood, Murray returned to star in this loud, mirthless holiday comedy "inspired" by Charles Dickens's classic *A Christmas Carol*. A special-effects-driven supernatural blockbuster in the

Scrooged, 1988

manner of *Ghostbusters*, *Scrooged* marked a return to box office form for Murray after the disappointment of *The Razor's Edge*. With the benefit of hindsight, that is hard to understand. This is easily the worst film of his career.

The screenplay for *Scrooged* sprung from the pens of Murray pals **Mitch Glazer** and Michael O'Donoghue, though O'Donoghue would later claim that less than half of what he wrote ended up on the screen. "The finished film was a piece of unadulterated, unmitigated shit," the dark-hearted genius known as Mr. Mike complained afterward. "The only good thing is that big checks came out of *Scrooged*, which allowed me to get a home in **Ireland**."

Murray's big check for agreeing to appear in the film totaled $6 million, or more than the salaries paid to the producer, the director, and the rest of the cast combined. But *Scrooged* did not start out as a money play. Murray loved the original script, which combined sentimentality with biting satire. Desperate to escape the treadmill of cranking out crowd-pleasing comedies, he saw *Scrooged* as a chance to "give the public a little food for thought. . . . There are moments in the Dickensian morality of *Scrooged* where you have the creepy chance to contemplate your ruin—the bottom of your future." To prepare for the role, Murray studied previous movie adaptations of *A Christmas Carol*. "I saw the Alastair Sim and the Albert Finney Scrooge. Mostly, I learned what not to do from them."

Unfortunately, not everyone on the *Scrooged* creative team shared Murray's vision for the project. Sydney Pollack was replaced as director early on. Murray chafed under the goading of his old-school replacement, Richard Donner, who encouraged the cast to play their parts as broadly as possible. At Donner's urging, Murray mugged and yelled through most of his scenes. Conceived as a devilish rogue who gains redemption through a glimpse at his wasted life, his Frank Cross comes off as a boorish jerk who gets what he deserves. There is little of the charm and none of the joy of Murray's previous performances, and the film is larded with product placements for Tab, Stolichnaya, and Budweiser. As a result, watching *Scrooged* is like being hit on the head with a hammer for 101 minutes—a cinematic crucifixion instead of a yuletide miracle play.

"That could have been a really, really great movie," Murray later confessed to Roger Ebert. "The script was so good. There's maybe one take in the final cut movie that is mine. We made it so fast, it was like doing a movie live. [Donner] kept telling me to do things louder, louder, louder. I think he was deaf." Even Murray's fabled powers of improvisation seemed to desert him on this one. He ad-libbed most of Cross's climactic monologue, in which the reformed creep pleads the case for kindness and good cheer, but the speech plays more rambling than inspirational. O'Donoghue, who was on the set at the time, likened it to a rant by the suicidal cult leader Jim Jones.

Whether it was creative fatigue or the pressure of headlining his first big-budget movie in four years, the *Scrooged* shoot turned out to be an arduous one for Murray. With no big-name costars, he was forced to carry the load by himself, on and off camera. He has described *Scrooged* as "a lonely movie for me to work on because I was really the only guy who was always there. I mean, there were all these people coming in, they drive in, then they drive out. And they're gone. And I'm still there. Like a schnook, you know? So I didn't get to have any developing fun with anybody." Things perked up for a while when Murray's brothers John, Brian, and Joel dropped by to film cameos, but most of the time Murray had no one to hang out with on the set. He spent much of the shoot in a blue funk, alternately restless, tired, and moody. Donner tried to lift his spirits by subjecting him to endless practical jokes, but they had limited effect. "Sometimes he was just wiped out," the director admitted. "You hadda keep the happiness level up around him, too. Sometimes you've got to artificially generate it, do silly things like print up T-shirts saying 'Where's Billy?'

after he had one of his few days off. It got him up again."

Even worse than Donner's mind games was the physical abuse Murray suffered at the hands of actress Carol Kane, who played the Ghost of **Christmas** Present. The script called for Kane to buffet Murray repeatedly about the head and ears during their scenes together. It was a task she seemed to relish. "She hurt me a lot," Murray later revealed. "She separated my teeth from my gums. She didn't even know. But she's such a time bomb. If you say, 'You hurt me,' she'd cry for six hours and break down. So you'd just put on protection, a catcher's cup, so the family heirlooms were covered."

There was one lighter moment on the set, courtesy of comedian Buddy Hackett. Playing Ebenezer Scrooge in a film-within-the-film production of *A Christmas Carol*, Hackett brought shooting to a screeching halt one day with a blasphemous tirade about the mother of Jesus. As Murray told the story in a 1998 interview with *Esquire*: "We're shooting in this Victorian set for weeks, and Hackett is pissed all the time, angry that he's not the center of attention, and finally we get to the scene where we've gotta shoot him at the window, saying, 'Go get my boots,' or whatever. The set is stocked with Victorian extras and little children in *Oliver* kind of outfits, and the director says, 'All right, Bud—just give it whatever you want.' And Hackett goes off on a rant. Unbelievably obscene. He's talking—this is Hackett, not me—about the Virgin Mary, a limerick sort of thing, and all these children and families . . . the look of absolute horror. He's going on and on and on, and finally he stops. It's just total horror, and the camera's still rolling. You can hear it, sort of a grinding noise. And the director says, 'Anything else, Bud?'"

NEXT MOVIE: *Ghostbusters II* (1989)

QUENTIN TARANTINO'S — TOP 5

Scrooged may not be Murray's best film, but it does have its supporters. No less a cinema geek than Quentin Tarantino has pronounced himself a fan of Murray's performance. "He's like W. C. Fields in *Scrooged*!" Tarantino once proclaimed. For the record, here are the *Pulp Fiction* auteur's five favorite Bill Murray movies:

1. *Lost in Translation*
2. *Groundhog Day*
3. *Stripes*
4. *Kingpin*
5. Tie between *Caddyshack* and *Scrooged*

SCTV

Murray was the special guest star on the 1982 season finale of this Canadian sketch comedy show. He impersonated Joe DiMaggio in a parody commercial for DiMaggio's on the Wharf Italian Restaurant, appeared as an out-of-breath wedding guest in an installment of the ongoing soap opera spoof *The Days of the Week*, and played a ne'er-do-well who insinuates himself into the inner circle of TV host Johnny LaRue (played by Murray's old **Second City** cohort **John Candy**).

SECOND CITY

Vaunted improvisational theater troupe based in Old Town **Chicago**, famed for churning out North American comedy talent since 1959. In 1973, Murray joined Second City at the invitation of his brother Brian. "Brian lived in Old Town, where all the hippies were, and I started hanging out at his place,"

S
T

TALES FROM
MURRAYLAND

Nº 22	The Night He Tried to Choke Martin Mull

   During a New York City performance of *The National Lampoon Show* in 1974, comic actor Martin Mull sat up front near the edge of the stage. He drank heavily and yakked loudly with his companion, actor Peter Boyle, throughout the show. After the final curtain, Mull went backstage to pay his respects to the cast. When Murray saw him, he flew into a frothing rage, grabbing Mull by the throat and attempting to strangle him. "I'll kill him! I'll kill that fucker!" Murray screamed. "He talked through the whole thing! I hate him!" John Belushi ended up having to pull Murray off Mull, who escaped the dressing room to accusatory cries of "Medium talent! Medium talent!"—a favorite Murray insult he would later use on his *Saturday Night Live* nemesis Chevy Chase. "I confess to having been extremely rude, though not quite as rude as Bill Murray trying to strangle me afterward," Mull remarked of his ill-fated evening at the theater.

he explained to *Rolling Stone*. "That's where I met **Harold Ramis** and **John Belushi** and Joe Flaherty and **Del Close**, who directed the show, and Bernie Sahlins, who ran Second City. They thought I was a riot—weekend hippie, you know, going back to my straight life in the 'burbs every night."

Sometime earlier, Murray had auditioned for one of the troupe's vaunted improv workshops—with disastrous results. "I was so bad I couldn't believe it," he confessed to *Cosmopolitan* magazine. "I was really depressed. I walked off the stage and just never went back." After time away, Murray had a fortuitous run-in on a street in downtown Chicago. "It was Christmastime," he later recalled. "Bells were ringing. There under the clock at Marshall Field, I met the head of the workshop, and he said, 'We'd like to offer you a scholarship, if you want to come back.' The bells were going bong, bong, bong, and I figured it was a miracle. I said 'Thanks, I will. Merry **Christmas**.'" He returned to find his skills as an improv performer markedly improved. "Somehow in the time I'd been away, I'd learned how to do it," he said. "All of a sudden, I seemed to have an aptitude for it."

Murray quickly worked his way up from the improv workshops to the main stage, where he spent a year honing his craft alongside the likes of **John Candy**, Betty Thomas, and Tino Insana (the future voice of Disney's *Darkwing Duck*). Murray developed a reputation as one of the troupe's most fearless and unpredictable performers. "You couldn't keep your eyes off Bill on stage," observed Second City director Sheldon Patinkin, "because there was so much going on inside the guy that you knew something would come popping out sooner rather than later. He emitted a true sense of danger."

Murray left Second City in 1974 to join the cast of *The National Lampoon Show* in New York. In interviews, he has often cited the guiding principle he learned at Second City as his surefire formula for show business success: "The reason so many Second City people have been successful is really fairly simple. At the heart of it is the idea that if you make the other actors look good, you'll look good. It works sort of like the idea of life after **death**. If you live an exemplary life, trying to make someone else look good, you'll look good, too. It's true. It really does work. It braces you up, when you're out there with that fear of death, which is really the difference between the Second City actors and the others."

SEINFELD

Though his brother Brian appeared in one of the show's best-loved episodes ("The Bubble Boy"), Murray admitted in a 2010 interview with *GQ* magazine that he had watched only one episode of comedian Jerry Seinfeld's 1990s sitcom. "I never saw *Seinfeld* until the final episode, and that's the only one I saw. And it was *terrible*. I'm watching, thinking, 'This isn't funny *at all*. It's terrible!'" In 2014, Murray told radio host Howard Stern that he had subse-

S
T

"BILL HAS LOTS OF
PERSONAL PROBLEMS. . . .
HE HOPES HIS EXPERIENCE
IN THEATRE, MOVIES, AND
TELEVISION CAN PERHAPS
GET HIM WORK AS A
PLAYGIRL CENTERFOLD."

—From Murray's official Second City bio

quently caught up on the series: "I've since seen some of it and I see what people like about it."

SHAME OF THE JUNGLE

DIRECTED BY: Picha and Boris Szulzinger
WRITTEN BY: Pierre Bartier, Picha, Anne Beatts, and Michael O'Donoghue
RELEASE DATE: September 14, 1979
FILM RATING: ☆
MURRAY RATING: ☆

PLOT: A henpecked he-man must rescue his sexually frustrated wife from the clutches of an evil jungle queen.

STARRING BILL MURRAY AS: An announcer reading the news on the radio

Murray supplies the voice of an unseen radio announcer in this mildly pornographic animated feature directed by Belgian cartoonist Jean-Paul "Picha" Walravens. Originally released in Europe under the title *Tarzoon, Shame of the Jungle* (and also known as *Jungle Burger*), the raunchy comedy parodies Edgar Rice Burroughs's Tarzan adventures. The film was completed in 1975 and then moldered on a shelf in France for four years before being redubbed by American actors and released stateside. In the meantime, the estate of Edgar Rice Burroughs sued, demanding that the title be changed and all references to Tarzan be removed. **John Belushi, Brian Doyle-Murray,** and Christopher Guest joined Murray in supplying voices for the redubbed *Shame of the Jungle*, which received a dreaded X rating from the Motion Picture Association of America. Johnny Weismuller Jr., son and namesake of the longtime big-screen Tarzan, plays Shame. In one representative scene, Shame's pet chimpanzee relentlessly masturbates while his wife is orally serviced by two penis-shaped creatures. Radio ads touting the film promised "You'll laugh your X off."

An unpleasant, unfunny film rife with sexist and racist stereotypes, *Shame of the Jungle* received mostly negative reviews and almost immediately disappeared into the cinematic memory hole. Writing in the *Village Voice*, critic Tam Allen called it "an uncomfortably accurate reflection of that civic eyesore known as toilet art." The *New York Times'* Vincent Canby derided the film's humor as "bland and exhausting." *Playboy's* reviewer was more kind, dubbing *Shame of the Jungle* "the most literate, prurient, and amusing challenge to community standards since *Fritz the Cat*."

The following year, Murray lent his vocal talents to Picha's next feature, the slightly less dreadful prehistoric cartoon *B.C. Rock*.

NEXT MOVIE: *Mr. Mike's Mondo Video* (1979)

ST

SHE'S HAVING A BABY

DIRECTED BY: John Hughes

WRITTEN BY: John Hughes

RELEASE DATE: February 5, 1988

FILM RATING: ★★

MURRAY RATING: ★

PLOT: Cutesy-pie newlyweds deal with the vicissitudes of marriage in the 1980s.

STARRING BILL MURRAY AS: Himself

Murray is one of several Reagan-era celebrities who do cornball cameos in the end credit sequence of this 1988 family comedy from director (and Illinois native) **John Hughes**. **Dan Aykroyd**, **John Candy**, Wil Wheaton, Matthew Broderick, and the cast of the TV sitcom *Cheers* also appear. The special guests, who were all friends of the director and/or working on the Paramount lot at the time, suggest names for the titular infant. Murray's contribution is: "Schwuk. I don't know what it is—I heard it on a bus."

    NEXT MOVIE: *Scrooged* (1988)

SHOTGUN GOLF

Madcap amalgam of **golf** and skeet shooting invented by gonzo journalist **Hunter S. Thompson** at his "fortified compound" in Woody Creek, Colorado, in the summer of 2004. In the final column he ever wrote, for ESPN's Page Two website, Thompson described pitching the idea for Shotgun Golf to Murray in a late-night telephone call. According to Thompson: "The game consists of one golfer, one shooter, and a field judge. The purpose of the game is to shoot your opponent's high-flying golf ball out of the air with a finely tuned 12-gauge shotgun." Thompson listed Murray as a "founding consultant" on his Shotgun Golf enterprise and credited the actor with teaching him "how to mortify your opponents in any sporting contest, honest or otherwise."

"SHOWER MIKE"

Seminal *Saturday Night Live* sketch, written and performed by Murray and **Gilda Radner** with guest host Buck Henry for the show's second season finale on May 21, 1977. In the sketch, Murray plays **Richard Herkiman**, a cuckolded husband who cajoles his cheating wife and her lover to join him in the shower as part of an impromptu nightclub act. "Shower Mike" was the crowning achievement of Murray's first season on *SNL*, capping a turnaround in his fortunes that began with the **New Guy Speech** two months earlier. Once relegated to playing the "second cop" in skits that featured the other cast members more prominently, Murray was now a force to be reckoned with on the show. "In the beginning of *SNL* I was angry a lot," he later admitted. "The writers weren't interested in writing for me. . . . If I hadn't written the Shower Mike sketch, I might have been off the show." The genesis of the skit came the week of the season's final episode, when Murray picked up a microphone-shaped bar of soap-on-a-rope given to him by **John Belushi**'s wife the previous **Christmas**. After hitting on the idea of transplanting his sleazy nightclub singer character to a shower setting, he and Gilda Radner went off and wrote the sketch together in twenty minutes. Murray reprised the role of Richard Herkiman in a sketch with guest host Jill Clayburgh the following season.

SHREK

In 1991, after Steven Spielberg acquired the rights to adapt William Steig's popular children's book as a hand-drawn animated film, he selected Murray for the role of the titular green ogre. Steve Martin was slated to play Shrek's companion, Donkey. By the time the movie was reimagined for CGI ten years later, Murray and Martin had moved on. Their parts went to Mike Myers and Eddie Murphy, respectively.

SIMON, KERRY

Murray is a longtime friend of this celebrity chef and restaurateur, widely known as the "Rock 'n' Roll Chef." Simon grew up in **Evanston, Illinois**, not far from Murray's hometown of Wilmette. The pair worked together at a **Chicago**-area **Little Caesars** pizza franchise in the early 1970s. Murray has often appeared as an emcee at charity events organized by Simon. In 1995, when Simon appeared on the Food Network cooking competition show *Iron Chef*, Murray and his wife cheered him on from a VIP box high above "Kitchen Stadium."

SIRENS OF TITAN, THE

In 1984, Murray was in talks to play the lead in a big-screen adaptation of Kurt Vonnegut's 1959 novel about a wealthy industrialist who gets caught up in a Martian invasion of Earth. For various reasons, the project never got off the ground.

A year earlier, Vonnegut had sold the rights to his trippy sci-fi opus to Grateful Dead frontman Jerry Garcia. Garcia then hired former *Saturday Night Live* writer Tom Davis to collaborate on a screenplay, which they pitched to Murray in June 1984, at the height of *Ghostbusters* mania. In author Robert Greenfield's oral biography of Jerry Garcia, *Dark Star*, filmmaker Gary Gutierrez—who created storyboards for the abortive film—recounts a meeting in Hollywood to discuss the project:

"It was Tom Davis and Bill Murray, and Jerry and me, and a bunch of attorneys and this guy from Universal [Mike Ovitz] sitting around this huge table, and during this very serious discussion about the deal, there was Bill Murray making his mouth like a billiard pocket at the edge of the table and Tom Davis was rolling gum balls across the table, trying to get them in Bill Murray's mouth."

SLEEPY

Murray's childhood nickname. "When I was a little kid playing baseball, my manager called me Sleepy. And only a few people, who know me from way, way back, call me that still. I used to drift off and that's why they made me the catcher, so I wouldn't fall asleep. That gift I have still."

SLICK CITY TRIO, THE

Murray was a member of this three-man folk music combo while a student at Loyola Academy in the late 1960s. The group covered material by singer-songwriter Bob Gibson, the Mamas and the Papas, and other folk-rock artists of the era. Murray's classmates John Heller and Larry Basil rounded out the trio, which re-formed in 2005 as a duo (without Murray's participation) under the name Basil and Heller.

SLOVENIA VODKA

In 2013, Murray lent his name and a chunk of investment capital to this high-end vodka made from "crystal clear water sourced at the foot of the Julian Alps in Slovenia." Ballet legend Mikhail Baryshnikov is a fellow investor in the company, which was cofounded by chef Peter X. Kelly of the Xaviar's Restaurant Group in New York's Hudson Valley. Kelly and his team created Slovenia to be "the culinary vodka, the perfect vodka for pairing with exquisite dishes; for use in the creation of these dishes; and for the creation of the most dramatic cocktails by chef mixologists."

A longtime vodka enthusiast, Murray rhapsodized about the charms of Slovenia in a 2013 interview with *Esquire* magazine: "Different vodkas have different effects. Some make you feel a little . . . poly-lingual. Some make you feel like you want to talk back to someone who's giving you a hard time. Some make you feel like lifting kettle bells. There's something about the taste of this vodka that takes the bad taste out of your mouth. I don't mean like a mouthwash, but if something bad is on your mind, this makes it go away. I have a quieter voice when I drink it. I drink gin, and once, when drinking gin, I made a large man cry. Not with this. This makes you kind of sweet."

SONG OF THE LARK, THE

Nineteenth-century oil painting by French realist Jules Breton that Murray has credited in interviews with saving him from suicide. At a 2014 press event for *The Monuments Men*, Murray revealed that he was so despondent after his disastrous **Chicago** stage debut that he contemplated walking directly into Lake Michigan. "I was ready to die," he admitted. "I thought, 'If I'm going to die, I might as well go over toward the lake and float a bit.'" On his way over, however, Murray took a detour to the Art Institute of Chicago, where Breton's 1884 oil on canvas was on display. The painting depicts a young peasant woman at daybreak holding a scythe. "I thought, 'Well there's a girl who doesn't have a whole lot of prospects,'" Murray said. "'But the sun's coming up anyway and she's got another chance at it.' So I think that gave me some sort of feeling that I too am a person and I get another chance every day the sun comes up."

SOUTH CAROLINA

Murray has lived part-time in Charleston, South Carolina, since the mid-1990s. "I didn't choose to go there," Murray told PBS gabber Charlie Rose in 2014. "Life took me there. That's where my sons are and that's where I am." As part of his divorce settlement with **Jennifer Butler** in 2008, Murray's ex-wife was granted ownership of the Murray family home on South Carolina's Sullivan Island. Murray continued to maintain a residence in Charleston to be near his children.

SOUTH PACIFIC

Murray played Luther Billis, a conniving Seabee, in a staged concert version of this classic Rodgers and Hammerstein musical, presented on May 22, 2000, at Lincoln Center's Vivian Beaumont Theater.

SPACE JAM

DIRECTED BY: Joe Pytka

WRITTEN BY: Leo Benvenuti, Steve Rudnick, Timothy Harris, and Herschel Weingrod

RELEASE DATE: November 15, 1996

FILM RATING: ★ ★ ☆

MURRAY RATING: ★ ★

PLOT: It's Bugs Bunny and friends to the rescue when a group of evil space aliens suck the life energy out of a motley assemblage of 1990s NBA stars.

STARRING BILL MURRAY AS: Himself

A mere fortnight after *Larger Than Life* blighted multiplexes, Murray wiped the bad taste from moviegoers' mouths with a spirited cameo in this highly successful basketball comedy mixing live action, cel animation, and CGI. One might think he would have leapt at the chance to share the screen with Bugs Bunny and NBA legend Michael Jordan, but Murray had to be talked into making *Space Jam* by producer **Ivan Reitman**. "I always have to convince him to work," Reitman told *USA Today*. In the end, Reitman was able to cajole Murray into doing two scenes for the film. In one, set on a **golf** course, Murray spoofs his *Caddyshack* persona; in the other, he takes the court alongside the Looney Tunes "Tune Squad" for the climactic face-off against the evil "Monstars" basket-

ball team. Murray's ad-libbing enlivens an otherwise lackluster cartoon feature weighed down by Michael Jordan's somnambulant lead performance. *Space Jam* also marks the first instance where Murray went "full meta" on the audience, riffing on his public image as a golf-loving eccentric. In another sign that Murray was now as much a personal brand as an actor, he insisted on wearing the cap of the St. Paul Saints—the minor league **baseball** he co-owned at the time—throughout his performance.

NEXT MOVIE: *The Man Who Knew Too Little* (1997)

SPACKLER, CARL

Demented assistant greenskeeper played by Murray in the 1980 film *Caddyshack*. A close cousin to **the Honker**, the sideways-talking drunk Murray dreamed up at **Second City**, Spackler is arguably the actor's most iconic creation. He does not appear in early drafts of the *Caddyshack* script, although an older caddy named Ray may be something of a proto-Spackler. Murray's role in the film was originally supposed to be a cameo—he was scheduled to be on set for only six days—and his character was virtually mute. "It was written like Harpo Marx, just not talking at all," director **Harold Ramis** later recalled. But according to Murray, the part "just kept growing like a mushroom. I'd go back to New York and work on *SNL*, and they'd call me up and ask if I wanted to come back down and do some more. I was good back in those days. Improvising about **golf** was easy for me."

While the Honker is almost certainly schizophrenic, and clearly an alcoholic, Spackler—who aspires to become head greenskeeper one day—is the more self-actualized character. "He's clearly damaged in some way, but he's not dumb," Ramis once observed. "His dialogue is as clever and inventive as any in the movie, really. To write even dumb or crude characters in a smart

TALES FROM
MURRAYLAND

Nº 23   ## The St. Andrews House Party

During a 2006 visit to St. Andrews, Scotland, for a celebrity golf tournament, Murray accompanied twenty-two-year-old Norwegian social anthropology student Lykke Stavnef—whom he had just met in a local pub—to a house party full of Scandinavian college students. "Nobody could believe it when I arrived at the party with Bill Murray," Stavnef said afterward. "He was just like the character in *Lost in Translation*."

Stavnef's Georgian townhouse was reportedly "overflowing" with chesty blonde coeds. Clad in a checkered shirt and brown vest, Murray drank vodka from a coffee cup and marveled at how drunk everyone was. "He seemed to be in his element, cracking lots of jokes," observed fellow partygoer Tom Wright. When the party was over, Murray personally washed all the dirty dishes in the students' sink. "The pasta was probably quite hard to get off the dishes because they had been sitting around," said one of the students.

way, that's the goal." "He had a vision of himself as holding a place of real importance in life," Murray told the *New York Post*. "It was just plugging into that desire to fall asleep to your own dream, as if you were slowly fading into the sunset at the top of the mountain. It was a beautiful thing."

SPEAKING OF SEX

DIRECTED BY: John McNaughton

WRITTEN BY: Gary Tieche

RELEASE DATE: October 5, 2001

FILM RATING: ★★

MURRAY RATING: ★★

PLOT: Farcical complications ensue when a bumbling marriage counselor sleeps with one of his clients.

STARRING BILL MURRAY AS: Ezri Stovall, bewigged Boise malpractice attorney

Undaunted by the law of diminishing returns, Murray re-upped for a third feature with **Chicago**-born director John McNaughton. In *Speaking of Sex*, he plays a sleazy lawyer virtually indistinguishable from the one he played in McNaughton's previous film, *Wild Things*. This time he wears a cowboy hat and a terrible toupee. The frenetic sex comedy languished in development hell at Fox for more than a year until French cable TV channel Canal Plus purchased the rights and gave McNaughton $11 million on the condition that he film it in Calgary, Alberta, Canada. Costars James Spader, Catherine O'Hara, Lara Flynn Boyle, Jay Mohr, Melora Walters, and Megan Mullally make the most of the subpar script, but any film that ends with a sped-up Benny Hill–style chase sequence is probably beyond repair.

In 2014, McNaughton announced plans for a fourth collaboration with Murray. Entitled *Counterfeit*, the new film would once again cast Murray as a disreputable attorney who comes to the aid of two young criminals.

NEXT MOVIE: *The Royal Tenenbaums* (2001)

SPLASH

Murray passed on an offer to play the lead in director **Ron Howard**'s 1984 comedy about a man who falls in **love** with a mermaid. According to actress P. J. Soles, when she presented Murray with the script, he proceeded to fling it across the room in disgust. Michael Keaton and John Travolta were also considered for the role, which wound up going to Tom Hanks.

> ## "I'VE PROVIDED WHOLE CAREERS FOR OTHER PEOPLE BY REJECTING MOVIES."
>
> —MURRAY, on the parts he let get away

SQUARE PEGS

Murray did a one-shot guest appearance on the February 14, 1983, episode of this high school sitcom created by erstwhile *Saturday Night Live* writer Anne Beatts. In the episode, entitled "No Substitutions," Murray plays Jack McNulty, a downtown **New York City** actor (founding member of the Greenwich Village Theater of Mime and Anger) who doubles as a substitute teacher. Sporting his unkempt *Ghostbusters*-era hairdo and wearing a billowy pajama top for much of the episode, Murray's character briefly upends the social order at suburban Weemawee High with a classroom experiment in which he pairs the students in mock marriages. Like most episodes of *Square Pegs*, "No Substitutions" plays best today as a time capsule of life in the early 1980s. In the episode's most memorable scene, Murray gets to boogie awkwardly with a young Sarah Jessica Parker to the tune of "Dancing with Myself" by Billy Idol.

SQUID AND THE WHALE, THE

Murray was director Noah Baumbach's first choice for the role of Bernard Berkman, a washed-up novelist going through a bitter divorce, in this 2005 indie comedy-drama. When Murray proved impossible to reach by phone, Baumbach gave up on him and offered the part to Jeff Daniels, who scored a Golden Globe nomination for his performance.

STALAG 17

This 1953 drama about a group of American airmen being held captive in a German prisoner-of-war camp during World War II is one of Murray's favorite films. "When *Stalag 17* comes on, I can't turn it off," he told film critic Elvis Mitchell. "I have to watch it. I have to go all the way with that movie. It's a Swiss watch. It's just a gorgeous movie." Murray is particularly enamored of **William Holden**'s Oscar-winning performance as Sergeant J. J. Sefton, the film's jaded, conniving antihero. "Even though I've seen it many times," he said, "I'm still fascinated at watching him turn the worm."

STAND-UP COMEDY

Murray has performed stand-up comedy only one time. "I did it once and it was fun," he said. "But I only had to do it once to realize I *could* do it, but I don't *want* to do it." In numerous interviews, Murray has pointed out that close observation of stand-ups early in his career left him with a bad impression of their mental health. "I saw them work, and they seemed so unhappy. If an audience didn't like them, they'd get so miserable about it. It looked too miserable."

STAR WARS

Legend has it that Murray was one among the legion of actors who auditioned for the part of Han Solo in George Lucas's 1977 space opera. Steve Martin, **Chevy Chase**, Perry King, Kurt Russell, Al Pacino, and Christopher Walken were all reportedly under consideration for the role, which helped make Harrison Ford a star.

STEWART, JIMMY

Murray had a brief, awkward encounter with this legendary actor at the thirty-eighth annual Cannes Film Festival in 1985. Murray was living in France at the time, and Stewart was in Cannes to be feted by the French government and watch a restored version of his 1954 film *The Glenn Miller Story*. "He had no fuckin' idea who I was," Murray said of the then-seventy-six-year-old screen icon. "Of course, I'm not sure he knew who his wife was. But I figured, well, shit, I'll walk up to him and say hello—'I'm so-and-so, I'm an actor, and I like your stuff.' And sometimes when you say you're an actor, they at least fake it—'Oh, sure, sure.' He couldn't even swing that."

ST. JOSEPH SCHOOL

Catholic grade school in **Wilmette, Illinois**, that Murray attended from 1956 to 1964. While at St. Joseph, Murray's class clown antics often got him in hot water with the nuns. "I was basically causing trouble all the time," he told an interviewer. "But not very serious trouble." He later described his experience at the school as "good practice for the entertainment business. I was constantly playing with danger and trying to get laughs out of an audience that doesn't think it's funny. That's what working with nuns was all about."

In 2004, Murray returned to St. Joseph for his fortieth reunion. He had to take time off from shooting *The Life Aquatic with Steve Zissou* to make it to the event, which he described as "a hoot." "I made an extraordinary effort to be there," he said. "I had to work extra-long days to get the day off to go. But it was worth it. The kids laughed at me at school and they still laugh today. I got the wish to play to an audience from them."

The Murray Report Card

During a 1984 TV interview, Murray awarded himself grades for his elementary school performance.

Neatness	D	Study habits	D
Effort	D	Getting along with people	B
Conduct	D-	Ambition	A

Teacher's comment: *Needs to practice self-control*

STRIPES

DIRECTOR: Ivan Reitman

SCREENPLAY: Len Blum, Harold Ramis, and Daniel Goldberg

RELEASE DATE: June 26, 1981

FILM RATING: ★★⟩

MURRAY RATING: ★ ★ ★

PLOT: A pair of shlubby New Yorkers join the army and keep its monstrous new weapon from falling into the hands of the Russians.

STARRING BILL MURRAY AS: John Winger, cab driver turned U.S. Army recruiting tool

Murray reunited with the *Meatballs* creative troika of **Harold Ramis**, **Ivan Reitman**, and Danny Goldberg to make this 1981 service comedy. The result was somewhat less successful, unless you look at it from the perspective of Murray's accountant.

"By the time I made *Stripes*, I'd made money from *SNL* and I was famous from *SNL*," Murray observed later. "That made it a lot easier to make the right decisions." In this case, the decision was to attach himself to a long-moldering vehicle for the comedy duo of Cheech and Chong, retooled for him and Harold Ramis at the behest of director Ivan Reitman. As Reitman told the *New Yorker* in 2004: "Bill is this great improv player, but he needs Harold, the focused composer who understands setting a theme and the rules of orchestration. So I told Harold, 'One, I want you to costar in my movie, and, two, I want you to rewrite it for two really intelligent guys—you and Bill.'"

Ramis obliged, cutting the creaky pot jokes from the Cheech and Chong script and convincing Murray to take on the new lead role of John Winger, a down-on-his-luck **New York City** cab driver who joins the army after his life falls apart. Ramis took the secondary lead as Winger's friend, laconic English as a Second Language teacher Russell Ziskey. Studio executives balked at the casting of Ramis, preferring the more seasoned Dennis Quaid for the role, but Murray insisted. Either Ramis was in or he was out. The suits relented, and *Stripes* ended up being Ramis's big-screen acting debut. A raft of newcomers who would go on to leave their mark on 1980s pop culture, including **John Candy**, John Larroquette, Sean Young, and Judge Reinhold, rounded out the supporting cast.

Production of *Stripes* took place during November and December of 1980, with Kentucky's Fort Knox doubling as the fictional Fort Arnold. For his first few days on the set, Murray tried getting up at five in the morning to go jogging with the real-life U.S. Army troops. But he quickly abandoned his plans to keep up the regimen for two full weeks. The rigors of day-to-day army life did leave an impression on the filmmakers, however, and that was reflected in the finished film. "It wasn't *Reds* or anything, but it captured what it was like on an army base," Murray later remarked. "It was cold, you had to wear the same green clothes, you had to do a lot of physical stuff, you got treated pretty badly, and had bad coffee."

John Winger wound up being one of Murray's most beloved fictional creations (and the inspiration and namesake of Joel McHale's Jeff Winger on the TV sitcom *Community*). Playing a character closer to his real-life personality than, say, **Carl Spackler** or **Hunter S. Thompson**, Murray inhabits the part in a manner not seen since *Meatballs*. Speaking to an interviewer about his experience on the film, Murray said he worked "more efficiently than I ever worked

before. The hard part with movies is to sit around and wait and still have yourself right there when you're needed for those three minutes a day they actually film. I really tried to keep control of myself for this one." Indeed, his performance is more restrained and less volatile than in his previous films. Winger's confrontation with Sergeant Hulka, the no-nonsense drill instructor played by veteran character actor Warren Oates, provides a rare early opportunity for Murray to show off his acting chops.

Although *Stripes* is maddeningly uneven—Ramis's soporific performance as Ziskey is a real lowlight—it does boast a number of bravura comic scenes. Murray gets to deliver another one of his signature improvised speeches—an oration exhorting his fellow army recruits to pull themselves together before the graduation ceremony—and the film briefly put the catchphrase "That's the fact, Jack" on the lips of every twelve-year-old in America. What holds *Stripes* back from classic status, however, is the toothlessness of its take on military authority. Strip away the sex and mud wrestling scenes and the film is virtually indistinguishable from the tepid service comedies of the 1940s and '50s. Even more problematic is the fact that *Stripes* goes completely off the rails in the final reel, an interminable chase sequence set in Soviet-controlled Czechoslovakia. The sequence's slapstick pratfalls and jingoist subtext seem jarringly out of sync with the rest of the film. "That was just Ivan grinding his anti-Communist ax," Harold Ramis later revealed. (The director's parents were Czech refugees who fled to Canada after

(CONTINUED ON PAGE 234)

Stripes, 1981

the Communists seized power.) Years later, Murray was still kvetching about some of the violent action scenes Reitman insisted on making him film. "I'm still a little queasy that I actually made a movie where I carry a machine gun," he confessed. "But I felt if you were rescuing your friends it was okay."

With a bombastic score from Academy Award–winning composer Elmer Bernstein and positive PR support from the Pentagon (who provided "technical assistance" in return for an advance look at the script), *Stripes* struck a chord with audiences in the emerging era of Ronald Reagan, G. I. Joe, and Rambo. It grossed more than $85 million and proved that Murray's name above a title could carry a movie. **Critics** were more divided. "*Stripes* will keep potential felons off the streets for two hours," wrote *Time* magazine in a decidedly backhanded rave. *Newsweek* called Murray "a funny original presence" but questioned his participation in the project. "Could it be that Murray himself doesn't give a damn that he's diddling away his talents on mediocrity?" the reviewer asked. "*Stripes* reeks of halfheartedness." The doyenne of American cinephiles, Pauline Kael, was even more cutting. Writing about Murray's character in *Stripes*, she opined, "I wouldn't want to be within fifty yards of anything he believed in."

NEXT MOVIE: *Tootsie* (1982)

ST. VINCENT

DIRECTED BY: Theodore Melfi

WRITTEN BY: Theodore Melfi

RELEASE DATE: October 10, 2014

FILM RATING: ★ ★ ★

MURRAY RATING: ★ ★ ★

PLOT: An adorable tyke teaches a grouchy alcoholic how to care again.

STARRING BILL MURRAY AS: Vincent MacKenna, irascible Brooklyn barfly

"I'm a sucker for hero roles," Murray once said. "The big brother parts, especially superheroes—providing they have flaws." He found just such a part in writer/director Ted Melfi's crowd-pleasing *St. Vincent,* which finds Murray fishing for his elusive Oscar in the brackish waters off Sheepshead Bay, Brooklyn. Playing an outer-borough grump who reluctantly befriends a single mother and her twelve-year-old son, Murray struggles mightily to maintain his Brooklyn accent. (At times he comes off as **Chicago** crossed with South Boston.) But his performance is so hammily charming it seems uncharitable to nitpick.

Jack Nicholson was Melfi's original choice for the title role, but he turned it down. (An interesting turn of events, since Nicholson had poached several parts from Murray's reject pile in the 1980s.) At Nicholson's urging, Melfi then embarked on a full-court press to convince Murray to sign on to the project. He secured the actor's secret **800 number** from Fred Roos, the legendary Hollywood producer, and cold-called it incessantly over two months in early 2012. When that proved fruitless, Melfi turned to Murray's attorney, David Nochimson, who suggested writing a letter and mailing it to a mysterious post office box somewhere on the East Coast. That seemed to get Murray's attention. He requested a script and then promptly cut off all communication.

Several months later, according to Melfi, Murray texted him out of the blue and asked him to meet up at the Los Angeles International Airport. So began an unusual rolling story conference, as Murray's chauffeured Lincoln town car took the actor and the would-be auteur first to **In-N-Out Burger** to pick up grilled cheese sandwiches and then on a three-hour drive through the Pechanga Indian reservation to Murray's mansion adjacent to a **golf** course about an hour north of San Diego. All the while, Murray gave Melfi notes on the script. As the afternoon drew to a close, he announced: "We should do this. Let's make a movie." And the deal was done.

Murray later revealed that he had been attracted to the project by the quality of Melfi's writing ("The people sounded like real people," he told Bloomberg.com) and by the chance to sink his teeth into a meaty role for the first time since *Hyde Park on Hudson.* "It is ambitious and it is larger," he said.

S
T

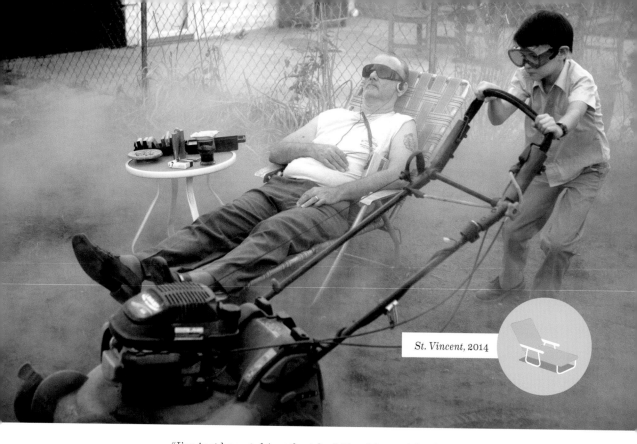

St. Vincent, 2014

"I've just been taking the jobs I like. I haven't had any kind of a plan, really. It really was a big, leading part. I thought to myself, 'God, I haven't had to be the leading part in a while.'" The revelation that there was a vegetarian option at In-N-Out Burger may have had something to do with it as well. "I didn't realize you could get a cheeseburger without a hamburger," he confessed to *USA Today*. "No meat."

Shooting for *St. Vincent* took place in Sheepshead Bay and surrounding Brooklyn neighborhoods over thirty-seven days in the summer of 2013. Murray bunked at a friend's house in the hipster enclave of Williamsburg the entire time, riding a ten-speed bicycle fifteen miles to and from the location each day. "I got myself in some kind of shape," he said afterwards. "People have been talking about Brooklyn for a long time, but I'd never really seen it. Williamsburg is hopping." On the set, Murray was his usual antic self, repeatedly tossing banana peels in the paths of passing crew members and periodically disappearing on impromptu walkabouts. One day Murray wandered off to chew the fat with a local military veteran who sat on his porch every day watching the shoot. Another time, he commandeered a golf cart and took costars Naomi Watts and Jaeden Lieberher for a joyride. The studio eventually hired a production assistant just to follow Murray around and record his whereabouts.

NEXT MOVIE: *Dumb and Dumber To* (2014)

SULLAVAN, MARGARET

Spitfire screen actress of the 1930s and '40s whose work Murray admires. "What a creature she was," he gushed to film critic Elvis Mitchell during a 2008 interview. "She could really do some funny physical stuff, which you didn't see in those old movies. Everyone was such a glamor puss. . . . This girl was really, really funny and beautiful. And to me that is fatal. I'm crazy about funny girls." Murray is especially enamored with Sullavan's performance in the 1936 screwball comedy *The Moon's Our Home,* in which she has a spirited pillow fight with her ex-husband Henry Fonda. "I love pillow fights with girls," Murray has admitted. "One of my favorite things."

"SUMMER BREEZE"

Murray loathes this 1972 hit song from pop duo Seals and Crofts. The soft-rock chestnut received so much AM radio airplay in the 1970s that the actor grew sick of it.

SWEET SPOT, THE

Golf-themed reality series featuring Murray and three of his brothers that aired on Comedy Central over five weeks in April 2002. The show followed Bill, John, Brian, and Joel Murray as they travelled the world, visiting exotic golf courses and teeing off against one another in pursuit of the elusive "Braggart's Cup." Interstitial comedy skits occasionally broke up the brotherly banter, which rarely rose above a "Dorf on Golf" level of humor.

S
T

TALES FROM
MURRAYLAND

Nº 24	## The Night He Went to His Own Ice Cream Social

In July 2014, Murray was filming *Rock the Kasbah* in Sherman Oaks, California, when neighborhood ice cream vendor Joe Nicchi decided to throw a "Bill Murray Ice Cream Social" in his honor. After parking his fully restored 1961 Mister Softee ice cream truck just off the set, Nicchi spread the word among the crew that he would scoop free cones in Murray's honor all evening long. To the ice cream man's astonishment, the guest of honor ambled over to test the wares. "When he actually started walking toward the truck, the crew members were following closely behind him," said Nicchi. "They seemed like proud parents excited to see this moment actually happening for me." On Nicchi's recommendation, Murray treated himself to a chocolate and vanilla twist with sea salt on the house. He took a few photos, asked Nicchi to deliver trays of ice cream to feed the rest of the crew, and then left.

TARZOON, SHAME OF THE JUNGLE

See Shame of the Jungle.

THAT'S NOT FUNNY, THAT'S SICK

National Lampoon sketch comedy album from 1977 on which Murray appears. The vinyl LP collects material from the recently canceled *National Lampoon Radio Hour* and includes performances from Murray's brother Brian, Christopher Guest, and Richard Belzer.

THERE'S SOMETHING ABOUT MARY

Two years after he made *Kingpin* for the Farrelly brothers, Murray was considered for the part of private eye Pat Healy in this high-grossing gross-out comedy. In the end, the brothers decided Murray was too old for the part and instead offered it to Matt Dillon.

THIS OLD CUB

DIRECTED BY: Jeff Santo

WRITTEN BY: Jeff Santo

RELEASE DATE: August 25, 2004

FILM RATING: ★★↙

MURRAY RATING: ★★

PLOT: A documentary about retired Chicago Cubs legend Ron Santo and his lifelong battle with diabetes.

STARRING BILL MURRAY AS: Himself

Murray is among a bevy of **Chicago**-area actors offering reminiscences of Hall of Fame third baseman Ron Santo in this reverent documentary directed by Santo's son Jeff. Dennis Franz, Gary Sinise, Dennis Farina, and Murray's brothers Brian and Joel also appear. Murray was recruited to the project by the film's narrator, Joe Mantegna. He filmed his segments in the summer of 2003 at a **golf** course on the outskirts of Chicago.

NEXT MOVIE: *The Life Aquatic with Steve Zissou* (2004)

S
T

THOMPSON, HUNTER S.

Iconic American outlaw journalist, best known as the author of *Fear and Loathing in Las Vegas*. Murray befriended Thompson in the late 1970s, when Thompson's sometime girlfriend, Laila Nabulsi, worked as a producer for *Saturday Night Live*. In the summer of 1979, the two men became inseparable as Murray prepared to play Thompson in *Where the Buffalo Roam*. After filming wrapped, Murray went through an extended personality crisis during which he adopted Thompson's voice and mannerisms.

> ## "I HATE TO ADVOCATE DRUGS OR LIQUOR, VIOLENCE, INSANITY TO ANYONE. BUT IN MY CASE IT'S WORKED."
>
> —MURRAY, as Hunter S. Thompson
> in *Where the Buffalo Roam*

Thompson committed suicide in 2005. Murray attended his memorial service, during which Thompson's ashes were blasted out of a cannon onto the heads of the assembled mourners, including Jack Nicholson, John Oates, and U.S. senator John Kerry. The alcohol- and drug-infused bacchanal that followed concluded with Murray swimming in Thompson's neighbor's swimming pool "somewhere between midnight and dawn." Murray later called it "the best funeral I've ever been to in my life."

See also Where the Buffalo Roam.

¡THREE AMIGOS!

In the early 1980s, when he was still attached as director, Steven Spielberg strongly considered Murray for the role of Dusty Bottoms in this Western comedy film. Steve Martin and Robin Williams were set to play the other two amigos. By the time the movie was made in 1986, only Martin remained. John Landis had replaced Spielberg behind the camera, with Chevy Chase in Murray's old role and Martin Short rounding out the trio.

TIPPING

Murray is known as a generous tipper, a trait that dates back to his early days working service jobs in support of his acting career. "Everyone I know is a waiter or waitress," he once said. "They're working hand to mouth, just trying to keep a gig where they have some cash coming in, so they can do what they want to do otherwise." During a visit to Maxim's de Paris Hotel in Palm Springs in 1989, Murray gave his bellboy a $20 tip (about forty bucks today). In recent years, Murray has been known to tip his limo driver with In-N-Out Burger coupons.

S
T

TOOTSIE

DIRECTED BY: Sydney Pollack

WRITTEN BY: Larry Gelbart and Murray Schisgal

RELEASE DATE: December 17, 1982

FILM RATING: ★ ★ ★ ★

MURRAY RATING: ★ ★ ★ ★

PLOT: A struggling actor impersonates a woman to land a part on a soap opera.

STARRING BILL MURRAY AS: Jeff Slater, playwright and roommate

Red hot following the success of *Stripes*, Murray could have named his price for his next project—provided it was another lowbrow comedy aimed at the *Animal House* audience. "I was some sort of movie star then, on a junior level," he said, "but not of an adult nature yet." Pigeonholed as the smirking comic lead, he longed to do more serious work. "I thought, 'If only somebody would hire me to be a second banana so I could play straight, then they would see that I can act." Determined to break out of the mold Hollywood had set for him, Murray lobbied hard for a supporting role in a prestige project whose script was already starting to generate buzz within the film community: director Sydney Pollack's *Tootsie*.

Murray won the part thanks to a fortuitous encounter with *Tootsie* star Dustin Hoffman at a birthday celebration for the wife of Columbia Pictures chairman Frank Price. Hoffman was so impressed with Murray's party banter that he recommended him to Pollack for the role of the main character's roommate. Pollack was reluctant at first, his impressions fixed from Murray's days as a cast member on *Saturday Night Live*. "My initial opinion was that Billy was just a strong sketch player," Pollack said. "It wasn't until I screened his films at Dustin's urging that I saw what a satisfying actor he could be. Even when those around him are merely filling their parts, Billy always gives a very sustained characterization. There's reality and candor, plus scene-to-scene growth. . . . He's got a complex and original range that puts him in a special category—a completely believable comic illuminator."

That skill set would be put to the test on *Tootsie*. Murray's character, playwright Jeff Slater—author of the soon-to-be-produced *Return to the Love Canal*—was a late addition to the *Tootsie* screenplay, courtesy of

uncredited script doctor **Elaine May**. Intended as a stand-in for the audience's point of view, Slater would have to be substantially improvised. That might have daunted another actor, but Murray relished the opportunity to put his personal stamp on the part. He accepted the role on one condition: that his name be excluded from the opening credits and all advertising for the film. He didn't want audiences to go see *Tootsie* expecting another *Meatballs* or *Caddyshack*. In another bold but ultimately shrewd move, Murray turned down a salary on the picture, opting instead for one of Dustin Hoffman's percentage points on the profits. *Tootsie* ended up grossing over $170 million.

Now regarded as a classic, *Tootsie* was in fact a very troubled production. When Murray arrived on the set, shooting was already a week behind schedule. Pollack and Hoffman were at each other's throats. "Dustin would throw a fit, and the crew just stood back and watched," Murray remembered later. "Sydney would have a go back and they'd be like these two prize fighters, with veins bulging in their foreheads. I still felt like the junior guy in movies, so I tried to lighten the mood." To break the tension, Murray threw his own on-set tantrum. "Everyone knew I was kidding," he said, "but it helped defuse one or two situations." He also needled Pollack about his predilection for cowboy boots, calling him "Tex."

As expected, Murray found his part totally underwritten, forcing him to ad-lib his way through scenes. "They kept on saying, 'Just react.' So I would come up with lines like 'That is one nutty hospital' or 'I'm just afraid you are going to burn in hell for all this.' Then they would write these down as scenes and say, after a few days, 'Come up with something else.' It was like that through the movie." Among Murray's signature contributions are a priceless monologue in which Slater pines for a theater that is "only open when it rains" and a strange scene in which he inexplicably munches on lemon slices while talking to Dustin Hoffman's character. "He was so good, we kept adding scenes for him," said Pollack. "I not only wanted to see more of him, but it was a fight to keep the cameras from jiggling when he was on because we were all laughing."

The second highest grossing film of 1982, *Tootsie* proved an enormous hit with audiences and **critics** alike, earning ten Academy Award nominations. Although it didn't propel Murray to the front ranks of "serious" actors just yet, it did serve notice on Hollywood that there was more to him than **Carl Spackler** and John Winger.

NEXT MOVIE: *Ghostbusters* (1984)

TOY STORY

Murray turned down an offer to provide the voice of Buzz Lightyear in this 2005 film from Pixar Animation Studios. **Chevy Chase** and Billy Crystal also passed on the role, which eventually went to Tim Allen.

TVTV (TOP VALUE TELEVISION)

San Francisco–based "guerrilla video" collective with which Murray was briefly associated in the mid-1970s. A pioneer in the field of "countercultural journalism," TVTV was known for sending correspondents equipped with handheld video systems (then called "portapaks") to cover live events such as political conventions. Correspondents were often recruited for their ability to improvise on camera. Christopher Guest, **John Belushi**, **Harold Ramis**, and Murray's brother Brian were all affiliated with TVTV at one time or another. The low-budget video films, which bear a formal resemblance to the fictional "mockumentaries" for which Guest later became famous, typically aired on public television.

Murray was first approached by TVTV cofounder Michael Shamberg in late 1975, shortly after the cancelation of *Saturday Night Live with Howard Cosell*. Shamberg was looking for correspondents for a documentary about the upcoming Super Bowl game in Miami, Florida. In the ensuing film, *TVTV: Super Bowl*, Murray and Guest pose as sportscasters and tailgaters in order to infiltrate the media horde surrounding Super Bowl X on January 18, 1976. Murray—billed as "Billy Murray"—provides color commentary for an impromptu touch football game featuring CBS Sports personnel and NFL legends Johnny Unitas, Sonny Jurgensen, and Paul Hornung. Harold Ramis served as a writer and producer on the film.

Buoyed by the success of *Super Bowl*, and with no permanent job prospects on the horizon, Murray decided to join the TVTV repertory company on a long-term basis. He moved to **Los Angeles** and spent the next nine months working on a variety of TVTV projects. In *TVTV Looks at the Oscars*, a backstairs glimpse at the 1976 **Academy Awards** ceremony, Murray appears briefly as a movie fan cheering Elizabeth Taylor on the red carpet. In *The TVTV Show*, the group's first pilot for network television, he plays a cameraman for the fictional WKTO Action News team.

In January 1977, Murray left Los Angeles to join the cast of *Saturday Night Live* in New York. He never worked for TVTV again. At the request of NBC, his part was largely edited out of *The TVTV Show*, which aired on the network in the *SNL* time slot on April 29, 1977.

TWAIN, MARK

This Missouri-born humorist and teller of tall tales is Murray's favorite author. "He's smart and funny," Murray observed of Twain. "*Huckleberry Finn*, especially the chapter all the purists hate, in which Tom Sawyer stages an elaborate rescue of Jim, is a writer having as much fun as possible." Murray performed a dramatic reading of a scene from *Huckleberry Finn* at a panel discussion marking the publication of a new "comprehensive edition" of Twain's masterpiece in 1996.

S
T

VAN DER POST, LAURENS

This South African storyteller, self-styled Jungian mystic, and confidant of the British royal family wrote Murray's two favorite novels. *A Story Like the Wind* and *A Far Off Place* tell the tale of a pair of European children who make a perilous journey across the Kalahari Desert with the help of an African bushman and his wife.

VEECK AS IN WRECK

In 1995, Murray was briefly attached to play the title role in this abortive biopic about flamboyant Major League Baseball owner Bill Veeck. *NYPD Blue* writer Ted Mann wrote the script for the film based on Veeck's 1962 autobiography. **Chicago** native John McNaughton, who had previously worked with Murray on *Mad Dog and Glory*, was slated to direct. Sigourney Weaver, Murray's *Ghostbusters* costar, was in line to play Veeck's wife, Mary Frances. The project never got out of the development stage.

Veeck as in Wreck might have been a tour de force for Murray, a lifelong **baseball** fan and Chicago sports aficionado. The peg-legged son of a former **Chicago Cubs** executive, Veeck specialized in devising outrageous publicity stunts. Among his many brainstorms: hiring a dwarf, Eddie Gaedel, to make a single plate appearance during a meaningless late-summer game; installing baseball's first exploding scoreboard; outfitting his players in short pants; and staging the infamous "Disco Demolition Night" promotion, during which a pyrotechnic protest against the then-popular form of dance music devolved into a riot. "Everything that I love about baseball is embodied in Bill Veeck," Murray once observed. "I met him the way everyone met him—he'd sit in the bleachers, take off his wooden leg and shirt, drink beer, and flick his cigarettes into the ashtray he'd built into his wooden leg. He'd just lay there in the sun, almost naked, talking to **fans**. That's how I'm going to play Bill Veeck . . . as the naked fan."

Murray was encouraged to take the part by Veeck's son Mike, his personal friend and co-owner of the Saint Paul Saints minor league team. "He thinks I'm similar in so many ways to his father," Murray remarked, "though he won't tell me how."

UVW

TALES FROM
MURRAYLAND

Nº 25   The Night He Saved the Sturgeon

In July 1994, Murray made a surprise appearance at the International Conference on Sturgeon Biodiversity and Conservation at the American Museum of Natural History in New York City. The two-day confab, organized by the Hudson River Foundation, brought together more than two hundred scientists and scholars to discuss solutions to the problem of overfishing. Murray was living in the Hudson Valley at the time and had been sensitized to the plight of Atlantic sturgeon. According to newspaper accounts, Murray cracked up the conference with an off-the-cuff speech playing off his purported ignorance of ichthyology. "How many of you are marine biologists?" he asked the audience. "How many are ichthyologists? How many are systematists? How many believe that the sturgeon is kosher?" He also remarked that he had to look up the word *sturgeon* in a dictionary from 1954, a time when "men were men, women were chicks or babes, and sturgeon were sturgeon." At the end of the evening, Murray crumpled up a signed blank check and tossed it to Kathryn Birstein, the wife of molecular geneticist Dr. Vadim Birstein, one of the world's leading authorities on endangered sturgeon. He then exited the building.

"I LOVE THE WEATHER CHANNEL. THE CHARM AND THE POWER OF THE FRONTS, YOU KNOW? YOU GET TO SEE SOMETHING REALLY IMPORTANT HAPPENING."

—MURRAY, on the joys of watching the Weather Channel

WAR OF THE INSECT GODS, THE

Unmade 1978 film project in which Murray was slated to star as Deadly Ed, an exterminator defending **New York City** from an invasion by giant cockroaches. *War of the Insect Gods* was the brainchild of maverick *Saturday Night Live* writer Michael O'Donoghue, who envisioned it as his directorial debut. O'Donoghue coauthored the screenplay with *National Lampoon Radio Hour* veteran Emily Prager, journalist and Murray pal **Mitch Glazer**, and novelist Dirk Wittenborn. From the start, O'Donoghue zeroed in on Murray for the lead role of Deadly Ed, the remorseless bug killer who figures out how to destroy the mutant bone-crushing roaches using bottles of ether. "Billy is who I want to play Deadly Ed," O'Donoghue gushed. "He's both a romantic lead and he's a little sleazy. He looks like that exterminator kind of guy. And yet he's a guy who can take on heroic proportions and look like an attractive American hero." Unfortunately for Murray, this proto-*Ghostbusters* star turn was not to be. NBC passed on O'Donoghue's pitch for a *War of the Insect Gods* TV movie. "Mr. Mike" then tried to raise money for a proposed theatrical version, but investors were put off by his demand that the film be shot in black and white and mortified by his habit of photocopying the corpses of squashed roaches into the pages of his script. When the film failed to acquire backing, O'Donoghue turned his attention to a new project, *Mr. Mike's Mondo Video*.

WATERS, JOHN

Mustachioed gay cult filmmaker who reluctantly allowed Murray to sing the "love theme" to his 1981 comedy *Polyester*. Murray's friend Chris Stein of Blondie recommended him for the gig, a suggestion the film's producers were eager to accept in the wake of *Caddyshack*'s success the previous year. Murray agreed to perform for free on the track, "The Best Thing," which was cowritten by Blondie frontwoman Debbie Harry. According to *Polyester* line producer Robert Maier in his book *Low Budget Hell: Making Un-*

> # "JOHN'S HUMOR WAS NOT DOOFUSY LIKE BILL MURRAY'S."
> —John Waters collaborator ROBERT MAIER, on why the two men didn't get along

U V W

derground Movies with John Waters, Murray came into the studio in a T-shirt and baseball cap and nailed the song in two takes, with Harry supplying backup vocals. The only person who was not pleased with Murray's performance was the notoriously prickly Waters. The outrageous auteur loathed Murray, whom he considered insufficiently edgy for his brand of envelope-pushing independent cinema. "He hated Bill Murray. He hated *Saturday Night Live*. He hated *Caddyshack*," Maier wrote. "Murray was a mass-audience TV phenomenon, while John was an underground and dangerous artist.... John was angry, gay, and shocking, and he didn't want it diluted." Studio bosses overruled Waters, insisting on Murray's participation as a way to generate buzz for a project with uncertain commercial prospects. (*Polyester* was presented in "Odorama," an evolutionary form of Smell-O-Vision that allowed moviegoers to use scratch-and-sniff cards to huff the flatulence of the on-screen characters.) Waters never got over having Murray foisted upon him and refused to thank the actor for his contribution. In the end, Murray's presence on the soundtrack did not generate the publicity producers had hoped it would. *Polyester* bombed at the box office and failed to launch Waters into the mainstream.

WEATHER CHANNEL, THE

This twenty-four-hour meteorological TV network is one of Murray's destination cable channels. "I've been a weather watcher for years," he told one interviewer. To a radio host, he confessed: "I was one of the first people to really devote my entire life to the Weather Channel." He boasts that he watches the channel "all the time. There's this guy from Wisconsin who's almost my personal savior." Murray prepared for his role as a TV weatherman in 1993's *Groundhog Day* by watching the Weather Channel almost nonstop.

WHAT ABOUT BOB?

DIRECTED BY: Frank Oz

WRITTEN BY: Tom Schulman

RELEASE DATE: May 17, 1991

FILM RATING: ★ ★ ★

MURRAY RATING: ★ ★ ★

PLOT: A multiphobic loon enrages his psychiatrist.

STARRING BILL MURRAY AS: Bob Wiley, needy psychiatric patient

Playing against type as a man with no self-confidence and precious little charm, Murray delivers one of the finest performances of his career in this delightfully dark comedy directed by legendary Muppeteer Frank Oz. As Bob Wiley, a neurotic shut-in with staggering emotional needs, Murray per-

U
V
W

What about Bob?, 1991

sistently bedevils a pompous psychiatrist played by Richard Dreyfuss.

According to Murray, the oil-and-water rapport he developed with Dreyfuss had its basis in their off-camera relationship. "[Dreyfuss and I] didn't get along on the movie," he once admitted. "But it worked for the movie. I mean, I drove him nuts, and he encouraged me to drive him nuts." Murray attributed the personality conflict to Dreyfuss's disciplined, theatrical acting style, which clashed with Murray's more freewheeling, improvisational approach. "He drove me nuts with his stage precision, so I returned the favor with anarchy," Murray said. "That's cinema verité you see up there."

> ## "IT'S ENTERTAINING— EVERYBODY KNOWS SOME- BODY LIKE THAT BOB GUY."
> —MURRAY, on the enduring appeal of *What about Bob?*

Considering that the film climaxes with Dreyfuss's character attempting to murder Bob by strapping dynamite to his chest, it is fortunate that the two actors managed to survive the experience. Apparently violent behavior was not unheard of on the *What about Bob?* set. When he wasn't driving Richard Dreyfuss to distraction, Murray was picking fights with the film's producer, Laura Ziskin. According to Ziskin, Murray "threatened to throw me across the parking lot and then broke my sunglasses and threw them across the parking lot." When those love taps failed to elicit the desired response, Murray reportedly picked up Ziskin and tossed her into a lake in full view of the crew. "I was furious and outraged at the time," Ziskin later recalled, "but having produced a dozen movies, I can safely say it is not common behavior."

NEXT MOVIE: *Groundhog Day* (1993)

WHERE THE BUFFALO ROAM

DIRECTED BY: Art Linson
WRITTEN BY: John Kaye
RELEASE DATE: April 25, 1980
FILM RATING: ★
MURRAY RATING: ★★

PLOT: Gonzo journalist Hunter S. Thompson drinks, smokes, and snorts his way through a series of magazine assignments in the 1970s.

STARRING BILL MURRAY AS: Hunter S. Thompson

Murray scored his first flop with this aimless 1980 comedy chronicling the exploits of gonzo journalist **Hunter S. Thompson.** Peter Boyle headlines the

U
V
W

cast—inexplicably, considering he is in only a
handful of scenes—as Carl Lazlo, a fictionalized
version of Thompson's lawyer and drug buddy
Oscar Zeta Acosta (known to his intimates as the
Brown Buffalo). As the hard-partying Thompson, Murray mumbles and shuffles and does a
lot of actorly gesturing with his cigarette holder.
If it were a three-minute *Saturday Night Live*
impression, his performance would have been
top-notch. Unfortunately the film goes on for an
hour and a half.

Loosely based on Thompson's 1977 magazine
article "The Banshee Screams for Buffalo Meat,"
Where the Buffalo Roam marks the directorial
debut of Art Linson, producer of the lowbrow
late-'70s hits *Car Wash* and *American Hot Wax*.
The film was shot in and around **Los Angeles**
over two months in the summer of 1979, just
as *Meatballs* was blowing up at the box office.
During filming, Thompson lived in a guest house
underneath the swimming pool in Murray's rented home in North Hollywood. "I'd work all day and stay up all night with him," Murray remembered.
"I was strong in those days." To give him something to occupy his time,
Thompson was kept on retainer as an "executive consultant" to the production—a gig he later said consisted
of wandering around the set firing
a machine gun.

Murray had reservations about
the script from the beginning. The
film seemed episodic and unfo-
cused. As shooting commenced,
he grew increasingly anxious that
he had a turkey on his hands. He
managed to convince Linson to al-
low him to rewrite entire scenes on
the set with help from Thompson.

> ## "I WANTED TO DO SOME ESCAPE WORK. IT WAS SUMMERTIME. IT WAS HOT."
>
> —MURRAY, explaining his decision to play Houdini
> games with Hunter S. Thompson

The duo continued to revise until three days before the film's release, adding
narration they hoped would fill the myriad holes in the plot, as well as the
dada monologue that buttons up the final scene.

None of their tweaks could render the movie's slapdash plot coherent,
however. When it opened in the spring of 1980, *Where the Buffalo Roam* was

U V
V
W

roasted by **critics** and shunned by audiences. Even Thompson disowned the film after seeing it. Writing about *Where the Buffalo Roam* for *Rolling Stone*, longtime Thompson associate David Felton called Murray's portrayal "spooky and accurate." But he dismissed the film as a hack job, "an embarrassing piece of hogwash utterly devoid of plot, form, movement, tension, humor, insight, logic, or purpose."

Rarely shown on television and never given a proper DVD release, *Where the Buffalo Roam* seems consigned to the cut-out bin of history. Its only lasting legacy is the plethora of Bill Murray/Hunter Thompson party stories that have been disseminated over the ensuing decades. In the most famous, Murray and Thompson spend a day drinking and carousing at the latter's ranch in Aspen, Colorado. They get into an argument over who is the better escape artist. Thompson ties Murray to a chair and throws him into his swimming pool. Murray almost drowns before Thompson fishes him out.

NEXT MOVIE: *B.C. Rock* (1980)

WHO FRAMED ROGER RABBIT?

Director Robert Zemeckis tried to offer Murray the role of Eddie Valiant in this 1988 comedy mixing live action and animation. The elusive actor proved impossible to track down, however, and the part went to Bob Hoskins instead. Murray has admitted that he regrets missing out on the gig.

WILD THINGS

DIRECTED BY: John McNaughton
WRITTEN BY: Stephen Peters
RELEASE DATE: March 20, 1998
FILM RATING: ★ ★
MURRAY RATING: ★ ★

PLOT: Two teenage sex kittens frame a high school guidance counselor for a crime he did not commit—or did he?

STARRING BILL MURRAY AS: Ken Bowden, sleazy South Florida lawyer

After headlining two stinkers in a row—*Larger Than Life* and *The Man Who Knew Too Little*—Murray returned to the safe harbor of scene-stealing character work in this high-gloss erotic thriller from *Mad Dog and Glory* director John McNaughton.

Like Cinemax softcore with a chewy Lifetime movie center, *Wild Things* sprays pheromones at the audience for nearly two hours to no discernible effect. It has garnered something of a cult following because of a steamy three-way sex scene featuring Matt Dillon, Denise Richards, and Neve Campbell—as well as a brief glimpse of Kevin Bacon's schlong—but the film's convoluted plot and some terrible performances undermine its effectiveness. Murray's character, an ambulance-chasing lawyer who inexplicably wears a neck

U V W

Where the Buffalo Roam, 1980

TALES FROM
MURRAYLAND

Nº 26	The Night He Left Sergio Leone Holding the Check

One night in the 1980s, Murray was having dinner in a New York City restaurant with a group of friends, including *Nothing Lasts Forever* director Tom Schiller and legendary spaghetti western auteur Sergio Leone. Toward the end of the meal, at Schiller's suggestion, Murray passed the word to the other diners to get up and leave the table one by one, as if they were going to use the restrooms. Then they would all meet outside and leave Leone with the check. "We were just a bunch of wise guys," Murray told author Michael Streeter. "It was such a novel idea to try and catch a real movie guy and stick him with the bill." Tom Schiller remembers Leone's expression when he caught on to the gag: "Kind of like Eli Wallach's look as Tuco during the duel at the end of *The Good, the Bad, and the Ugly*. Priceless."

brace in half his scenes, was added by McNaughton to provide comic relief to the noir goings-on. It is one of many weird tonal shifts that do not serve the picture well.

Despite mixed reviews and lackluster box office returns, *Wild Things* spawned three straight-to-video sequels—none of which included Murray. By 2013, director McNaughton was musing publicly about a possible fourth sequel, set at the same Miami high school, revolving around the offspring of the original characters. "Maybe there is a child and maybe Bill Murray's character had a child and they're exchange students and things get out of hand," he told Hollywood.com.

NEXT MOVIE: *With Friends Like These . . .* (1998)

WILLIS, BRUCE

The *Die Hard* star worked with Murray on *Moonrise Kingdom* in 2012, but they had met much earlier. In the late 1970s, Willis worked as a page at NBC headquarters in **New York City**. His duties included refilling the M&M bowls in the dressing rooms of the *Saturday Night Live* cast members. Nearly thirty years later, Willis told Murray that he and **Gilda Radner** were the only two actors on the show who ever treated him "like a human being."

WILMETTE, ILLINOIS

Suburban village fourteen miles north of **Chicago** where Murray grew up. Although Wilmette is often cited as his birthplace, in fact he was born in nearby Evanston. Incorporated in 1847, the village is home to the world's oldest surviving Bahá'í House of Worship. Other notable Wilmettians include actor Charlton Heston, entertainer Ann-Margret, and Chicago mayor Rahm Emanuel.

In his autobiography *Cinderella Story*, Murray described Wilmette as "a neighborhood of front lawns and sidewalks. . . . People had money there, but we weren't among them." Murray's brother Andy once described it as "a fabulous place to be a kid." The Murray home was located at 1930 Elmwood Avenue, a quiet, tree-lined street across from the Sisters of Christian Charity convent. "Our house was a wreck—a constant claustrophobic mess," Murray once observed of the three-bedroom, 2,000-square-foot home where he and his eight siblings jockeyed for space.

> "I REMEMBER SPENDING MY LAST DOLLAR ON SOME FRENCH FRIES, AND I JUST WANTED TO GET OUT OF WHERE I WAS."
>
> —MURRAY, on his decision to leave his hometown of Wilmette, Illinois

U
V
W

WIRED IN

Unaired TV documentary series about the tech trends of the 1980s for which Murray contributed a bizarre antitechnology monologue. In the presumably improvised rant-to-camera, Murray rails against digital watches ("People have hands. Watches should have hands"), decries the advent of worker robots, denounces "talking dashboards" in cars, and extols the virtues of Kenny Baker, the "fine actor" who played R2-D2 in the *Star Wars* movies. Lily Tomlin also appears in the program—excerpts of which live forever on YouTube—playing a Pac-Man-addicted housewife in a parody of antidrug public service announcements.

WITCHES OF EASTWICK, THE

Murray was director George Miller's first choice for the role of Daryl Van Horne in this 1987 dark comedy based on John Updike's novel. But Murray was in the midst of his four-year **sabbatical** from Hollywood at the time. Jack Nicholson got the part instead.

WITH FRIENDS LIKE THESE . . .

DIRECTED BY: Philip Frank Messina

WRITTEN BY: Philip Frank Messina

RELEASE DATE: September 10, 1998

FILM RATING: ★ ★

MURRAY RATING: ★

PLOT: Four small-time actors vie for a part in a Martin Scorsese movie.

STARRING BILL MURRAY AS: Maurice Melnick, cheese-hoarding Hollywood bigwig

Murray has a one-scene cameo as a penurious TV producer who steals cheese from people's party platters in this obscure late-'90s curiosity, also known as *Mom's on the Roof*. An inside-Hollywood comedy about four friends who find themselves at odds when they all are up for the same part in a new Martin Scorsese movie, *With Friends Like These . . .* played briefly on the festival circuit and then moldered on a shelf for seven years before resurfacing in theaters in 2005. Scorsese, Garry Marshall, and Michael McKean also have cameos in the film.

NEXT MOVIE: *Rushmore* (1998)

WOODWARD, BOB

Legendary journalist and coauthor of *All the President's Men*. Murray despises Woodward for his depiction of **John Belushi** as a degenerate drug addict in the 1984 biography *Wired*. "I read that and said, 'Holy shit, this Bob Woodward is a total fraud,' Murray once said. "The people he interviewed for his

U
V
W

story were all in the outer circle, four degrees of separation removed from John's life and the truth." In an interview, Murray accused Woodward of having a vendetta against his old *Saturday Night Live* costar. "Woodward had a mean bent from the beginning, and I know why," he said. "Bob Woodward is jealous: he is only the third most famous person from Wheaton, Illinois. The first is John Belushi, the second is Red Grange, and the third is Bob Woodward. And Woodward is a distant third and is never going to get any closer."

WORK

Before committing full-time to a show business career in the mid-1970s, Murray performed numerous odd jobs. As a young man, he hauled concrete blocks, sold hot dogs from a cart, and caddied at the Indian Hill Club in Winnetka, Illinois. He worked as a rod man on a surveying crew, a pizzaiolo at a Little Caesars, a landscaper, and a marijuana dealer. "I had no idea what I was going to do," he once observed of his checkered work history. "I had trouble holding jobs because they want you to be on time. That wasn't going to work." The life of the theater appealed to him, he said, because "you didn't have to get to work until nine o'clock at night."

In many interviews, Murray has bemoaned his lack of a strong work ethic. As he has grown older, he claims, he has just gotten lazier. "Life interferes, you know. When you're young and all you have is your career, some of your life can be in second place. And then you want your life to take first place, and other people don't see it that way. They see it that your life has to take second place, and it's hard. Life is really hard, and it's the only one you have. I mean, I like doing what I do, and I know I'm supposed to do it, but I don't have anything to bring to it if I don't live my life."

> ## "I DO ABSOLUTELY NOTHING. I GO HOME AND STAY THERE. I WASH AND SCRUB UP EACH DAY, AND THAT'S IT. ONE MONTH I ACTUALLY GREW A MUSTACHE, JUST SO I COULD SAY THAT I'D DONE SOMETHING."
>
> —MURRAY, on what he does when he's not working

U
V
W

YEAR OF LIVING DANGEROUSLY, THE

During a 2014 interview for *Grantland*, Murray revealed that this politically charged 1982 melodrama, set amid the tumult of 1960s Indonesia, was the one film he wishes he had gotten the chance to make. Murray was never offered a role in the film because, he said, he was not considered a serious actor at the time. Mel Gibson ended up playing the romantic lead opposite Murray's future *Ghostbusters* costar Sigourney Weaver.

TALES FROM
MURRAYLAND

Nº 27	## The Time He Read Poetry to Construction Workers

On May 1, 2009, Murray visited the future home of Poets House, a 60,000-volume free poetry library in Lower Manhattan. While on-site, he took time out to do an impromptu poetry reading for the construction workers at work on the new building. To the general befuddlement of his audience, Murray read three poems aloud: "Another Reason Why I Don't Keep a Gun in the House" by Billy Collins, "Poet's Work" by Lorine Niedecker, and "I Dwell in Possibility" by Emily Dickinson. When he finished, he informed the assembled hard hats: "You have about three minutes left on this break, so smoke 'em if you got 'em." Then he posed for some photos and left.

Nº 28	## The Time He Put Some Mayhem in the Pro-Am

In 2007, at a celebrity golf tournament in Utah, Murray decided to forgo the traditional cry of "Fore!" and instead throw a Coke bottle into the crowd. It ended up being his most unfortunate drive of the day. He hit a spectator in the face, shattering the man's nose and causing him to bleed profusely. A mortified Murray ended up apologizing to the injured golf fan and autographing the offending soft drink container for posterity.

ZIMMERLI OF SWITZERLAND

This Swiss luxury underwear purveyor "makes the best undershirts," according to Murray.

ZOMBIELAND

DIRECTED BY: Ruben Fleischer

WRITTEN BY: Rhett Reese and Paul Wernick

RELEASE DATE: October 2, 2009

FILM RATING: ★ ★ ⯨

MURRAY RATING: ★ ★ ★

PLOT: Four survivors of a zombie apocalypse travel across America.

STARRING BILL MURRAY AS: Himself

In a career studded with memorable cameos, *Zombieland* might be Murray's most impactful. Working in a full-on fright wig for the first time since *King-pin*, lampooning his own off-screen persona with a zest not seen since *Space Jam*, he adds a welcome dash of surreal humor to this violent, meta zombie comedy. The quick-and-dirty performance provided a respite for Murray as well, coming on the heels of his second divorce and the long, cold, unpleasant *Get Low* shoot in rural Georgia. Murray later described his appearance in *Zombieland* as something of a blessing. "It was like putting on an old coat and finding a couple hundred dollars in it," he told *Esquire*.

It almost did not happen at all. Murray was the tenth choice for the role of the movie star who plays host to four zombie hunters in his **Los Angeles** mansion. He got the offer only after Patrick Swayze, Sylvester Stallone, the Rock, Matthew McConaughey, Jean-Claude Van Damme, Joe Pesci, Mark Hamill, Kevin Bacon, and Dustin Hoffman all turned it down. With shooting on the scene scheduled to begin in just forty-eight hours, director Ruben Fleischer enlisted *Zombieland* costar Woody Harrelson to approach the notoriously reclusive Murray. "Pal, would you ever like to play a zombie?" Harrelson asked upon reaching Murray on his **800 number**. Murray asked to have pages faxed to him at a Kinko's near his home in New York.

After reading the script, Murray decided he was not too keen on playing a zombie after all. But he did want to be in the movie. He asked that the part be rewritten so that his "character"—a bewigged, heightened version of himself—was only pretending to be a flesh-eating creature. That set up the scene's unforgettable conclusion, in which Murray is shotgunned in the chest by a jittery Jesse Eisenberg. Most of Murray's dialogue was improvised on the set, including his final quip about *Garfield* being his biggest regret. Test audiences loved Murray's surprise appearance, although some were disappointed at seeing him come to such a gruesome end. "In the feedback on the film, people were actually sad that Bill Murray dies," Fleischer told *Entertainment Weekly*. "They felt such a strong connection to him, and they were so glad he was in it that they didn't want to see him go."

NEXT MOVIE: *Fantastic Mr. Fox* (2009)

THE QUOTABLE BILL MURRAY

MURRAY ON . . .

ALCOHOL

"I like alcohol but I don't have a favorite drink, which is probably why I'm not an alcoholic. If I had a favorite I'd probably be a drunk."

ART

"It's hard to be an artist. It's hard to be anything. It's hard to be."

CHICAGO

"Chicago actors are more hard-nosed. They're tough on themselves and their fellow actors. They're self-demanding."

CHILD ACTORS

"Most kid actors should be taken out and shot, let's face it. And their parents too."

COMEDY

"When Clint Eastwood teaches the girl how to shoot a gun, he says: 'Just squeeze it. Don't pull it. Squeeze it.' It's like that with comedy. You don't have to push it. You squeeze it. And it goes off. And it kills."

DRAMA

"I've always maintained that it's easier to make people cry than to make them laugh. Sadness is always so much easier to evoke in people because they're closer to it most of the time."

FAILURE

"I made a lot of mistakes and realized I had to let them go. Don't think about your errors or failures. Otherwise you'll never do a thing."

FAME

"I think everyone becomes a jerk for about two years when they become famous. So I give people two years to figure it out and pull it together. But you end up behaving poorly because there's just no training for it. There's nothing your parents ever did no matter what kind of people they are because everything just gets different. The information coming to you becomes differently—comes differently, and people treat you differently sort of and everything changes for us. So it takes you a little while to figure it out."

FAMILY

"I was kind of formed early on. People go, 'Oh, you act like that because you're a big shot.' No, I always acted like a jerk. I came from a big family."

GHOSTS

"I believe there are ghosts, but most of them are just waiters in restaurants. They take your order and then they vanish."

GOALS

"The first thing that happens when you announce your goals is that these demons start spilling out of manholes to thwart you. I mean, if I say I want to do a movie about the Shroud of Turin, some guy in Ohio who doesn't like my movies will set fire to the Shroud of Turin."

HIMSELF

"People say I'm difficult and sometimes that's a badge of honor."

HIS DAILY ROUTINE

"It would be too embarrassing to tell you a typical day in my life. I don't do a fucking thing. I couldn't tell you that I scrub my teeth every day. I mean, I probably do, but I couldn't swear to it."

HOTELS

"It's nice to have a date in a hotel but being alone in a hotel is kind of a sad kind of thing, isn't it? You feel like a traveling salesman or something like that. It's kind of sad to be in a hotel by yourself."

IMPROVISATION

"I think that good actors always—or if you're being good, anyway—you're making it better than the script. That's your fucking job. It's like, 'Okay, the script says this? Well, watch this. Let's just roar a little bit. Let's see how high we can go.'"

INDEPENDENT FILM

"I love independent films, but it's fun to do studio movies too. You should do both. You don't want to be like, 'Oh, he's an independent film guy.' It sounds like he makes his own dresses or something, you know? It just doesn't sound right."

LIFE

"As I once said to one of my brothers, 'This is your life, not a rehearsal.' Somewhere there's a score being kept, so you have an obligation to live life as well as you can, be as engaged as you can. The human condition means that we can zone out and forget what the hell we're doing. So the secret is to have a sense of yourself, your real self, your unique self. And not just once in a while, or once a day, but all through the day, the week, and life. You know what they say: 'Ain't no try, ain't nothing to it but to do it.'"

MELANCHOLY

"Melancholic and lovable is the trick, right? You've got to be able to show that you have these feelings. . . . A melancholy can be sweet. It's not a mean thing, but it's something that happens in life—like autumn."

MOATS

"A moat can be a pretty good thing. It can be lovely. It keeps rodents away from the castle. It can have fish in it. Even fish that talk."

MONEY

"Whenever I think of the high salaries we are paid as film actors, I think it is for the travel, the time away, and any trouble you get into through being well known. It's not for the acting, that's for sure."

MOVIES

"Movie acting suits me because I only need to be good for ninety seconds at a time."

PARTIES

"Parties are only bad when a fight breaks out, when men fight over women or vice versa. Someone takes a fall, an ambulance comes, and the police arrive. If you can avoid those things, pretty much all behavior is acceptable."

PRIVACY

"I can deal with losing my own privacy, but it affecting my kids is what I regret. No one can prepare you for what happens with fame."

PUBLICITY

"I think your best publicity is the work you do. My personal life shouldn't be of interest to anyone, and to garner publicity with a picture of me and my dog or my barbecue, that makes no sense to me."

RELAXATION

"The more relaxed you are, the better you are at everything: the better you are with your loved ones, the better you are with your enemies, the better you are at your job, the better you are with yourself."

RETIREMENT

"I've taken a couple of breaks. I've retired a couple of times. It's great, because you can just say, 'Oh, I'm sorry. I'm retired.' And people will actually believe that you've retired. There are nutters out there that will go, 'Oh, okay!' and then leave you alone."

RICHES

"I always like to say to people who want to be rich and famous, try being rich first. See if that doesn't cover most of it. There's not much downside to being rich, other than paying taxes and having your relatives ask you for money. But when you become famous, you end up with a twenty-four-hour job."

RULES

"Whenever you hear somebody has rules, you should run for the hills."

SUCCESS

"I remember reading that success is when the people in your village come to you for one thing they need done. I thought that made sense. You've got to find a village where they're missing something and do it. Because in this town—I heard this joke—in New York, even if you're one in a million, there are ten people just like you."

TELEVISION

"I can only take so much TV, because there is so much advice. I find people will preach about virtually anything—your diet, how to live your life, how to improve your golf. The lot. I have always had a thing against the Mister Know-It-Alls."

VICES

"When you become an adult and get to pick your pleasures. They should be worth picking."

WORK

"I'm basically lazy. I work really hard when I work, but I try to avoid work."

WHAT ABOUT BILL?

A SELECTION OF QUOTES FROM FRIENDS AND CONTEMPORARIES ABOUT BILL MURRAY

"Bill's whole life is in the moment. He doesn't care about what just happened. He doesn't think about what's going to happen. He doesn't even book round-trip tickets. Bill buys one-ways and then decides when he wants to go home."

—Ted Melfi, director of *St. Vincent*

"The most unkempt, fucked-up looking human I'd ever seen."

—Sean Kelly, *National Lampoon Show* writer, on his first impressions of Bill Murray

"*All* the Marx Brothers rolled into one: He's got the wit of Groucho, the pantomimic brilliance and lasciviousness of Harpo, and the Everyman quality of Chico."

—Harold Ramis

"There's a charming assholeness to Bill, and it's how he really has gotten through life. When I knew him, that was kind of how I thought of him, as this charming, always seducing, asshole-y kind of guy. But asshole in the sense of old-fashioned asshole. Like, a jerk willing to make a fool of himself—willing to do anything in order to get the girl. And there's something admirable about that, and there's something that makes you want to punch somebody about that."

—Betty Thomas, actress, director, and Second City alum

"He's the best comic actor in the world by a mile."

—George Clooney

"He's a god to comedians. He's like what a cow is in India."

—Nick Kroll

"I love Bill, but mostly I feel compassion because he has such a hopeless and profound crush on me."

—Janeane Garofalo

"I have nothing but admiration and affection for Bill. He still can be a surly character, to say the least. But ultimately, he's a good guy."

—Chevy Chase

"He's got a complex and original range that puts him in a special category—a completely believable comic illuminator."

—Sydney Pollack

"He was a force of nature. He was a movie star when he came onto this planet."

—Michael O'Keefe

"He has a certain rare animal—snow leopard—quality. Kinda dangerous as well as exotic."

—Tilda Swinton

"If you were reincarnated and had to be reborn into mortality, the Dalai Lama would probably be the most desired embodiment to be reborn in. I'd imagine that coming back as Bill Murray would be second."

—Del Close, legendary improv teacher

"He can be difficult, but he's worth it. You get so much bonus."

—Ivan Reitman

"He's a nutcase! He is a nutcase! If we were doing another [*Garfield* movie], Bill Murray would do it again."

—Jim Davis, creator of "Garfield"

"He's a dark guy. He's a black hole in which many of our spaceships have been lost."

— Michael O'Donoghue

"When Bill was onstage, he didn't much care whether they liked him. Because of that, he had enormous integrity. When Bill's good, it's the same as when De Niro's good."

—Lorne Michaels

"Wherever he goes, he's leaving a trail of hysteria behind him."

—Naomi Watts

"I think he's really attractive. Bill Murray is hot."

—Sofia Coppola

"He wasn't the pain in the ass I had heard he was. I expected a bad boy, but what I found was a really intelligent man who loved his work and expected everyone to give one hundred percent."

—Andie MacDowell

"Bill is a smart man. Much smarter than some of the movies he's done."

—Tim Robbins

"He's very mysterious."

—Wes Anderson

"One of the world's most appealing hipsters."

—David Denby, film critic

"He would come on as a guest and I'd watch him from the sidelines, thinking, 'How can he be so cool?'"

—Will Ferrell, on Murray's *Saturday Night Live* hosting appearances

"He has a genuine outré gift: he makes you feel that his characters are bums inside —unconcerned and indifferent—and he makes that seem like a kind of grace."

—Pauline Kael

"Bill is a dangerous brute with the fastest reflexes in Hollywood, but he is suave, and that is why I trust him even more than I trust all his brothers."

—Hunter S. Thompson

"If Frank Capra had taken a little acid, he probably would have come up with Bill Murray."

—John Byrum, director of *The Razor's Edge*

"There was always a certain danger with Bill. You just never were exactly sure where he was going to go."

—Andrew Alexander, CEO of Second City

"The big part of his appeal for grown-up men is that he personifies the wish to get away with everything. It's disruption for the cosmic good."

—Howard Franklin, director of *Quick Change* and *Larger Than Life*

"Bill is kind of a depressed guy, except when the camera's rolling. Then he puts it all out there and tries to be funny and witty and a genius, but otherwise, he's not that funny."

—P. J. Soles

"Being a fan of Bill Murray never gets boring because he's not bored. He's more mercurial and yet somehow more available than ever. In a world where most careers are xeroxes of each other, his is uniquely his own."

—Cameron Crowe

"Bill Murray is definitely the most creative improvisational actor I've ever worked with."

—Bob Tischler, producer of *The National Lampoon Radio Hour*

"The beauty of Bill is if he sees something he doesn't like, he will rip into that person. I have seen him go off on people, but I've never seen him go off on someone who didn't deserve it."

—Peter Farrelly

"Bill Murray is to me what calculators are to math. I never knew math before calculators, and I never knew life before Bill Murray. Being a child of the '80s, his movies were always around me, and I can't remember a time when there wasn't Bill Murray."

—Jason Schwartzman

"I used to feel guilty about behaving badly, and I met Bill, and it feels so much better."

—Harvey Weinstein

"He's truly a godlike, iconic hero to me."

—Quentin Tarantino

"Bill is a social anarchist."

— John McNaughton, director of *Mad Dog and Glory*

"Some people photo-bomb pictures. Bill Murray photo-bombs life."

—Anonymous Internet commenter

BILL MURRAY FILMOGRAPHY

Next Stop, Greenwich Village (1976)

Meatballs (1979)

Shame of the Jungle (1979)

Mr. Mike's Mondo Video (1979)

Where the Buffalo Roam (1980)

B.C. Rock aka *The Missing Link* (1980)

Caddyshack (1980)

Loose Shoes (1980)

Stripes (1981)

Tootsie (1982)

Ghostbusters (1984)

Nothing Lasts Forever (1984)

The Razor's Edge (1984)

Little Shop of Horrors (1986)

She's Having a Baby (1988)

Scrooged (1988)

Ghostbusters II (1989)

Quick Change (1990)

What about Bob? (1991)

Groundhog Day (1993)

Mad Dog and Glory (1993)

Ed Wood (1994)

Kingpin (1996)

Larger Than Life (1996)

Space Jam (1996)

The Man Who Knew Too Little (1997)

Wild Things (1998)

With Friends Like These . . . (1998)

Rushmore (1998)

Cradle Will Rock (1999)

Hamlet (2000)

Charlie's Angels (2000)

Osmosis Jones (2001)

Speaking of Sex (2001)

The Royal Tenenbaums (2001)

Lost in Translation (2003)

Coffee and Cigarettes (2004)

Garfield: The Movie (2004)

This Old Cub (2004)

The Life Aquatic with Steve Zissou (2004)

Broken Flowers (2005)

The Lost City (2006)

Garfield: A Tail of Two Kitties (2006)

The Darjeeling Limited (2007)

Get Smart (2008)

City of Ember (2008)

The Limits of Control (2009)

Zombieland (2009)

Fantastic Mr. Fox (2009)

Ballhawks (2010)

Get Low (2010)

Passion Play (2010)

Moonrise Kingdom (2012)

Hyde Park on Hudson (2013)

*A Glimpse Inside the Mind of
Charles Swan III* (2013)

The Grand Budapest Hotel (2014)

The Monuments Men (2014)

St. Vincent (2014)

Dumb and Dumber To (2014)

Aloha (2015)

Rock the Kasbah (2015)

BIBLIOGRAPHY

BOOKS

Boyle, Deidre. *Subject to Change: Guerrilla Television Revisited*. New York: Oxford University Press, 1997

Carroll, E. Jean. *Hunter: The Strange and Savage Life of Hunter S. Thompson*. New York: Dutton, 1993.

Cohen, Karl F. *Forbidden Animation: Censored Cartoons and Blacklisted Animators in America*. Jefferson, NC: McFarland & Company, 2004.

Davis, Tom. *Thirty-Nine Years of Short-Term Memory Loss: The Early Days of "SNL" from Someone Who Was There*. New York: Grove Press, 2009.

Fruchter, Rena. *I'm Chevy Chase . . . and You're Not*. London: Virgin Books, 2013.

Greenfield, Robert. *Dark Star: An Oral Biography of Jerry Garcia*. New York: William Morrow, 1996.

Griggs, Jeff. *Guru: My Days with Del Close*. Chicago: Ivan R. Dee, 2005.

Gurdjieff, G. I. *Beelzebub's Tales to His Grandson*. New York: Penguin, 1999.

Hill, Doug, and Jeff Winograd. *Saturday Night: A Backstage History of "Saturday Night Live."* New York: Vintage Books, 1987.

Johnson, Kim Howard. *The Funniest One in the Room: The Lives and Legends of Del Close*. Chicago: Chicago Review Press, 2008.

Karlen, Neal. *Slouching toward Fargo: A Two-Year Saga of Sinners and St. Paul Saints at the Bottom of the Bush Leagues with Bill Murray, Darryl Strawberry, Dakota Sadie and Me*. New York: HarperCollins, 2000.

Karp, Josh. *A Futile and Stupid Gesture: How Doug Kenney and National Lampoon Changed Comedy Forever*. Chicago: Chicago Review Press, 2008.

Levy, Shawn. *De Niro: A Life*. New York: Crown Archetype, 2014.

Lidz, Frank. *Fairway to Hell: Around the World in 18 Holes*. New York: ESPN Books, 2008.

Maier, Robert. *Low Budget Hell: Making Underground Movies with John Waters*. Davidson, NC: Full Page Publishing, 2011.

Martin, Scott. *The Book of "Caddyshack": Everything You Ever Wanted to Know about the Greatest Movie Ever Made*. Lanham, MD: Taylor Trade Publishing, 2007.

Murray, Bill, with George Peper. *Cinderella Story: My Life in Golf*. New York: Doubleday, 2000.

Nugent, Benjamin. *American Nerd: The Story of My People*. New York: Scribner, 2008.

Patinkin, Sheldon. *The Second City: Backstage at the World's Greatest Comedy Theater*. Naperville, IL: Sourcebooks, 2000.

Perrin, Dennis. *Mr. Mike: The Life and Work of Michael O'Donoghue*. New York: Avon Books, 1998.

Rubin, Danny. *How to Write "Groundhog Day."* Gainesville, FL: Triad Publishing Company, 2012.

Rush, George, with Joanna Molloy. *Scandal: A Manual*. New York: Skyhorse Publishing, 2013.

Shales, Tom, and James Andrew Miller. *Live from New York: An Uncensored History of "Saturday Night Live," as Told by Its Stars, Writers and Guests*. New York: Back Bay Books, 2003.

Shields, David. *Enough about You: Notes toward the New Autobiography*. New York: Simon & Schuster, 2002.

Simmons, Matty. *Fat, Drunk, & Stupid: The Inside Story behind the Making of "Animal House."* New York: St. Martin's, 2012.

Stein, Ellin. *That's Not Funny, That's Sick: The National Lampoon and the Comedy Insurgents Who Captured the Mainstream*. New York: W. W. Norton, 2013.

Stone, Steve, with Barry Rozner. *Where's Harry? Steve Stone Remembers His Years with Harry Caray*. Dallas: Taylor Trade Publishing, 2001.

Streeter, Michael. *Nothing Lost Forever: The Films of Tom Schiller*. Albany, GA: Bear-Manor Media, 2005.

Whitmer, Peter O. *When the Going Gets Weird: The Twisted Life and Times of Hunter S. Thompson*. New York: Hyperion, 1993.

PERIODICALS

Borrelli, Christopher. "Sister Act." *Chicago Tribune*, April 23, 2009.

Breznican, Anthony. "Zen and the Art of Casting Bill Murray in Your Movie." *Entertainment Weekly*, August 20, 2014.

Brownfield, Paul. "What about Bill?" *Los Angeles Times*, February 29, 2004.

Chase, Chris. "Bill Murray: More Than Just a Funnyman." *Cosmopolitan*, December 1984.

Conrad, Harold. "At Large with Bill Murray." *Smart*, July–August 1989.

Coyle, Jake. "No Worries: Bill Murray Reflects on Life, Career." *Detroit Free Press*, October 7, 2014.

Crouse, Timothy. "The *Rolling Stone* Interview: Bill Murray." *Rolling Stone*, August 16, 1984.

Elder, Robert K. "Bill Murray on Sky Diving, Movie, Politics." *Chicago Tribune*, October 9, 2008.

Felton, David. "Bill Murray: Maniac for All Seasons." *Rolling Stone*, April 20, 1978.

———. "When the Weird Turn Pro." *Rolling Stone*, May 29, 1980.

Friend, Tad. "Comedy First." *New Yorker*, April 19, 2004.

Grossberger, Lewis. "Bill Murray: Making It Up as He Goes." *Rolling Stone*, August 20, 1981.

Kelly, Richard. "Bill Murray: In Cold Blood." *Sight & Sound*, August 1999.

Labrecque, Jeff. "Bill Murray: The Curious Case of Hollywood's White Whale." *Entertainment Weekly*, August 27, 2013.

Madigan, Andrew. "'It's like looking in a mirror—a pretty funny mirror': I Was Bill Murray's Stand-In." *Salon*, September 25, 2014.

Markoutsas, Elaine. "Bill Murray on *Saturday Night Live*." *Chicago Tribune TV Week*, July 22–28, 1979.

Martin, Brett. "This Guy Could Be President." *GQ*, January 2013.

Meyers, Kate. "Triumph of the Bill." *Entertainment Weekly*, March 19, 1993.

Pearce, Garth. "Old Stone Face Cracks." *Guardian*, October 21, 2005.

Rowland, Mark. "Hey! C'Mon, We Love You, You Knucklehead!" *Playgirl*, August 1981.

Schussler, Steven. "Inside the Wondrous Mind of Bill Murray." *Minnesota Business*, April 2010.

Smith, Bryan. "House of Cards." *Chicago*, June 2005.

Solman, Gregory. "The Passion of Bill Murray." *Film Comment*, November–December 1993.

Stabiner, Karen. "Bill Murray: I'm a Nut, but I'm Not *Just* a Nut." *McCall's*, October 1984.

Steadman, Ralph. "Gonzo Goes to Hollywood." *Rolling Stone*, May 29, 1980.

Wloszczyna, Susan. "Larger Than a Laugh." *USA Today*, December 3, 1996.